Rising on Water

Water Play Therapy

Yael Livneh

To protect their privacy, the names of the patients appearing in this book have been changed
Photos in the book showing children were approved by the parents in writing, waiving their legal rights to privacy and confidentiality.

Photo art by Sezen Vatansever

Translation: Haim Haviv

Copyright © 2014 Yael Livneh

All rights reserved.

ISBN: **1500749486**
ISBN-13: **978-1500749484**

CONTENTS

Chapter 1 Water in Our Lives...2-27

Chapter 2 The Sink 28-53

Chapter 3 Color..54-85

Chapter 4 Game Playing 86-105

Chapter 5 Preservation...106-119

Chapter 6 Depths Discovered in Water Therapy...................120-132

Chapter 7 The Inner World of Images..................................133-144

Chapter 8 Archetypes, Myths and Symbols..........................145-178

Chapter 9 Memory..179-209

Chapter 10 The Role of the Therapist..................................210-231

Chapter 11 Water Treatment: Diagnosis and Evaluation.........232-254

Chapter 12 Trauma and Birth Trauma..................................255-286

Chapter 13 Subject - Adoption 287-293

Chapter 14 Selective Mutism..294-309

*Dedicated with love
to my husband Muky and my boys*

Introduction

At first I didn't believe the data rising of the water, appearing as a child would create "a water world" in the sink.

How is it possible that a therapeutic encounter associated with water could so easily unlock the sub-conscious mind, shorten treatment and heals a variety of predicaments?

Take for instance the case of Oren, a nine year old, who arrived at treatment following unsuccessful psychological intervention that consisted of an attempt to extinguish eye twitching in both eyes, appearing after he had fractured his arm.

After four sessions, during which Oren built a 'water world,' played and formed a narrative, the eye twitching disappeared. The water brought to the conscious surface an old, untreated trauma, that occurred when Oren was five, when a tree branch poked his eye, which was now healed as a result of the water treatment.

I was determined to try and comprehend the secret of water in relation to emotional healing. the result, is this book, which is about an innovative emotional psychotherapy treatment of children (though it may also be applied to adults), using water in art expressive therapy and as a form of play therapy.

I invite you to dive into the book, it describes dozens of case studies portraying the use of this unique method of treatment.

Just as this method rose from the field or, to be more exact, from the water, it is brought to you so as to serve in simple and effective manner in actual practice, intended to reduce suffering in the world and help children live with a heart that is whole.

Dedicated with love to all children and all therapists.

Water Therapy

"Water is the principle, or the element of things,
All things are water."

Thales of Miletus
(As quoted in *Placita Philosophorum* by Plutarch c. 620 BCE – c. 546 BCE)

Chapter 1

WATER IN OUR LIVES

From water all things come into being and it is their essence.

Water is a fluid element and life would not exist without it.

Water surrounds us here on earth: oceans, lakes, rivers and springs; it falls on us from the sky, converging on mother earth in forms that are either soft as a dawn blanket or harsh as a blizzard.

Water is central to our world, and is found at all parts of the planet, playing a major role in every religion and culture, folk stories and mythologies.

People have found water to be a source of joy and holiness, especially when encountered in conjunction with great forces of nature. The need for water on one hand, while fearing it on the other, have served as a fertile ground for numerous creations of art, legends, stories, poems and beliefs that endlessly fill our lives either with a trickle or as a constant flow.

Due to its central role, water has served as a source of living and livelihood throughout the evolution of our civilization, as communities and cities rose around water resources. The very same reason led, throughout history, to disputes and wars as attempts were made to gain control of water resources. People were ready to die in order to gain access to or control over water, for there is no life without it.

Moreover, water is the basic fluid that enables us to form into human beings. Indeed, all forms of life manifest themselves in a body of fluids: sperm and egg join together and fertilize, leading to the creation of an embryo in a mother's womb [in a fluid environment]. Likewise, in mammals, and in other animals, such as reptiles or birds, life develops in a fluid environment inside an egg.

After birth and throughout life, water constitutes about 70% of human body contents, and it is found in every cell in our body, blood vessels, interstitial spaces and internal organs.

Since water plays such a vital role in our body, spirit and awareness, most people have experienced meaningful events related to water. Some are worthy and stimulating, while others can be traumatic and daunting. Experiences that accumulate in our brain and body, pass through the senses. These are perceived, register, and become etched in our consciousness and sub-consciousness. In our everyday language we call them memories. Water is a memory carrier; thanks to water, memories are present in each and every cell of our body.

WATER: A PRIMARY AND THERAPEUTIC MATTER

Water, H_2O, is one of the four basic elements of nature: earth, air, water and fire.

Water's central features are fluidity, expansion, saturation, constant shifting, the ability to contain or hold, carry and transport, and alter its state of matter (solid, liquid and gas).

In therapy settings, dreams, prose, poetry and the arts, water represents the human soul. The soul, like water: it aspires to find balance, sometimes the psyche feels inundated, and a corresponding need to be held, contained; seeking a cleansing and a change of its emotional state. Emotional change is attainable from a place of inner, invisible motion, as if rising from the depth of the sea to the surface and the seashore, the so-called "real world."

The idea, wrote Ken Wilber, is not to create an accurate map of your objective world, but to let go of your resistance, sink into your inner depths and learn to report on these depths more sincerely, to others as well as yourself. This allows your inner self to start synchronizing with your behaviors. Words and reactions will start to synchronize each other, so that you would live what you believe in, and your left hand will know what your right one is doing.

THE GOALS OF WATER THERAPY

Water therapy is focused on shaping a positive shift in the patient's life. The goal is to float up and give expression to unsolved emotions, cope with painful issues that surface and heal them. Therapy enables improvement of self image, boosting of confidence and increasing self awareness, all of which contribute to a transformation in the realty

WATER: A PRIMARY AND THERAPEUTIC MATTER

Water, H_2O, is one of the four basic elements of nature: earth, air, water and fire.

Water's central features are fluidity, expansion, saturation, constant shifting, the ability to contain or hold, carry and transport, and alter its state of matter (solid, liquid and gas).

In therapy settings, dreams, prose, poetry and the arts, water represents the human soul. The soul, like water: it aspires to find balance, sometimes the psyche feels inundated, and a corresponding need to be held, contained; seeking a cleansing and a change of its emotional state. Emotional change is attainable from a place of inner, invisible motion, as if rising from the depth of the sea to the surface and the seashore, the so-called "real world."

The idea, wrote Ken Wilber, is not to create an accurate map of your objective world, but to let go of your resistance, sink into your inner depths and learn to report on these depths more sincerely, to others as well as yourself. This allows your inner self to start synchronizing with your behaviors. Words and reactions will start to synchronize each other, so that you would live what you believe in, and your left hand will know what your right one is doing.

THE GOALS OF WATER THERAPY

Water therapy is focused on shaping a positive shift in the patient's life. The goal is to float up and give expression to unsolved emotions, cope with painful issues that surface and heal them. Therapy enables improvement of self image, boosting of confidence and increasing self awareness, all of which contribute to a transformation in the realty beings. Indeed, all forms of life manifest themselves in a body of fluids: sperm and egg join together and fertilize, leading to the creation of an embryo in a mother's womb [in a fluid environment]. Likewise, in mammals, and in other animals, such as reptiles or birds, life develops in a fluid environment inside an egg.

After birth and throughout life, water constitutes about 70% of human body contents, and it is found in every cell in our body, blood vessels, interstitial spaces and internal organs.

Since water plays such a vital role in our body, spirit and awareness, most people have experienced meaningful events related to water. Some are worthy and stimulating, while others can be traumatic and daunting. Experiences that accumulate in our brain and body, pass through the senses. These are perceived, register, and become etched in our consciousness and sub-consciousness. In our everyday language we call them memories. Water is a memory carrier; thanks to water, memories are present in each and every cell of our body.

experienced by the patient in his everyday life.

All of these factors improve the quality of life of the child and enable one to find a meaning in his or her life.

The therapeutic process is structured so that each action taken by the therapist – be it physically, mentally or spiritually – serves to support and contain the patient.

The human soul is in a constant, dynamic search for balance. Unconsciously, children undergoing therapy act on, or provide hints about, their emotional state. It is important to be attuned to and read these signals, in order to ascertain which would be the most appropriate reaction, at a given moment, in relation to a particular child.

Focused therapy with water is very powerful and requires sensitive and concrete use, as each child that arrive at the therapy room has a different rhythm and ability to move from one state to the next, within the room's space, and is also affected by personal traits and personal rhythms which may vary.

Violet Oaklander says in her book, *Windows to Our Children: A Gestalt Therapy Approach to Children and Adolescents*, that, focused methods help save time and shorten therapy. They also insure coverage of other needs of evaluation and therapy. Still, there is a risk that it may rush kids into a painful confrontation which they cannot yet tackle.

KEY FEATURES OF WATER AND WATER THERAPY

Being a substance, water can serve as a means for therapy, similar to other substances known from the arts such as clay, paints, puppets, etc. In using water for emotional treatment of children, the unique features of water allow direct and rapid accessibility to the pathways of the child's senses: Water can be sensed through vision (sight), audition (hearing), gustation (taste) and tactition (touch).

Furthermore, water sets in motion regressive psychological mechanisms that help in the emotional healing of those children who, for whatever reason, avoided such regressive experiences in their early stages of development.

FLEXIBILTY AND ALTERATION

Water is characterized by its ability to alter both shape and state of matter, as a result of changes in temperature. In its natural state on earth it is liquid. As the temperature rises it vaporizes and when the temperature dips below zero (centigrade) it assume a solid state. Despite the dramatic alterations of its state, chemically, water does not change its composition.

As a substance that sets the tone during therapy, water facilitates change in human being. It affects us and we have an effect on it. Water meets the senses head on, when it is encountered by a sensing organ. Various studies have proven that the molecular structure of water allows it to accumulate "memories" of places it came into contact with. Despite its amazing capacity for flexibility and transformation, water is an element which has more anomalies than any other substance found in nature.

HOLDING and EQUILIBRIUM

Water takes the shape of the vessel in which it is held, and always strives for equilibrium (the law of communicating vessels). Emotional Therapy with water deals with holding and equilibrium. Emotional therapy imitates a vessel within which the therapist holds the patient, and where the therapy occurs is a vessel that contains them both.

In water therapy there are several instances where holding is duplicated, since the sink in which water therapy takes place is the container of emotional contents that rise up and surface, and concurrently the therapist is present and holds the contents surfacing up on the water, as well as the patient's emotional reactions. The therapeutic space, while at the therapy area, holds all three.

MOVEMENT and FLOW

Water can flow in different directions, overcome obstacles or drain into lower basins; conversely, it can flood and sink unto itself various objects. This is a substance that, as it flows, it is capable of overcoming impediments. It can assume, on one hand, the shape of the vessel it is in and lie there inert and still. On the other hand, it can dynamically rush and sweep, affecting loss of control, causing frustration or bursting intensity. Accordingly, the flow of water can afford interaction, through methods of work and play, with children, as it presents a technical challenge and, at times, allows frustration and aggression to surface and be experienced in a non-harmful manner, allowing coping with these emotions metaphorically, symbolically, as it is facilitated through enjoyable playfulness. Flow and movement, which coexist in emotional therapy, allow for both internal and external movement, enabling the overcoming of mental and emotional hurdles, it also allows emotional cargo to either surface or be internalized.

LAND and SEA

Water therapy has two aspects: (i) internally, i.e., working inside a sink, the "water world," and (ii) externally – the "solid ground" surrounding the sink. Each aspect of the treatment strives for balance; there is also a dialogue between them all the while, reflecting the dialogue between our inner world and external reality, between consciousness and sub-consciousness.

TRANSPARENCY

Water is unique in that it is inert. It is transparent thus can be looked through to a depth; it allows light to come through; it can acquire ambient colors. Water can also be actively colored, which would instantaneously affects the visual cortex in the brain. Water therapy, has emotional expression on several different levels: submerged worlds with deposits, memories and repressed emotions, as well as unconcealed contents surfacing on top.

REFLECTION and MIRRORING

Adding objects, figures and artistic or recreational activity to water allows the transfer of contents – till then stored in memory – into the water sink which will now serve as a detached holding reservoir. The picture forming there, mirrors memories (see chapter 9, entitled, "Memory") is now transferred to what feel as a safe place, enabling the child to observe the situation from a different emotional perspective, forming a different feel toward it, allowing a different plot to take shape: a shift in the power dynamics, enabling empowerment by the scene reflected to the child from the sink.

The visual picture that forms is taken from a given emotional-mental experience. The transformation it underwent in the sink, allows its placement back in the mind in a visual-experiential manner, an event that directly affects the process of selectivity by the emotional and mental memory.

MUSICAL SOUND

As it flows, water creates sound, which is either monotonous or is varied in its intensity. When it is still, however, it is silent. Sound therapy complements the elements of senses-oriented, inter-disciplinary therapy. Utilizing the sounds water makes, sound dynamics and empowerment may be produced, ranging between the vibration created by water that is forcefully tossed and that caused by a soothing flow or a gentle trickle. Accordingly, the water can serve as a sound conductor in the process of according emotional therapy to children.

PRESERVATION PRINCIPLE

At the end of the client's visit at the "water world," where he had played a creative and imaginative game, he would choose certain elements he would opt to keep. He would choose a transparent container to hold the colored water from the "water world," as well as objects or figures used in his playing with the water. The preservation principle enables focusing on the contents of therapy kept in a small container that may be used in later stages of the therapeutic process. It is vitally important to create, at every stage of the process, a pleasant, protected therapeutic space and ambience, where children would encounter a friendly environment, of familiar games and materials they have previously met in their experience at home, kindergarten or school. Water is in concert with this notion, being a familiar element they relate to daily, which thus facilitates for the therapist a smooth association with the children.

KEY ELEMENTS IN THERAPY

TIMING

The timing chosen by the therapist to use water therapy plays a key role in the process. Precise timing will result in an optimal outcome and vice versa. Indeed, timing is everything, as is the case with a random encounter that turned into a meaningful relationship or that moment of the Big Bang creating the universe we inhabit. Likewise, think of those harrowing "almost" moments, where we were saved from a dangerous situation and could breathe a sigh of relief in its aftermath. There are those who would say that nothing is coincidental, and some believe that a guiding hand is present in our lives. Either way, timing plays an important role in the outcome revealed in our lives and it affects the way we feel.

Timing in therapy translates into the ability to read the emotional and mental state of the patient at work in a given situation and at a given moment. It allows the therapist to understand and analyze the personal and collective cultural context in which the patient functions and his mode of expressing it, while concurrently becoming aware of herself as a therapist and feeling its effect on her.

Therapists can practice and refine their sense of timing, reaching an integrated mental/intuitive capacity that will serve to guide their therapeutic intervention so that, with perfect timing, they will shift to water therapy with a particular patient.

ATTENTIVENESS

In art therapy there are so many rich and diverse moments, as it simultaneously utilizes imagination, thought, play, creativity and verbal expression. Therapists are required to absorb, sort and analyze this input, while segregating the meaningful and exciting moment, highlighting it by some act undertaken together with the patient by way of listening as well as responding: choosing to either say the right thing or say nothing at all.

MOTION in SPACE

Motion toward the patient, to create closeness and motion away, to create spaciousness: the former can be in the form of looking him in the eye or placing a hand on his shoulder and the like, which can a play a significant role in the healing process. On the other hand, it has been my experience, that some children would say the most meaningful and sensitive thing during a session only when they did not see me, for instance when I moved to another corner in the room where there was a curtain. Conversely, others would express feelings of excitement when I reached closely to the child's face, in a gesture of sharing a secret.

MATERIALS

The therapist should either offer the right materials for promoting expression so as to enable the creative process itself, or allow the materials to facilitate the experience. The therapy room has various and sundry materials to offer, such as fabrics, feathers, sand, clay; nature supplied ones: leaves, branches, dries flowers; hard materials such as boards of wood or small metal objects; and materials from daily life, such as keys, utensils, pegs, threads, wires, yarn, straws, etc.

Often, I ask the child to look around and choose the material he wants to work with on the occasion. At other times, imagery scenes the child presents dictates the material that will be chosen. For example, if he talks about "a nestlings' nest", I would ask "what is the nest made of?" A six year old once told me that the nest was made of iron, but was very soft inside. He chose to make the nest of aluminum foil, padding its interior with colorful downy feathers.

SPIRIT

The therapist endeavors to enable the patient to experience acceptance and belonging, absence of judgment and to endow him with comprehension, sensation and love. People who enter the treatment room are not impressed just by the sight of the room, the colors on the wall or the furniture. Invariably, they react to the energy in the room and the emotional quality conveyed by the therapist. When the child first enters, he quickly scans the place and can sense whether the surroundings are pleasant or unpleasant, in his experience. It is important to relate to the child at "eye level," treat him with respect, accept him as he is. We must not to allow perceptions to cloud our view. These include the difficulties he brings along, what his parents, teachers and friends think of him, or his own negative slant on himself. As a therapist, I always find worthy qualities in the person before me, accepting him as he is with love and warmth. More often than not, humor always helps create positive interaction with children, it also frees them of tension and allows them to feel comfortable with themselves.

Therapy is a kind of a development graph in which parallel processes occur. On one hand there is openness, trust; it is where inner contents and emotions are revealed. The psychological layers of resistance and alienation start to peel off like an onion. Conversely, as trust and personal connection between patient and therapist grow, and a process of empowerment, a sense of security and healing of broken, aching aspects of the self begins.

The following case delineates and highlights certain elements of the therapy process. These aspects may be observed: Spatial movement in a relationship that contains both closeness and detachment, use of control enabling materials, as well as the matters of acceptance and holding during therapy, which is characterized by the ability exhibited by the patient to stay with his difficulties as a kind of a game where aggression is legitimate, has other rules and is not harmful to its object.

A Glimpse into the Therapy Room

Dalit, a 7 year old girl, arrives at the treatment room. She has wise black eyes and black shiny hair. She is very serious while with me, glancing around suspiciously while continuously checking the holding limits the therapy has to offer.

During the first few sessions the girl avoided soft materials and used only markers for drawing with much precision. The same drawing repeats time and again: a pirate ship with two pirates on board, and a treasure island at the corner of the page. Every now and then she would defiantly throw the markers at me and check for my reaction while the drawing "slipped" toward me at the table. Her aggression gradually escalated until one day a pillow hit me squarely in the face!

Dalit – one of the early therapy's pirate ships drawings. Notice the single pirate and the relative paucity of what is drawn on the page.

I felt I was being tested each and every session, despite the discomfort, I decided to maintain an approach of love and acceptance. The turning point occurred during a sessions in which she "sought to kill me" while Playfully wrestling. She knocked me down time and again on a big bean bag at the center of the room, an accomplishment that never failed to fill her up with satisfaction. The moment I was defeated and crushed, she allowed herself to come close, gently hold and embrace me as if saying: I create moments of defiance that generate a brawl, and through such violence I admit intimacy and closeness.

Note:

That day was a turning point where Dalit could unveil softer aspects of herself and, in fact, laid aside seven years during which she had struggled with primary figures. Now she could relinquish the incessant fight and take the time to become focus on and become acquainted with herself. Now, it was opportune time to move on to our interaction through the medium of water.

Dalit – Pirates and a treasure island, a drawing made at mid therapy

Towards the end of therapy Dalit went back to drawing the pirate ship. I asked her casually: "Why aren't the pirates reaching a shore?" She responded: "Yael, don't you see? If they reach shore then you and I are through."

Note: In Dalit's mind, when the pirates shall have reached a safe harbor and no longer need to fight on their way to finding the treasure, there will be no more conflicts to solve by way of therapy, thus, the therapy would come to an end.

Dalit(age 7) – Building a Pirate ship model (see Chapter 8, Archetypes, Myths and Symbols, p. 145).

Pirate's ship at the end of therapy: One can see that the ship came ashore, accompanied by two other boats. The cannon disappeared, and instead there is a yellow flag. Note the size of the ship and the clarity the drawing depicts – there are no clouds.(more on the water therapy with Dalit in the Chapter 5, Preservation, p.98)

A Glimpse at the Therapy Room

A boy at play in a sandbox, presenting strong emotional experiences including loneliness, aggression, anger and fear. When ends playing, he asks for paper to draw on. The drawing nearly always includes, among others, a depiction of a house, the sun, flowers and the sky.

Note:

Drawing after emotional catharsis, following playing or engaging in art-related activities, does not always contain the emotional contents that came to the fore during those activities. Sometimes the expression is, "I've landed," communicating the message that "now everything is alright."

On other occasions the opposite effect will manifest, as was the case with that child who built a garden using small trees, paths, a greenhouse, garden beds, all in a highly symmetrical manner, doing it with bated breath.

When done, he asked for a sheet of paper, took crayons and scribbled one big chaotic mess on the whole page. Only then did he resume breathing regularly.

Note: When using focused treatment with water, one has to take into account that the therapist has come to know the patient to such a degree that he could recognize the different psychological mechanisms the former is utilizing, and that there is a safety net in place, one of trust and communication between patient and therapist.

Six-year old Daniel's well-ordered garden creation

ACTIVE FACTORS IN WATER THERAPY

Sixty percent of our body weight is fluid and 70% of planet Earth is covered with water. We are born into this world out of a womb, which is a hydrous environment; many of our experiences are related to water. Hence, this is a highly familiar and natural substance to us all. Water has a dimension of depth that, combined with its transparency, allows for therapeutic work at different levels of various elements of consciousness that, consequently, would surface from subconscious levels, from the deep. Being fluid, not solid, water requires coping with situations that are uncontrollable and require creative solutions, while dealing with frustration and loss of control.

Therapeutically, water is a neutral environment where the patient and therapist meet, creating a "transitional space"[1], which is one of the child's developmental stages; it subsists throughout life. This "transitional space" enables integration between imagination and reality,[2] between the inner and the outer world and, to a degree, between the self and others, as well. It allows building relationships in different aspects of life: family, work, society and others. The transitional world has significant importance in art therapy, for the arts and creative processes enable presence in a "transitional space."

As a therapeutic medium, water symbolizes the human psyche, through which the patient can project his emotions and experiences. The patient, assisted by the therapist, would transfer to water contents clutched in a deep inner dimension, enabling a process of exploration, handling the playing experience and emotional contents that surfaced as the "water world" is formed. This is followed by a process called

---

[1] See, Transitional Objects and Transitional Phenomena — A Study of the First Not-Me Possession. International Journal of Psycho-Analysis, 34:89-97 (1953). Winnicott explored the phenomenon of the 'intermediate area', a transitional phenomena, an area of human experience, i.e., an area where experience transpires. This area bridges inner and external reality and connects between subjective experience and objective reality.
[2] Id.

introversion.

Here, inner occurrences, that surfaced as the water world was formed, then were observed, sorted out, named and defined – more than any internal experience of the patient's other experiences that have assumed shape, sound and color – can now be re-internalized, permeating in a processed form and becoming embedded in the of the patient's consciousness.

The therapeutic model using water includes elements of other expressive therapies, as well as elements of play therapy,[3] among other reasons, because this model employs techniques and materials used in those forms of therapy, e.g., objects, play-acting, creativity, colors, storytelling and the like. This model differs, in that it allows focused intervention in the treatment of various cases, for it enables surfacing of psychological contents by way of a simple, creative and enjoyable experience.

Amit, 6, relationship between siblings

---

[3] Generally, play therapy is employed with children aged 3-11. It provides them with an avenue by which they can play out experiences and emotions via a self-healing, self-guided and a natural procedure. Since children often communicate through play, it is a valuable venue enabling them to become acquainted with and accept themselves and, consequently, others.

WATER REMEMBERS

A Japanese researcher, Masaru Emoto, performed an amazing experiment and wrote a book, "Messages form Water and the Universe,[4]" bringing us evidence of the influence of human energy, thoughts, words, ideas and music, on the molecular structure of water. He visually documented molecular transformation in water by using different filming techniques. He froze drops of water then photograph them with a special microscope. His work documents in a clear way the variety of molecular structure of water and influence of environment on these structures.

Playing of different kinds of music to distilled water from same source, shows the difference in crystallization of that water – according to the type of music played.

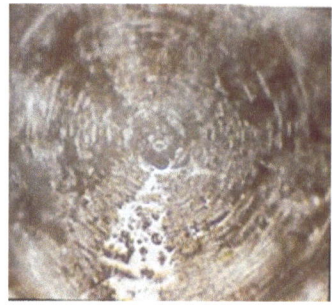

Playing Heavy Metal to water

Playing Beethoven to water

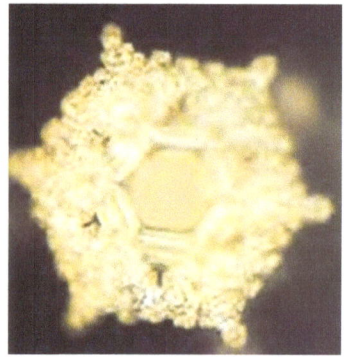

Love and appreciation

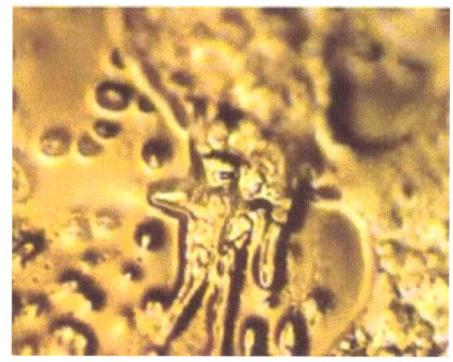

"You make me sick, I'm going kill you!"

---

[4] Hay House, 1st ed. 2010.

"These pictures represent the amazing reaction of water to ... feelings and thoughts. It can be clearly seen that water absorbs frequencies and energy from the environment."

Masuro Emoto, in Messages from Water and the Universe.

WATER THERAPY- THE PROCESS

Water therapy combines several techniques including: art therapy, play therapy and free associations. Thus, water therapy is an integrative therapy.

The process of water therapy constitutes a focused stage in comprehensive expressive therapy. Water treatment takes place in the regular therapy room, thus incorporating the same qualities of healing found in emotional therapy in general, as well as unique qualities stemming from the medium itself and the form it utilizes.

Water Therapy Has Six Stages:

The therapist and patient stand together by the sink, and the latter fills up the sink with water.

1. The patient colors the water;
2. The patient print the colors;
3. The patient empties the sink out;
4. The patient build a "water world" in the sink using a particular color (a new choice);
5. At the end of the process, the patient created aquariums in order to preserve parts of the "water world;"
6. The patient renders the sink empty.

Therapy by water has – from the moment the patient stands by the sink and fills it up with water – an immediate effect on our senses: the water is heard, seen as it flows and, when splashed around, it, tactually, feels wet. Our sensory system awakens by this familiar substance. There is sensory reception of stimuli that is transmitted to the brain, which ties together the sensory input with emotional contents stored in memory. These memories are usually associated with contents trapped deeply in the subconscious, relating to the patient's past experiences. Contact with water enable such past experiences to surface, as a result of the patient's contact with water. These contents manifest in the water world, which is a creative game, as well as through the use of metaphors and texts, stated in the proximity of the sink.

Water therapy occurs in a sink or any a similar container. Water, by its nature, strives for equilibrium, as does the human psyche. The emotional therapy by the sink calls for therapy using multiple containers: The first container is the therapy room, the second is the sink and the therapist is the third.

When emotional contents are "poured" by the patient into the sink, the latter gains a great deal of holding (containment). Equilibrium is reached when the sink is filled up with projected emotional and imaginative content. This is followed by emptying it by the patient, as a signal that the 'game is over; time to go back to reality.'

Since water is transparent, it is possible to see deeply through it, in more ways than one. Light that penetrates through water is reflected back to the retina. When the patient paints the water with colors, there is an immediate impact on the visual cortex of the brain, thus affecting various centers in the brain and, consequently, the patient's state of mind.

Building the water world allows the application of symbolism to emotional contents, to the point of creating an entire visual picture. When unveiled, it gives both the patient and therapist an opportunity to relate to the emotional contents that surfaced, define them, sort them out and observe their influence on the patient's life. By playing in the water world the patient can alter the original picture and process emotional contents while encountering intimidating emotions such as fears, threats, conflicts; solving problems for the figures found in the water world, thus resolving and curing constrained aspects of his life that are in need of such healing.

WATER THERAPY: THE BEGINNING

During the many years I treated children, I have always felt great deal of respect for choices they made at the therapy room. I intuited that they had the key to their own therapy within; that, unconsciously, they know what they needed in order to heal. Therefore, I helped them express their feelings in any manner they opted for, even if it seemed illogical or implausible. I believed (and still do) that each child makes a personal journey of self-discovery and growth. Out of such trials, with a variety of expression techniques, I was able to develop the treatment and produce impressive results with treatments that last, relatively speaking, short periods of time.

Water therapy is a method that evolved in the therapy room, as children honed in on it on their own. It turned out, as a rule, to be both efficient and highly therapeutic. Throughout the years of using water as therapeutic means, it proved to be one that opens up emotional blockages, facilitates the emergence of contents from subconscious layers and enables freeing energy and its flow, and I found it worthy to reduce my impressions and experience to writing and organize them as a structured therapeutic model that will allow other therapists, of different disciplines, to utilize it in helping both young and adult patients to dislodge trapped issues wedged in their inner world, thus create emotional emancipation, energetic flow, exuberance and passion the patients ought to have in their lives.

How Did the First Water Treatment Start:

A Glimpse into the Therapy Room

Noam, a 6 year old kindergarten student arrived to my clinic one day.

He was from a kibbutz at the center of Israel, with two penetrating black eyes and cropped black hair. Noam was referred by his parents, who were separated at the time. He exhibited distance in his relationship with his father. The parents reported social difficulties and low self-esteem. They described the child to be very sensitive, witty, logical, likes to hug and cuddle, creative, highly imaginative, competitive, sensitive to sensations, does not like to get dirty and impulsive. Consequently, they expressed concern that he might suffer from Attention Deficit Disorder (ADD). They also described excessive crying and anger responses.

Noam commenced with expressive arts therapy, an initial introductory meeting that led to building a relationship with me as therapist. He was very creative and changed the therapeutic medium several times: He worked with clay, painted, made puppet show characters of paper on sticks, and more. During therapy, Noam brought up the difficulties he had in kindergarten and at home, the communication between his parents, and, mainly, his feelings of frustration and loneliness that accompanied him wherever he went.

Noam painted an aquatic scene:

Then, he asked to work with water. It was the first time a child made such a request during these therapy sessions.

Having missed two weekly meetings, he then arrived with his mother, who reported difficulties, much crying and tantrums since our last encounter. At the start of the session he wanted us to build a ship, "like a real ship," he said. As we worked on it, he asked that the ship should also sail "like a real one". Being faithful to my young patients' visions, I filled a small sink with water, and we placed a Styrofoam ship in it. He then took a turtle figurine, placed it on the ship and, as he drowned the turtle in the sink's water, he said: "The turtle is drowning, the turtle is drowning," and then, "The crab is coming to the turtle's rescue", then grabbing a small crab and had it dive from the edge of the sink straight into the water.

Turtle: "Oh, thank you."
Crab: "You are welcome."

Then Noam turns the crab on its back while floating on the water. Noam: "Blood is oozing. A hunter came, short the crab and killed it." He then forms a lifebuoy of Play-Doh in red and white (as he switches roles to become the storyteller): "The lifebuoy saves the turtle," he declares and wraps it around the turtle's mid-section.

Noam: "And he wants to enter his quarters on the ship but there is no entrance." Now, the turtle floats about, helpless, not knowing where to turn.

Noam then thinks for a moment and finds a solutions – he puts golden sequins in the water.

Noam: "And everyone found treasures! The turtle noticed that he had a treasure." He continues to churn the water and golden sequin surfaced, coloring the water gold, then he states: "I don't have treasures", as he empties the water from the sink, his entire body exuding acceptance.

The session ends with us keeping the ship, turtle and life float and, of course, "the treasures."

Note:

In a later conversation we talk about " life's treasures," what they accord us and why we don't always notice them. Noam shares with me his deepest sentiments, his desire for his life to improve, to be rescued.

Following the event at the sink, I had a feeling that a momentous event had just occurred. On one end, the scene was akin to a puppet show, with figures conducting a dialogue, and there is a scene that could relate to his life experience at home and with other children. Yet, there was something in Noam's involvement and the way he was able to refine his difficulty and strengths through the medium of a water-filled sink, and the interesting way he interacted with it. The notion captivated me in its simplicity, earnestness and depth of affect it had on Noam, combined with the insight that surfaced, using the treasures.

At the end of meeting with Noam, I intuited that water had the capacity to facilitate raising deep, delicate issues to the surface in a simple manner, from an inner, buried location to one that is out in the open. The water, so I assumed, is a special, powerful expressive modality. In days to come, this assumption opened a door to a whole new world – the unconscious world of delightful children who, like water, endeavor to achieve inner balance and release issues that disturb their flow, expression, vivacity and inner and external joy.

Chapter 2

THE SINK

Beginning Water Treatment

Therapist to Patient is Akin to Water in a Vessel

A child is a human being, a soul, having the features of one vessel or another. At times, the vessel is transparent, at others, opaque. Sometimes it is chipped or has an end broken, it could be tall and narrow, straight or twisted like a pretzel, and occasionally the vessel is plate-like, easily flooded by contents flowing out of one's inner world, threatening to spill over.

There are small vessels and large ones, some looking rather strange others seemingly empty. And there are those that appear smooth on the outside but are rough and jagged on the inside; some look lackluster and meek.

Be that as it may, each vessel can hold water.

The therapist, as water would, adjusts to the vessel – he is in touch with every aspect of it, he strokes, becalms and accords the vessel its primary purpose.

The law of communicating vessels, that liquid will balance out at the same level in all of the linked containers, regardless of the shape and volume of each), demonstrates that liquid changes its form in agreement with the shape of the container that holds it. According to this law, the surface level of fluid in different parts of the communicating vessels will seek to even out among them all. An example of this law is observed at sea level, which is nearly equal in all seas that are connected one to the other on earth. Hence, melting of the glaciers at the poles will cause a rise of sea level all over the planet – coral islands in the tropics, whose elevation is only a few centimeters above current sea level, will become submerged due to the ensuing upsurge. On the other hand, inland seas, each self-contained, have different levels, for they are not "communicating" (connected), for example, the difference of surface level between the Sea of Galilee and the Dead Sea (separated only by a distance of 204.3 kilometers) is hundreds of meters.

Water therapy involves a process that evokes the law of communicating vessels: The patient is a vessel that holds water, while the therapist surrounds him, forming a metaphoric container; she, too, is a body holding water, thus she contains the patient, as does water when enveloping an object submerged in a tub: the two touch one another and play together. A mutual balance synthesis is enabled in such therapeutic range.

Since water, while being played with, conducts emotions and awareness well, it is possible to float up memories and suppressed emotions. The presence, attention and acceptance of and holding by the therapist bring balance into the therapeutic process. The child feels he can (and does) unload all the "muck," burden, pain and anger, that will then dissolve in clean, fresh water; at a place that will help him with his inner cleansing.

CONTAINMENT

The concept of containment is taken from the psychodynamic theories of mother-infant relationships. The psychoanalyst Wilfred Bion stressed the mother's role of infant's containment, providing attention and psychological support, at which junction she can suspend the infant's sense of anxiety, only to restore it in a manner with which it can cope. She does it through a process called *projective identification*. How the mother would hold the infant, both physically and emotionally, has great importance when the infant cannot understand what transpires either in his environment or his body, e.g., when it is undressed or held in either uncomfortable or unsuitable manner. "Holding" means the correct and suitable manner of gripping the infant, with an emphasis on soothing the infant's anxiety and related sensations. The infant needs protection and the feeling of being held both physically and emotionally.

"Containment" is the mother's ability to place the infant's sense of anxiety on hold, in such a manner that it would be able to accommodate the feeling. Its containment occurs by way of projection: as the mother enjoys external support, such as family presence, combined with the availability of internal resources, necessary for providing requisite care for and containment of the child, where the mother can also feel contained, which helps her in containing her offspring.

The experience of containment, according to Bion, allows the infant to grow a psychological "thick skin" which protects it when the mother is absent from its immediate vicinity. Bion anticipated that at stressful moments the infant would lose the ability to sense itself, becoming "flooded" and would have a need for intervention by an adult, who could contain the emotional difficulties it is undergoing.

If the mother contains the stress, comforting the infant and removing its cause, the infant would project its stress on the other (the mother) and will re-acquire the experience in a processed form, which he is able to contain. This way, the world is experienced as a brighter, more pleasant place and the infant can better relate to itself and the objects around it.

According to Child Development Psychoanalyst Daniel Stern, initial experiences are the beginning of the mental-symbolic activity, i.e., the infant senses that it contains within concrete components of his reality such as its mother's smile, her voice, touch, holding, etc., exactly the same way they exist in its external reality. These experiences are stored in memory and connect directly to the maternal-infant bond. They are stored in the form of images of the external reality.

CONTAINMENT IN WATER THERAPY

Emotional therapy through water occurs at the sink, the physical receptacle that contains the water, and where the therapeutic activity will ensue. The sink is also a therapeutic metaphor of a vessel, a container, for during therapy the patient would experience containment, nurturing, support and a sense of being protected. Linette McMahon, a play psychotherapist, believes that the therapist should offer the child a sense of containment and a mental space where she would treat the communication ability of the child and reflects for him these abilities by symbolism incorporated into the playing he would be engaged in.

Many children create or play with containment symbols during therapy. In these cases, the therapist can learn much about the child's feelings, which are associated with containment – does he, for instance, feel contained and enfolded or does he feel a need for protection.

A Glimpse into the Therapy Room

Children use symbols of containment, such as a house, a tent, a nest, an egg with a chick in it, a belly pregnant with a infant inside, a cradle or a box with a slumbering tot in it, etc. These symbols reflect a child's need for containment and security, and are indicative of the different stages of interaction between therapist and patient in a healing process, reflecting its various phases. For example, children building a house with figures in it are opting to bring to the fore the subject of family and relationships at home, bringing our attention to such and seeking a healing for the situation through therapy.

Noga, at age six: "I'm home"   Noga, six months later: "my family"

Children who choose a container with a single figure in it, usually opt to deal with matters related to their emotional defensiveness vis-à-vis support and containment they are in need of, which, typically, are lacking in their life. When the child undergoing therapy asks to create a given container form, I, as a therapist, understand that he is guiding me toward a deep emotional need he has for support, containment, boundaries and trust. Through the process of creating different kinds of containers, I have the privilege to be part of building a "sheltering emotional skin" for that child. Most often, the creation of a container will bring progress and improvement in the therapy process. It is as if the child is saying: "After I have built a container that will protect me, hold me and contain all those hardships, shielding me from myself, I can now bring you, the therapist, into my inner world where storms, confusion, helplessness and fear may reside."

1

DIVORCE :Nir, age six – a house with a hole at its base. In other words, the container he depicts is not whole.

2

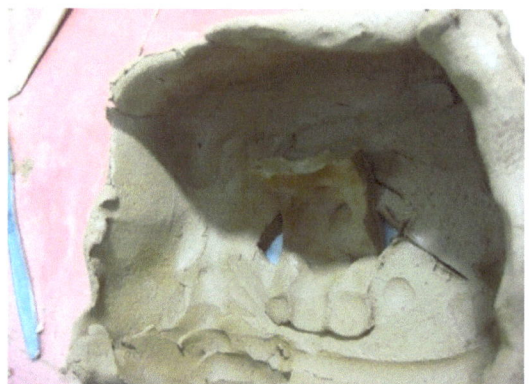

Nir "patches up the hole" at the base of the house, an act representing Nir's need to' fix' the house.

3

Nir "grows" supportive columns at the base of the hole. These look like figures that are turning their back on each other.

This creation describes Nir's feelings regarding occurrences at home.

Note: the dwelling does not have a roof, i.e., there is no protection, everything is wide open, resembling an archeological site, broken and deserted, a hint about its past.

4

Nir's self portrait by the "fixed" house.

Nir placed himself outside the house, sitting on an armchair and looking away. This phenomenon, of emotional detachment from a broken home, manifests at times in the experience of children of divorced parents. Their emotional experience is one of sensible, clear observation of the breakup of their former home and family. More often than not, they are bright enough to take note of the deeper characteristics of the event which their parents cannot or do not want to see.

Note: Nir's therapy continued throughout the protracted divorce of his parents. Because he did not feel protected or having a stable base, using a big cardboard box, he created a trailer car in the therapy room in which he put a comfortable couch and a wheel. Inside the trailer he had clothes, and refreshments offered him during therapy. Nir created for himself a symbolic 'container' with which he was traversing the distance between his mother and father's homes.

The children create most of the symbols from materials found in the therapy room: soft pillows, beanbags, blankets, fabrics and more. Sometimes, the children's artistic creations clearly reflect symbols: drawing or building a scale model of a house from cardboard, clay eggs with small animals in them, little dolls well wrapped in fabrics to keep them warm.

Noga ,at six and a half – parents' bed

CONTAINMENT IN A SINK

Maya, a second grade student, was carried away with the imagery of protection and containment as she was immersed in water. She created a water world in the sink that had animals and plants, then took thick, light blue fabrics and covered the water thus sheltering her world from above. She said, "There are only dolphins and whales in the water, all are asleep now. In the morning there are the guards present, [at night] the fabrics hide the animals from people that don't love them.

The therapist's presence with the child serves in and of itself as a "sink," a container. As a result of creating a sense of security, freedom, affection and a secure space, the child feels he can "place" in this sink just about anything he wishes to. This is akin to being allowed to put any color, figure or material in a physical sink. Therefore, the therapist should encourage the child to express any emotion, thought or idea, even if it is otherwise considered one that is purportedly "inappropriate." The therapist enables the child to be who he is, free of any masks he might have gotten used to wear, designed to shield himself, and enable him to come forward and express his anger, fears, innermost secrets and any deep-seated questions boring into his mind or heart.

A house constructed of the sofa's cushions in the therapy room – an example of using soft materials ,that symbolize containment.

Containments Occurs in Several Stages:

Initially, the therapist allows the child to choose as she invites him to go on a joint excursion. The therapist asks, "Would you like to work with water today?"

The invitation brings with it two conditions: **First**, collaboration and mutual support in building the 'common space' that will form a corridor between reality and imagination: the use of water allows the formation of a mock reality, the "water world."

The second condition is the use of water – a material in regular use in daily life that is familiar, accessible – which facilitate openness.

Throughout the process, the therapist both projects the notion and provides guidance to the effect that *there are no rules* in the space occupied by the two. Everything is possible. In other words, the choice of water as a medium allows the child to express himself in any which way he so desires.

More often than not I allow children in the therapy room to choose any material they wish to work with, even if such materials are regressive in nature. I believe in spontaneity, creativity, intuition, and their synergy, as long as it yields healing.

Though the therapist comes with knowledge and experience in child's therapy modalities and therapeutic theories, especially regarding art therapy, each therapist is responsible for attuning to her intuition. It is the intuition that, more than any existing theory, could provide information during a session and in it is the key to actual healing. Moreover, one must keep in mind that children tend to possess a sharp, powerful and finely attuned intuition and, if we just listen to the child, we are liable to discover that he knows how to help himself quickly, effectively and spontaneously. The child can actually guide us to find the means and paths to his heart through stories, colors, intonations and subtexts.

Using water as a substance, with the addition of color and playing, allows the child to open up to an array of experimentations, sense experience and interests, and to emotional contents that surface in natural fashion. The therapist should be careful and insure that these contents are neither criticized nor blocked by her.

A Glimpse to the Therapy Room

There is a knock on the therapy room's door. I open the door and a child is standing there. I welcome, relate to and esteem the child as a whole person, body, personality and spirit. He has strengths, abilities, inner autonomy and individuality. I invite him to enter the work area, which is a sheltered space that enables 'magic' to happen.

While doing so, I say in my heart, "Welcome you are as you enter. You, too, can. Your growth and development are unbound. You are welcome to discover your own capacity and use it to the greatest extent you can. I am devoid of any judgment or criticism, I am filled with love and acceptance."

Note: Most kids arrive at therapy with difficulties in certain aspects in their lives: in school, the company of other children and intra-family relationships. Some make it even worse for themselves. Being stuck emotionally hurts their quality of life, and backfires in their close and distant environments, which not always are sympathetic.
Sometimes the reasons that bring them to therapy are just byproducts of an inner cause lying deep in their emotional memory
I believe and find out over and over again, that children know what they need for healing. Therefore, by far and for most, what they need is a supportive environment, containing, attentive and empathetic, that will allow them to heal themselves.

A child's soul is made from a complexity of expressive forms , consequently, creative arts therapy enables the use of different expressive forms in a different artistic medium, such as music, dance and movement, theatre, play, writing, arts and crafts, speech, etc.

Throughout the therapy the child should be allowed to express himself anyway he wishes to. When we get to know his forms of expressions, we can map the wider array of his soul and create a new internal order. Parts that have not been expressed, yet, can now be revealed and grow, whereas other parts that might not be effective, or are even harmful, can lose strength and occupy less space.

When a child chooses marker pens, for example, he declares," I have a need for control, it is important for me to be clear to my environment." Adolescents tend, many times, to use pencils and markers to lock reality (as it is perceived by them). Other forms of drawings, which tend to be 'soft', such as oil pastels, water paints , washable paints or chalks represent a different mode of dealing with things. For example, a child who needs control in his life and chooses oil pastels allows himself a regressive experimentation with materials that do not tend to be exact. Many times, reactions such as "oh, it went off line", "I've failed," will serve as a prolific launching pad for treatment and emotional endurance for the patient.

A Glimpse to the Therapy Room

Noga, 6.5, reached therapy as she was having difficulties forming social interactions and would get temper tantrums each time her parents refused her for something. She was described by them as rigid and stubborn.

Therapy with Noga was fascinating. She opened up slowly, and gradually developed trust in the process and in me as the therapist. Her rigid approach marked her throughout the beginning of the therapy process. She would use only markers for drawings, pointing, depicting her need for control, and always knew what she was going to draw. Through different times of playing, she would repeat the same pattern – always the same game, which she always had to win. Noga repeated a certain order of activities in the room, as a ritual, and when we played a game that required an involved interaction opposite me, she would get "stuck." On one hand, Noga could not play any "make believe" games, while, on the other hand, she had exhibited imagination and inner world that were extremely well developed but would be expressed just when she was by herself, and only by artistic means.

I felt it would be right to work on her difficulties from a place where she felt strong and confident. I used color drawing. First, I let her choose colors and draw whatever she liked, so that she could gain a sense of control. In the encounters to follow, I gave her abstract instructions, such as drawing different kinds of lines, sometimes crossing each other, sometimes drawn apart, painting small and large stains, painting with two paint brushes to the sounds of music, like a conductor of an orchestra and, finally, finger painting. Each of these instructions was carried out throughout a whole meeting, and Noga was working cautiously and slowly. At first, Noga was responding in a heartbroken manner to each line that would not be "right," and turned a lot of anger and frustration towards me. But I had contained the anger and helplessness, and cheered her up for her trying and for the artistic and creative experience. As a result, Noga learned to contain the imperfection and her "errors" and started to even enjoy the parts of the drawing which seemed scrabbled and not understood. Every time the line would not work out in the painting, she would repeat the same words I had told her in order to comfort her: "Art has no rules – everything is possible and allowed."

After a long time, when there was a significant progress in her social interaction ability and in the processes taking place in the therapy room, I allowed myself to offer her to work with water.
Water posed a challenge for her. She chose three colors: white, purple and blue. She had a hard time organizing the water environment, and was mainly exploring the substances and materials: what would float, what would sink and so on. She would repeat the phrase "it doesn't make sense," but in spite of her difficulty, she would not 'call it off' and she was actually enjoying touching and playing around with water.

Note: Children that react or respond in fixed patterns, need to train with gradually and diversely on new experiences. Only so can they allow themselves to overcome the fear of change and develop spontaneity. Laughter, physical activity, change of rhythm, stimulation of curiosity, etc., promote expansion of their inner repertoire. When there is resistance, the therapist has to "disarm" it gently and softly, and understand that rhythm, timing or ripeness for change has not been reached. Sometimes, there is a need for "negative" exposure to allow the patient to survive the unpleasant situations and acknowledge that he had survived and walked through his fear. Being able to sense and act upon it requires sensitivity and skills, experience, intuition and creativity.

The same way a multi-facetted expression is recommended for children, it is even more so recommended for therapists. The larger and more liberated is the array of expressive modes, the more containment space there will be as a result. It is in such a space that children sense it and dare break their walls, their habits and their limiting casts. The therapist should be free, creative and not set in his responses, inviting the child to do the same ,literally and practically.

A Glimpse to the Therapy Room

When I opened the therapy room's door that day, there was a mother standing there. A five year old, red head boy wearing glasses, was hanging on her shoulder, head down, feet kicking up. He was screaming: "I don't want to come in!" as he was struggling to free himself from his mother's clutches.

His mom put him down cautiously and made sure the door to the room was locked so he wouldn't try to run out. The little guy went on screaming as loudly as he could. The mother sat down helplessly, her eyes asking, "what can I do?"
After a few minutes, during which he wouldn't calm down, I stood by him and screamed my lungs out in concert with him. He fell silent, and looked at me through his glasses, as if amazed and wondering: "Is there anyone in the world that can scream louder than I"? Therapy started that very moment. He calmed down, stopped

screaming, and sat down to chat a bit and then play. Ever since that day he came willingly and therapy worked well.

THE CONTAINER

The form of the sink and its color

The start of the therapeutic encounter with water takes place at the sink. The sink has a set size and form. Sometimes it is round-edged, sometimes square, it may be made of different substances such as metal or porcelain. Most sinks are white, which increases the sense of cleanliness or of tingeing, formed inside during play.

A Glimpse to the Therapy Room

Ky, a five and a half year old, used to start his sink encounters with coloring the water in different colors, then pulling the plug out and cleaning the sink rather vigorously. Instead of playing, he would be occupied with coloring the water, then cleaning; focusing on cleaning was the center of his engagement. It practically became a ritual.

Note: In this case, filling up, messing up, emptying and then cleaning, forms the emotional basis upon which the treatment evolved. The more "mess" there was to clean up, the more vigorous the cleaning actions were. Each time Ky worked at the sink, it would raise emotional contents that, as time went by, multiplied and intensified (including fears, aggression, helplessness and the like), his need to clean "the (emotional) mess" increased. It allowed him to express his soul's innermost secrets on one hand, while controlling the feeling of being overwhelmed or, more accurately, gaining back control that he felt he had lost when his deep secrets of the heart bubbled in the sink of the water therapy.

Ky, five and a half, "How to clean dirty water with soap!"

Boundaries of the Sink

Each sink has counters, whether narrow or wide. Kitchens' sinks may have also a larger attached counter, which may add additional therapy space. Such space offers creative work potential outside the sink, also, and it is very significant to the process (as we will later see). The boundaries of the sink, which separate the inner part of the sink and its depth from the outside, symbolize the inner world of the person while the counter, the world outside. The relationship between these two worlds can be seen in the sink.

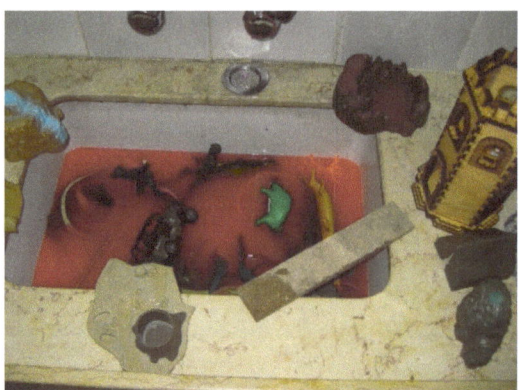

Omer, eight year old. Water world. Anger.

Arrangement of the sink – internal and external. The inner part of the sink is packed with detail, disorganized, forming an irregular picture. The external side of the sink is defined by a small number of details – mountains, castle, bridge.

A Glimpse to the Therapy Room

A 12 year old teenager boy who worked at the sink arranged two worlds: inside the sink, in a white world, were a few plants, a sea turtle, two dolphins and a starfish. On the counter, he set predatory animals, with their mouths full of teeth wide open, and some soldiers turning their weapons toward the water; he then said: "Inside it's all quite, no noise, no predator. Life is in harmony. Outside there are predators, roaring, attacks and killing."

This child had experience violence in school during first and second grade, and his way of dealing with confrontations at home was to lock himself in the closet. He did not have friends and did not try to make any, being so fearful.

12 years old. White water world.

Note: This work points to the fact that he feels better within himself, having harmony inside his inner world, while outside he is threaten by something he does not want confront.

When a child feels contained and able to share, his whole world will be reflected in the sink, literally and practically, allowing for healing. This is yet another example of the counters of the sink allowing for interaction between the inner world of the child and the outer one.

Several researches have demonstrate that, the connection between these two worlds' influences, extensively affects the development of the child while still an infant. British Psychotherapist Melanie Klein, who specialized in play therapy, found that infant's perceptions are influenced by processes of *introjection* and *projection*. According to her, an infant's development depends on the complex interaction between his outside world and inner one – the physical and psychological. Her research shows that an infant is active in creating his close social environment and his inner world.

Psychoanalyst Donald Winnicott, specializing in children therapy, saw the act of infants, who put things in and out of their mouth, as a way to explore parameters in the relationships with their mother and the filling of their worlds with meaning. To him, "the space between the mother and child is a symbolic one. There is something of the mom in this space, something of the infant, and something common to them both." As per Winnicott, this 'togetherness' in this space is created from the beginning of life. The act of playing allows the little child to create new containers to his feelings, as also to expand his relationships. It also support the infant by reducing the intensity his mom is carrying as a container and his first mediator to the external world.

There is a great importance to the way children use the space of the sink and the relationship between the two worlds- inside and outside of the sink. Some children fill the sink with figurines of animals and plants but leave the counters empty. Their play dynamics points that the internal contents are those that pre occupy them. The sink serves as a magnifying glass to meet these contents. There are also other kids that fill the counters with symbols of plants and animals while their water world is poor, or a sink which is "calm" as opposed to the happenings outside. Some kids put a lot of energy to arrange the external world and to keep the different elements from falling to the water and drown, while others build bridges and fences. Each of these options has a meaning behind it. The essential meaning can be provided by the child himself, if asked. Other interpretations can be provided from knowing the child and his expressive patterns, the images he is using or those that he had used in the past.

Pictures of Different Sink Counters

A 13 years old introverted boy. The outside is ideal, with some female figurines, a small life boat and a transparent house. The inner sink is very 'clean', with one fish and one plant.

This work brought to the fore the loneliness experienced by this boy who lived with his mother on their own.

Oren, . There is much disparity between the red water world, assuming a meaning of fear and terror (trauma), opposite the world outside which seems like a conservation park. (See more in Chapter 12, Trauma and Birth Trauma, p. 232)

David, 10. Dealing with bullying in school.

A Glimpse to the Therapy Room

Shai an eight and a half year old ,was a third grade student, the oldest of three brothers. His parents divorced two years earlier, when his mother "came out of the closet "and moved in with s female spouse. Ever since then Shai had moved several times, moved to a different school, and had reached therapy because his mother felt his self image had to be reinforced. Her feeling was supported by his dearth of friends and his constant need to be in control.

Shai formed an immediate connection with me, told me about his school affairs, and once in a while raised topics about home, where he described a complex connection with his dad, and a complex one with his mom's spouse and her son, who was two years older than him and who lived with them. Shai felt close to his mom, but she had to share her attention with his two siblings, the spouse and the spouse's son. He expressed the need to be on good terms with all parties, while actually he had complex feelings toward them. He did not want to lose his place with his mom and dad and kept all his frustrations and anger to himself.

A concentrate of his emotional world can be seen in his water world. Shai chose to work with light blue, which symbolizes the need to express himself. He put a shark in the water, an alligator, a fish and a frog.

Note: The predators in the water represent aggression and anger he feels.

On the counter around the sink he put on the right side a figure referred to as 'Jane' (the female figure from Tarzan and another female figurine, who he called 'guest.' It seems that the guest symbolized his mother's spouse. On the left side of the sink, on the counter, Shai placed a masculine male figurine, Clayton' (the name of a figure from Tarzan), which represented his father, who was a sports teacher. One can see the clear separation between the man and the women in the outside world on the counter. Inside the water, close to the right, there was a drowned tree, its edge sticking slightly above water close to the female figurines.

Note: It's important to note that Shai mentioned that he identifies better with the female side, and he felt his mom understood him better than his dad, who kept demanding him to be "a man."

Shai put a giraffe on the counter in front of the sink, close to where he stood, between the counters on both sides of the sink. The giraffe symbolized him and his relative position between the existing figures. He then said: "If I had to choose what to be, I would choose a giraffe. She is sad. Her tree drowned in the water." Saying that, Shai is actually commenting on the fact that the solid ground that is his family is being taken away, and the tree, which serves as a nurturing source to the giraffe, is in the process of disappearing. "I am sad because of this situation of divorce," he went on. "These water is poisonous to people."

Note: Water symbolizes feelings, emotions, and Shai feels they are poisonous, meaning: if you feel, you might die!

Also, the conflict between the figures can be seen, there is a visually clear physical separation between the parents, with a main theme of divorce.

Shai identifies with the giraffe. When a patient chooses an animal to represent him, he distracts the real figure, and via it he can represent feelings, saying "it's sad."

Many children of divorced parents represent their life via drowned trees, as if saying "my growth stopped". One child asked me once, after his parents announced their separation, "Can trees grow on water?", trying to understand if one can grow in a place with no ground and stability.

Noya, 10:" Trees growing in water."

Her parents divorced when she was 3. The counter around the sink was full with family figurines.

Among children of divorced families, relationships are a main theme around the sink.

Noya, 10. Relationships in the family. The children are at the center and the family surrounds them.

Rising on Water

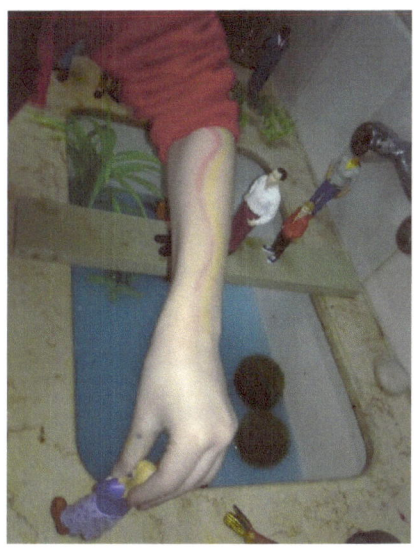

Rona, a seven year old.
An example of working with water. Subject, divorce.

Rona, a seven year old.
Father and daughter. Subject, divorce.

STAGES OF WATER THERAPY

Empty Sink

Working with water starts with an empty ,clean ,plugged up sink. (See below on filling up and emptying the sink.)

The child stands facing the sink. If the sink is too high, use a stool or a chair, in a safe way. It is important that the child has a comfortable access in order to place his hands in the sink, to turn on the faucet and to freely move his upper body. It is similar to a blank paper handed for drawing when nothing has been drawn yet, and it a *tabula rasa,* a blank board for artistic genesis.

Statement of Initiation

The child's interest in "playing" with water needs to be verified before initiating the process. Therefore, he should be asked: "Do you want to work with water today?" If he answers, "no," he should be asked what substance he would rather play with. If however he answers, "yes," the therapist could announce, "Today we will play with water."

Filling the Sink with Water

The water is turned on , filling up the sink to about a fourth of its height. The noise the water flow makes, immediately influences the therapy experience. Children's response to the sound and power of water is diverse. It can raise excitement, interest or withdrawal. The therapist is standing by the child and helps him turn the water on, and is present as a partner to the excitement of early encounter with water. Through the process of water therapy, the position of the therapist may change. (Read more in the chapter on the Therapist Role- part 1).

To most children, standing by the sink is enjoyable. They are full of anticipation and curiosity, as the sink is part of the kitchen and adult world .

A Glimpse to the Therapy Room

Some kids will immediately say: "in my house I help in washing the dishes," or, "I would very much like to wash the dished, but mom doesn't let me. She is afraid I will break a glass and get hurt."

"Once Grandma let me help her with an expensive coffee set. My mom would never let me!"

Note: In this very early stage we can already detect details of the child's home dynamics and the emotional place of the child in the setting: how he is being treated, how he is being perceived, how he perceives himself and what is his perception on how others perceive him.

Empty sink- before adding color to the water.

Chapter 3

COLOR

Color is the key. The eye is the hammer. The soul is the piano with its many chords. The artist is the hand that, by touching this or that key, sets the soul vibrating automatically. Wassily Kandinsky

Children relate to colors from a deep and natural place. They actually fuse their emotions within with the color they perceive from without. Children's experience with colors is much more intense than adults'. Their high sensitivity to color affects an emotional tuning, they align with the colors they work with. A given color might form a relaxed, pleasant sensation with one child while causing discomfort in another.

In the previous chapter we focused on work at the sink. However, on our way to the water world we will first traverse the world of color.

CHOOSING COLORS

Water play therapy: first graders in Kenya

Choosing colors by the patient is done in a flowing manner – as the patient and therapist walk together towards the sink. The therapist would ask the patient to stop by the drawer containing the paints and have him choose three colors that "he finds both suitable and attractive, today." After the child made his choices, we proceed toward the sink and place the three bottles of color on the surface by the sink.

Next, once the water has filled the sink to about a quarter of its volume, we take a clear jar, pour in a little from the first paint bottle chosen, fill the rest with water and stir, to create a "color extract/concentrate."

A Glimpse into the Treatment Room

Adi, a wondrously sweet and gentle six and half year old girl said: "This is like stirring tea. I am excellent at stirring tea; I drink tea all the time, morning and evenings."

The child pours the extract into the sink. At this magical moment, a thick cloud of color ripples through the water, its expanding motion coloring up the sink. Usually, the first initial reaction of the child is a shout of excitement.

While the paint languorously twirls and spreads, I ask the patient to dip his hands into the color and complete the process of mixing of it up in the water. While his hands meander in the mix, I ask him: "What does this color you have picked remind you of?"

It is important to write down the association that each color brings up, for it holds a deeply seeded emotion that propels the child, meaningfully contributing to the reality he shapes.

A Glimpse to the Treatment Room

Noa, a 10 year old girl, chose yellow and said:" I choose with my left hand, which is the one connected to my heart. I choose an intense tint of yellow that resembles the sun, which reminds me of summer. In the summer I like the most to be in the pool, where the sun is present, really yellow and strong.

Miri, a 7 year old first grade student, chose red. After uttering a cry of excitementin reaction to its intensity, she said: "it reminds me of lips and blood." Later, the association with blood was discovered. (See Chapter 12, Trauma and Birth Trauma, p.255.)

Benny, a 12 year old sixth grader, was a freckled, red head, tall and rather slender boy. His parents divorced when he was three and his father was in a wheelchair due to a work related accident. Benny reached therapy after being bullied by his classmates.

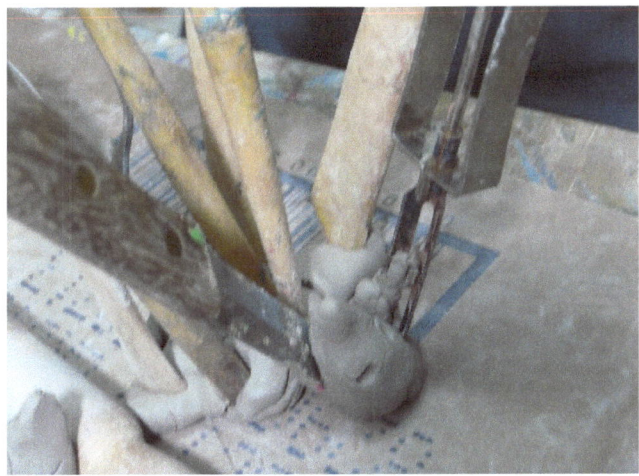

Abuse. A 12 year old expressing anger and vengeance: a work in clay, done during a session prior to commencing water therapy.

*He chose the color **orange**, saying: "It reminds me of my dad; he has dark orange color hair. It also reminds me of hot lava– whatever goes in it burns! I'd have liked to dunk the kids at school who hurt me in lava!"*

Note: With these three sentences Benny brought to the fore his copings with the incidents in school, as well as his sense of identity and self-image vis-à-vis his environment.

Subsequently, Benny went on in his water therapy and built a water world with two main figures, whose names were the same as the bullying kids.' Those figures were pushed, drowned and burned in scorching lava over and over again, Benny feeling great pleasure as a result; he was feeling powerful, in control, healing the injustice inflicted on him.

Orange: a 12 year old who experienced bullying at school

Mixing colors in the jar, pouring it into the water in the sink and triggering associations is a process we would repeat three times, before draining the water first poured in. Thus, different shades and colors are formed just from blending one color with another. The various colors formed also elicit reactions from the children. The younger ones, who do not know what would happen when, for instance, blue mixes with yellow are thrilled with the magic transpiring before their own eyes; others, however, may be disappointed when the color in the jar does not precisely replicate itself in the sink.

At that juncture, the therapist would echo the child's words, toning them softly; for instance, "It did not turn blue. I really wanted it to be exactly that blue!" The echoing of the patient's words, in response to the visible manifestation, serves as an anchor, holding the therapeutic container in place while, concurrently, reflecting issues that literally surface from the water, to be sorted out and discussed in therapy, subsequently. (Read more on the echo and reflection process. See, Chapter 10, The Role of the Therapist, Listening and Reverberation, p.223)

I often ask the patient this question: "If this particular color was in your body, where would it be, in what part of your body?"

The incorporation of a question on the location of a given color in the body, is the upshot to the relationship between body and soul, more common in far-eastern cultures and gaining a foothold in certain current psychotherapeutic perceptions, which stress the strong relation between the inner world and the physical imagery of a given feeling.

There are children who, in terms of awareness, are detached from their body, becoming unaware of their body's signals, as it reacts to their emotional state. The relationship between color and body allows them a renewed interaction with the physical body. It also unlocks for the patient the language of metaphors, which would surface from their activity in the therapy room and then serve as a system of signals for them and the therapist.

As therapy progresses, association of different organs with particular colors often shifts. One boy told me, "I have black in my belly." When we talked about the color black, he explained why it took residence in his abdomen. He described a black whirl which, monster-like, is gyrating in his belly, has denied him peace of mind, constantly reminding him of that which frightens him. Later on, the color changed to deep purple, deep blue and, finally, to light brown. The language of colors gave me the leeway to ask him directly, without resorting to the medium of creative activity, "How is your stomach today? What is its color?" the healing process progressed in correspondence with the shifts of his abdominal coloration.

The association between colors and the physical body also enables therapy to focus specifically on different organs, either with guided imagery, through the use of deep breathing or by exercising physical movement.

A Glimpse to the Therapy Room

Ohad is a handsome, intelligent five and a half year old boy, who loved go through water therapy and each time chose a different color.

Towards the middle of the therapy process he chose silver, and as the color was shimmering in the water, making the water s translucent, he said: "The color silver – it's in the mind!"

Ohad arrived at therapy after his mother miscarried at an advanced stage of pregnancy. At the beginning of therapy we dealt with the loss of his brother and how the strenuous event affected him and his family. After going through mourning, he started to relate to the issues that affected him, personally. He suffered from recurrent constipation, which could last days at a time; he refused to use the bathroom independently and would resort to disposable diapers, exclusively.

Interpretation: The silver color, in his case, meant a sterile, futuristic color. Its inclusion of grey and black shades is indicative of pessimistic and gloomy feelings, symbolizing alienation and sadness. Matte silver transmits inflexibility and stubbornness.

Ohad chose transparent water, on which the color silver floated unevenly. The transparent water symbolizes authenticity, and the silver lining is a kind of self-reflecting mirror. The transparency of the water stands for understanding, hope and the courage to open one's heart and eyes to new things, to things buried in the subconscious depths.

Ohad's choice of silver on the transparent water is consistent with the therapeutic process of removing blocks and emotional inhibitions. It enables him to self-reflect unreservedly and have new insights into his emotions. Silver also relates to sterility and mental rigidity. Since Ohad pointed out that silver is in the mind, one can deduct that there are some rigid predispositions related to mental contents and mental processes that concerns regarding the ability to release, let go, and fluidity.

Ohad, a five and a half years old, made a yellow elixir for the belly. The elixir was produced at the water world in the sink (notice the face appearing in the scribble on the bottle).

COLORS AND THEIR MEANINGS

Color is all around us: it is everywhere, it pops up in our neighborhoods, clothes, food, our eyes' color, beddings and the dreams we dream as we lie on them; and though they affect us consciously, mainly their effect is subconscious. Our choices in life, aesthetic perceptions, attraction and mood are all affected by colors. Therefore, one's mood can be altered with the use of color. Similarly, ambience can be molded and healing brought about by employing color. Colors contribute to the formation of internal and external reality both on the micro level, in each person, and on the macro one, in society. Every person may be attracted to a preferred color, be it momentarily, periodically or for an extended period that would last for years.

Color serves as an important tool in water therapy. Therefore, one of the first questions in the therapy room should be "what is your favorite color?"

WHAT IS COLOR?

Color is a form of radiation, occupying certain range of the electromagnetic spectrum.[5] Visible light falls at the middle of this spectrum and contains the eight colors of the rainbow. Wavelengths of visible light are as strong as sun rays reaching earth. In research conducted on effects of sunlight on the human body, it was discovered that, among others, light affects enzymes and hormones, sometimes

---

[5] The electromagnetic spectrum may be defined as the entire range of wavelengths or frequencies of electromagnetic radiation, extending from gamma rays to the longest radio waves, including visible light.

causing strong physiological reactions. Since reflected colors (pigments) are forms of radiation, they can affect the body as well, though in more subtle ways. Other research shows that shining different colors affects different parts of the brain and have an immediate effect on our moods.

HEALING WITH COLORS

Healing with colors is most likely an ancient form of healing; prehistoric man's knowledge of nature and the food he consumed, as he lived in caves in natural settings, and was ruled by the seasons, high the tides, his activities subject to the dictates of light and darkness – all of these serving as sources of color, tints and shades.

There are also writings, traced to ancient Atlantis, describing how, during those days, physical, mental and emotional ailments were treated with crystals which were used in order to radiate colored lights. healing in Atlantis took place at a vast temple of healing that had a capped ceiling made of colored quartz[6] arranged together in the shape of ancient symbols. The temple of healing also had individual rooms of different colors, used for individual treatment. (See, Colour Therapy by Pauline Wills).

The ancient Egyptians, too, had diagnostics rooms in their temples, where sun rays entered and were refracted into the colors of the rainbow. A patient would be placed in a room with single ray of the color considered the one suitable for his treatment. The Egyptians also healed using precious stones, they believed held the colors of the universe in a concentrated and pure form. Ibid.

Since, vast research was undertaken in an attempt to prove the power and significance of color in our inner world. In 1666, Sir Isaac

---

[6] Colored varieties of quartz include citrine, rose quartz, amethyst, ametrin, smoky quartz, milky quartz, agate, onyx, jasper, carnelian, prasiolite, tiger's eye, rutilated quartz and others.

Newton already discovered that light rays may be refracted, individually. Scientists thus started to notice a connection between light and color and the latter's effect on human being. Other research showed that a change in one part of the sensory system affects its other parts as well as the emotional state of the subject. For instance, an office painted blue caused employees to complain that the ambient temperature is too low. When it was repainted yellow, the complaints stopped. In fact, it was exactly the same temperature.

Colors have a very significant effect on our sensory system. Each color has a different wavelength and characteristics of its own, Each activates certain systems in the body. The German Philosopher Goethe claimed "color is a live entity," believing color has a spiritual value.[7]

Just like Goethe, Rudolph Steiner, who, in 1919, founded the Anthroposophist society, believed colors have momentous effect on human health and consciousness. Steiner believed that illness is created as a consequence of the separation of material awareness from higher perception, which may be cured by artistic activity and color therapy.

In Switzerland during the early twentieth century, Dr. Max Lüscher explored the effects of color on human nature. (Lüscher argues that a subject's choice of color shows the state of his psychosomatic and emotional status and how he feels about himself.) Lüscher conducted his research on patients in psychiatric wards and discovered that different personality structures and mental illnesses, or the risk of incurring such, can be psychologically diagnosed by the patient's choice of a particular order of a given number of colors.

As a result of a many other studies it is possible to ascertain that color

---

[7] Goethe outlines his method ((original German title *Zur Farbenlehre*) in his essay, *The experiment as mediator between subject and object* (1772).

has an effect on plants, animals and human beings and that different chemical reactions are created by different colors. All in all, current findings show that matching the ambient colors to the person may have a far reaching effect on the individual's degree or rate of concentration, relaxation, healing, pleasure, joy and appetite. Consequently, choices regarding color are made nowadays at work sites, hospitals, clubs, restaurants, schools, kindergartens, prisons and elsewhere.

Examples of Different Colors in the Sink

The Magical Sea. Elian, a seven year old girl.

Clouds. Yaron, a 10 year old boy.

CHARACTERISTICS OF COLORS

Each color has unique qualities that can help the therapist in diagnosis and enable healing. Many theories associate color with its effect on man in both its physical significance and psychological one. My experience as a therapist shows that choice of color is unique to each individual. Accordingly, each color's symbolic meaning is individual as is its effect. There are numerous perceptions and I have chosen to present one which, as a result of observing therapeutic processes in water, I have found to be most suitable. It is detailed below.

COLOR CHARACTERISTICS IN ORIENTAL CULTURES

Healing processes in oriental cultures are based on the assumption that all colors are in harmony in all aspects of the human body, i.e., the physical, mental, emotional and spiritual. The lack of one color would disrupt the balance and cause illness. Therefore, that which is wanting has to be made whole through exposure to the missing color.

According to these perception, the chakras[8] are major centers of life force energy, placed along the "ethereal spine." They serve as transfer points of the life force (chi) to the physical body. There are seven such energetic centers associated with the human body. When all chakras are open and energy flows through unvaryingly, a white aura forms and wraps the person up. The Indians discovered that energy in these energetic centers swirls from the center outwardly to the aura – an electromagnetic field enveloping us.

---

[8] Literally, chakra means a wheel in Sanskrit; these are centers of consciousness and *prana* (the raw substance that feeds one's life force) in a person's being; they are sensed at major plexuses of arteries, veins and nerves (e.g., the one at the solar plexus), or in the vicinity of major glands (e.g., the pineal gland) though they are not physical in nature.

The following is a detailed depiction of the body location corresponding to each of the seven main chakras, their characteristics and effects:

Table 1 – The Chakras

Name and Location	color	Characteristics	Organs influenced by this Chakra	Psychological and Energetic Influences
Root Chakra Muladhara Between the lower body orifices	Dark red, black	Low vibration, rounded, connected to vitality, physical energy, relays stability and security	soles, bones, colon, spine, nervous system, secretion and sex glands	Libido. When imbalanced - a need for survival, stability and acceptance will rise
Sacral Chakra Swadhisthana Between sex organs and the navel	Orange	Emotions, social interaction, force of life. The color orange relates to intuition, creativity, change and growth. It relates to the immune system and its expression reflects inner strength and sexual prowess.	Skin, female reproductive organs, kidneys, bladder, blood system, lymphatic system, the adrenal gland.	Affinity to self- and social awareness. Enables participation in group activities while enabling individuality. Relates to water; affects bodily fluids. When imbalanced, emotions of fear and anxiety will awaken.
Solar Plexus Chakra Manipura At the solar plexus	Yellow	Self-identity, knowledge, intelligence, elation, optimism, quality communication.	Respiration, diaphragm, abdomen, duodenum, gall bladder, liver, pancreas	Identified with active intelligence. Relates to will power, logic and deeds. Energetic deficiency causes mood swings, difficult in transitions, depression, fatigue, introversion,

Table 1 – The Chakras

				increased need of control, digestive difficulties.
Heart Charkra Anahata Between the ribs	Green	Identified with the element of air and the somatosensory system (tactile sense), emotions, compassion, need for balance, love and empathy.	Heart, blood circulation, lungs and the respiratory system, immune system, arms and hands, Thymus gland (plays a role regarding T-cell).	It has affinity to sensitivity to touch, love and higher levels of consciousness. When imbalanced, there are difficulties in giving and acceptance.
Throat Chakra Vishuddha At the center of the throat.	Blue (light blue, and, at times, appearing turquoise)	A center of purification. Related to various aspects of communication as well as emotional expression. Linked to responsibility, faith and imagination.	This center governs the nervous system, ears, vocal cords, thyroid gland, which plays an important role in metabolism during childhood.	It is a creativity and communication center. It is sensitive to colors, voices and shapes, it is especially active in people active as to all forms of expression. When imbalanced, there are expressive difficulty, attentiveness is lacking and emotional outbursts are not uncommon.
Third Eye Chakra Ajna Between Eyebrows	Purple, indigo	Characterized by its affinity to all things related to spiritual consciousness; enables inspiration and relates to the seeking perfection.	Eyes, nose, ears, brain, pituitary gland. When dysfunctional fatigue, nervousness, confusion and stilted thinking ensue. Imbalance may lead to sinus problems, rhinorrhea, hay fever and migraines.	It is a center of prediction and insight. Relates to mental stress and insomnia. Imbalance may trigger defense mechanism of rationalization, detachment, day dreaming, insecurity, indecisiveness, stress and cynicism are.
Crown Chakra- Sahasrara At the tip of the head	White (with gold above it)	Symbolizes eternity, infinity; pure, unbounded consciousness.	Biological clock. Regulation of puberty	Affects mood and the will to sleep. Helps in healing and love. When dysfunctional - confusion, existential qualms, life becomes disharmonious.

RELIGIOUS AND CULTURAL SYMBOLISM OF COLORS

Certain ancient culture and various religions regard color as revelation of light, i.e., the divine source whence all that is emerges. Colors have taken a central place in rituals and formed a significant element in mysticism and alchemy.

Each color symbolizes a certain quality and more often than not, there is a common characteristic associated with a particular color among different cultures, religions and beliefs across the world, even when separated by great distances. (Though, due to local proclivities, a certain area or culture might associate a different quality with a given color, than the one it has attained in most other parts of the world.)

The therapist should be attuned to how the child describes color, and explore its origin in the child's psyche. When working with children from different cultures, awareness to cultural contexts of colors is required. Some of the issues that surface during therapy arise from the child's sub-consciousness, which is tied to the collective consciousness,[9] where symbols and archetypical connotations, that may have sprung from various origins (such as cultural, religious, etc.), or that may have been derived from different sources worldwide, have been assembled.

Occasionally, understanding the source of images where the child draws upon, may lead the therapist to a whole world of experiences, beliefs and emotions, which drive the child from the inside out and have no equivalent in the child's outer reality.

---

[9] "My thesis then, is as follows: in addition to our immediate consciousness, which is of a thoroughly personal nature and which we believe to be the only empirical psyche ..., there exists a second psychic system of a collective, universal, and impersonal nature which is identical in all individuals.... It consists of pre-existent forms, the archetypes, which can only become conscious secondarily and which give definite form to certain psychic contents." C. G. Jung, *The Archetypes and the Collective Unconscious* (London 1996) p. 43.
Mary Kelsey, sociology lecturer in the University of California, Berkeley, used the term to describe people in a social group, mothers for instance, becoming aware of shared traits, conditions and values and, consequently, acting as a community and reaching solidarity. People come together – instead of operating separately – as dynamic groups and share resources and knowledge. It has also developed as a way of describing how an entire community comes together to share similar values. See, John D. Greenwood, The Disappearance of the Social in American Social Psychology 2004, p. 110.

THE MEANING BEHIND THE CHOICE OF COLOR

When children choose the colors themselves, they reflect to the therapist the stages of healing they need to go through and the direction they therapy should focus on. Accordingly, when an there an energetic blockage occurs, it might assume expression through the use of a particular color. For example, children who suffer difficulties in their emotional expression often choose to color the water world blue, which relates to the throat (see Table 1 – The Chakras, at pp. 67-68. This choice demonstrates their need for healing in that specific area. My experience with treating children suffering from selective mutism shows that choosing blue during water therapy had a major importance and, indeed, helped healing that particular impediment. (For more on therapy of selective autism see, Chapter 14.)

The Choice of color is entirely individual. Some children insist on certain hues and tones of color; I often feel the colors chosen represent an emotional area they wish to address.

Ohad, the five and a half year old boy who lost his unborn infant brother, was brought in for therapy in order to handle his grief. Early on in the treatment he chose the color green, which stands for life, growth and healing of the heart.

Gali, a eight years old girl. Social difficulty,
red water – here, red stands for anger.

The Effect of Color on Emotional Processing

Researchers from the Brain Mind Institute at École Polytechnique Fédérale de Lausanne in Switzerland studied the immediate influence of light and its colors on sensory processing of emotions in the brain, using functional magnetic resonance imaging.[10] The research demonstrated that there were significant effects of spectral colors (caused by refraction of light) on the way the brain processes emotional stimuli. Brain activity of healthy volunteers was recorded while listening to "angry voices" then to "neutral voices," while exposed, alternatively, to either green or blue light. It was determined that exposure to blue light increased reaction to emotional stimulation in the hippocampus, the "voice area" of the brain, which is also significant in memory processing. Exposure to the blue light also formed a strong interaction between the amygdala, a key organ in

---

[10] Functional magnetic resonance imaging or functional MRI (fMRI) is a functional neuro-imaging procedure that uses MRI technology measuring brain activity by detecting associated changes in blood flow. The technique relies on the fact that cerebral blood flow and neuronal activation are coupled. When an area of the brain is in use, blood flow to that region increases concurrently.

generating emotion, and the hypothalamus, which is vital to regulation of biological rhythms using light.

That research proved that the functional organization of the brain is significantly impacted by blue light. Consequently, ambient light appears to distinctly affect emotional processing and have long term effect on one's mood.

The Effect of Color on Emotional Memory

Research that examined the relationship between color reception in the retina and its effect on the brain, specifically the lobes related to the sensory system, emotions and central nervous system, ascertained that the way we see the world and perceive it through our sensory system is the way we will remember information, emotionally. Thus, if we experience a pleasant event where a certain color is dominant in the setting, the color will fuse with the emotional experience as it registers, through the sensory system, in the brain and will be etched there as a pleasant memory. When, on adifferent occasion, we see the same color we will immediately associate it with a pleasant feeling. (For more on the relationship between the sensory system and emotional memory see Chapter 9, Memory, p. 179.)

Another example illustrating the relation between mental state and choice of colors can be seen in the yellow period of Dutch painter Vincent Willem van Gogh (1853-1890). Nowadays Van Gogh is considered a major Dutch Impressionist, however, during his life he suffered poverty and privation, never becoming either successful or celebrated. Most of his works were drawn and painted during the ten years preceding his suicide, that followed a depression he had suffered. It was only after his death that he achieved recognition for his artistic expression. There was extensive use of yellow during the time he suffered from depression, highlighting the severity of mental state.

Bedroom in Arles (1888)　　　At Eternity's Gate (1890)

Vincent Willem van Gogh

A Glimpse into the Therapy Room

While I interned as an expressive arts therapist at a psychiatric hospital in Israel, I treated a group of female patients in the closed ward. At one of the encounters, I let each choose a color for the day then draw anything which the color represented to her. One of the participants was an 18 year old Jewish orthodox girl who suffered from catatonic depression and would rigidly sit in a chair, like a statute, neither talking, moving or making eye contact with those around her. Each patient chose a color and started drawing on paper.

I then approached that girl, trying to persuade her to try. I offered her to choose one that suited her the most, that day, from a small basket with colored pencils in it. Many moments later, her hand reached in and picked the yellow one. While checking on the others, I glanced at her every so often and saw her just holding it still, seemingly forever frozen in that posture.

I made a round, asking the patients to show me their drawings and explain the choices they made. Then came the girl's turn. She did not speak up; when all the other patients left, she stayed back, unmoving. I approached her and asked: "What did you paint with the yellow pencil?" She did not raise her head, the sheet of paper looked as blank as ever, then she whispered: "A yellow dot." I looked carefully and, indeed, practically invisible, there was the yellow dot close to the edge of the sheet. I turned to her and said : "I see you, yellow dot!" She raised her eyes, there was a smile nested in them. That was the first time she talked since she had arrived at the facility. The use of color and art allowed her to express her feelings, as though saying: "I am transparent, nobody sees me, I feel like a tiny, yellow dot."

So, since patients' autonomous choice of colors, in a specific order, points subconsciously to their emotional and mental state, it directs the therapist to the manner and color of healing they are in need of at that juncture.

COLOR PRINTS

First Print

After choosing the color, stirring it in and placing hands inside, the sink is being emptied out. This latter event changes the picture entirely. Some of the kids wish to put their hands in and touch the remnants of color stuck to the bottom of the sink. Ask them to wait, take a sheet of paper, not too thin, that would approximately correspond the size of the sink's surface. After the water had drained completely, place the paper at the bottom of the sink and tighten it down with your palms. At this stage, allow the child to participate.

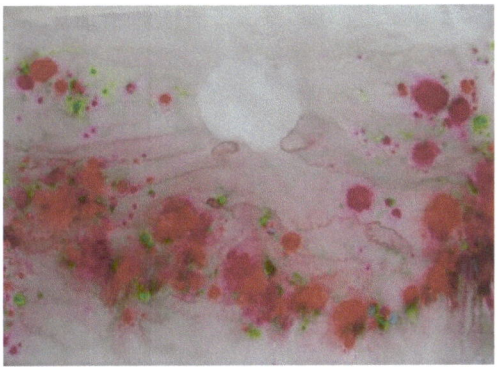

Tomer, a nine years old. Flowers.

A Second Print

After the print is made, the children can touch the paint's remnants left in the sink and smear that joyfully on the edges of the sink. A second print can then be made.

Tomer, nine years old. A man drowning.

Additional Prints

The process can be repeated several times, as long as there paint remnants left in the sink and the child finds interest in the magical prints being produced.

A Glimpse into the Therapy Room

These pictures show the work process of Daniel, a six year old boy. He arrived at therapy following social difficulties in kindergarten. During therapy it became apparent that the family system and inter-parental relationships were in a state of crisis, which festered beneath the surface. These are three prints made and named by Daniel.

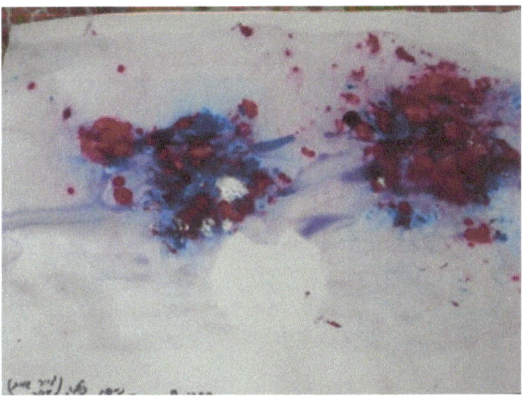

Convergence

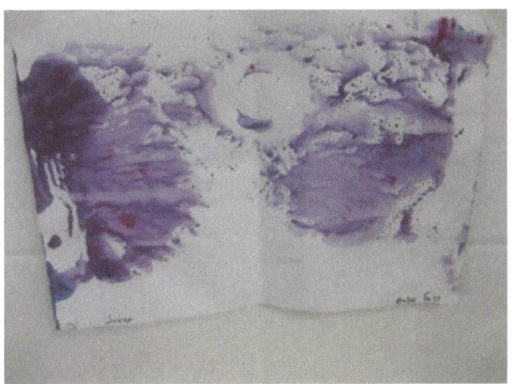

Turbulence

Avalanche

This is how such prints are made – lumps and smears of paint, stuck to the bottom of the sink, are adhered to a sheet of paper. This technique is well known and is often used in plastic arts. It was added to water therapy by another art therapist, a colleague of mine named Yael Shalom. Yael Shalom reached art therapy from plastic arts, and specialized in treatment with color, from a creative orientation that is enabled by such medium (the sink).

Another example to how prints are formed. Stains and lumps of paint that remained in the sink, imprinted on paper.

A Glimpse into the Therapy Room

A six year old boy who was treated by Yael, used to repeatedly play the same board-game, rebuffing any attempt to have him play any other game or engage with any other media in the therapy room. After a few weeks, during which the phenomenon repeated itself, Yeal felt the treatment reached an impasse. Any and all advice given her by colleagues, in order to resolve the predicament, was to no avail. In a discussion we had, I suggested she have a go at water therapy. to her great delight, the boy agreed to try and found it agreeable. While working with paints in the water, Yael suggested that he might want to print the remnants left in the sink after draining the water. The result was remarkable. a stain that looked like an embryo appeared on the paper, surrounded by a circle as a background.

A Glimpse to the Therapy Room (by Yael Shalom)

Gill, a five and a half years old boy, arrived at art therapy after a debate ensued as to his readiness and mental maturity to cope with transitioning to first grade. His parents also reported he had behavioral patterns that hinted at a deep seeded fear: intense nightmares, bed-wetting and nail-biting.

During our first few encounters, Gill opted, for the most part, for board-games and avoided, almost exclusively, any contact with any other materials in the room. Later on, however, he chose to play inside a Playmobil^R house, placing various furniture and human figurines in the different rooms. When He finished placing these, he would repeatedly improvise plays about a masculine "Mr. Sleepy" and a little infant that, time and again, would end up being thrown in the garbage. This game repeated in different variations throughout the next few encounters.

Note: The combination of various components that included Gill's repeating playing the same game over and over again and avoiding contact with other materials, as well as his avoiding counter-transference sensation from me, led me to feel that there is a need for therapeutic intervention in order to mobilize and open up the issues with which Gill was struggling. At that stage I adhered to the advice of my colleague, Yael Shalom-Bar'am, and resorted to water as a means of therapy.

Initially, work above the sink included preparation of various extracts of color for any number of uses. Gill was excited by the different materials: glitter, water, color paints, glue, all of which would be blended together in a jar and form a "concoction."

Note: The technique of forming a "container within a container" generates a sense of safety and protectiveness, and allowed Gill to feel as if in an intimate, secure surroundings. The kitchenette is located in the larger space of the therapy room, which "contains" it, the jar into which the materials are poured is located in the sink, and within all of these, Gill finds a place that enwraps, holds and protects him.

"The next few meetings were characterized by much ado by Gill around the sink, paints and water. Each meeting would start by picking five paint colors that Gil would then stir into the water with which we had filled up the sink. At times, though not always, Gill added figurines in and around the sink."

Note: "Emptying out the water" constitutes a significant part of working at the sink. This activity might be accompanied with a feelings of relief, well-being, change, dynamic movement and more. Also, when emptying the sink, residue of paint colors left unmixed appear in remaining puddles of water. These puddles comprise the essence of the whole of process conducted at the sink that day. This residue leaves a sampling of material imprint from a process that would eventually be washed away by tap water. At this stage a sheet of paper, comparable in size to the sink's surface, may be place there on the residual puddles of color and an imprint made of the leftover colors in the sink, a process that may be repeated several times.

"Gill was very enthusiastic about making these imprints. It led him to make assorted images in the sink, then imprint them on paper."

Note: The free style entailed while working with color paints in water gives room to creating pliant, amorphous, fluid works, yet one that yields spectacular and surprising esthetic results.

"Gill was moving on to experiencing a new and interesting medium, a process through which he reached greater and greater depths. At one of the sessions he expressed a desire to be 'a real painter.' We hung sheets papers above the sink, and, using observation, Gil painted the figures of Tarzan and Jane with a brush.

"In another encounter, Gill created a murky swamp and buried in it all kind of things. His mother, who was present at the session, was asked to guess what was placed inside the swamp, then to fish out whatever was in it.

"In yet another meeting, Gill created a whole project out of paper, color paints and water. He started out by folding small pieces of

paper, immersing them in a small container of liquid paint, opening the folded papers, creating an element of surprise, for there is no way of knowing how the color settle in the folded areas. Gill folded, dipped and opened many pieces of papers in this manner, until they all made one large unified work of art.

Stage 1: the prints are placed on a large sheet of paper. Gil was very excited about creating the prints.

Stage 2: evolution

Stage 3: Transformation

"This creation was accompanied by feelings of value, seriousness, responsibility and purpose. Not once did Gill say: 'I am working very hard,' and continued pursuing the goal he had set for himself."

Note: Working with water and imprinting led to Gill opening up and to a transformative behavioral shift in him. It took a few months of internal, deep, emotional work. During this time, Gill courageously coped with numerous fears that surfaced. Working with water allowed him to dive deep into the unknown and manage fears that lied deep in 'the swamp,' while also creating small fragments of safe harbor in the form of immersed pieces of paper, which together formed the entire landscape.

Some children tend to make the smear color the heart of a session. This choice is, also, significant for the return to a sensory-regressive developmental stage, that serves to complete their unfulfilled needs and experiences. At times, smearing the colors and the joy of this experience allow the child to express chaotic feelings, even loss of control, which may not be allowed within the framework of daily life.

The papers are hung up to dry and then the important stage of cleaning up the sink is arrived at.

Choosing Titles

The prints already formed are laid flat on a horizontal surface, to prevent dripping and smearing. The therapist and child stand by the print, and the therapist asks: "How would you like to call this painting?" The name given to it can be written down on the art piece, and this process repeats itself with the next painting.

Cleaning up the Sink

After printing is complete, the sink is cleaned jointly by the therapist and child, to bring it back to the same condition it had before the session commenced. Cleaning the sink enables a release of emotions that have accumulated during the previous stage, whether positive or negative. Cleaning the sink allows the energy withheld to be released through a concrete act. Some children start singing energetically while engaged in the act of cleaning, some talk about what occurred just prior to the clean-up. Cleaning allows a "time of transition" to bridge between the two stages of water therapy. The therapist should be able to sense if the patient is ready for the next stage of playing in the water world or whether to settle at that juncture for the first stage.

Cleaning the sink brings about closure of one phase and beginning of another in the therapeutic process.

This concludes the first stage of water therapy.

Colors open higher and dormant worlds in our mind and vision. Their powerful force serves the therapy by opening a window to the child's psyche. The use of color could serve to unearth the child's thoughts, reflections, desires and dreams, as well as hidden corners of his personality.

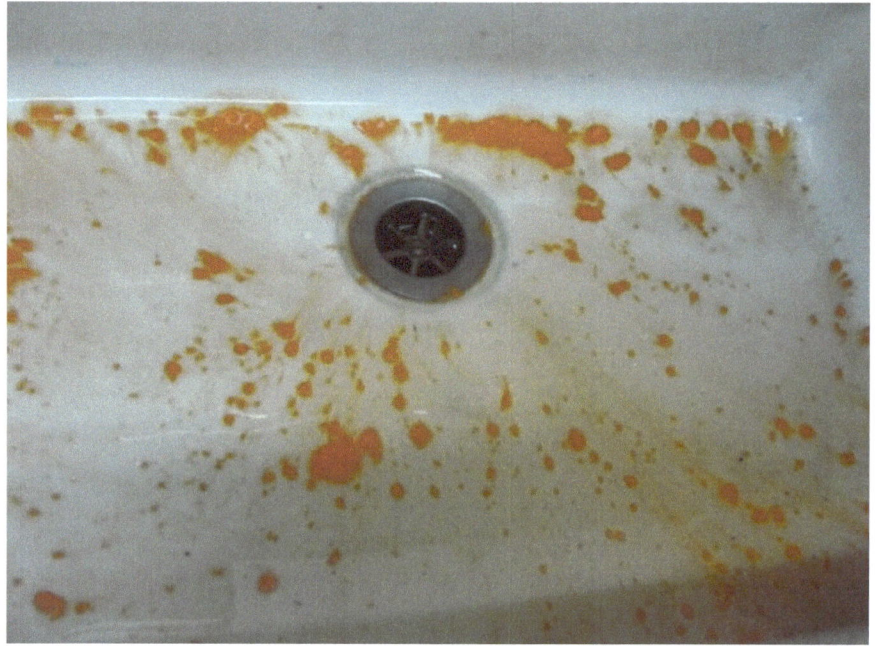

The sink– at the end of the first stage of using paints, just before making an imprint.

THE TOOLBOX

Color as Means of Diagnosis and Healing

The patient chooses 3-4 colors, then stirs them in water one after the other and tells his association each time a new color is stirred in.

Main question in the process:

1. What is the order of colors chosen (see Table 1, pp. 67-68)

2. What are the associations stated in relation to each?

    a. What were associations formed between a given color and a particular body part(s)?

    b. Where could a significant energetic expression or an emotional response be detected? For instance, what color was the most difficult for the patient to associate with? Which association led to further verbal articulation?

3. What was the emotional response to the formation of color stains in water?

4. What was the emotional response to making an imprint of the color remnants in the sink?

5. What was the emotional response to emptying and cleaning the sink?

Chapter 4

GAME PLAYING

Since becoming a mother, game-playing has become an inseparable part of creative and effective means of communication with my children. Such communication resolves many situations where conflict could develop into various stages of rebellion. Using game playing diverts threatening 'blocked' energy into a mode of humorous communication which opens the door for various potential solutions.

A PEEK THROUGH THE PEEP HOLE

In a bathtub full of soap bubbles, my two boys bathe together, accompanied by an army of plastic soldiers, sea animals and plastic cups full of sparkling "soap ice cream." When I come by, to fish them out, I apprehend that my fears have been realized: the bathroom floor has become the floor of the town's swimming pool, the bathroom cabinet turned into a slippery breakwater, and in the midst of this tsunami sail different clothing parts with the bath mat laying peacefully among them. While still contemplating whether to hold my anger or call the Coast Guard for rescue, the shower curtain opens up and a familiar voice shouts: "invader! attack!"

"Right", comes the other voice in rejoinder, "let's wipe out it out!"

At once I am hit by two "water and soap bombshells" that were prepared in advance to counter such eventuality of an assault by a foe. At this stage, my head is wet, my cloths drenched in lukewarm water, I am furious, raging, yet I can still somehow contemplate what to do next. I take a big towel, spread it with both hands, making sounds of a

World War II fighter plane and say: "And then the plane lowers down to its destination to save the surviving heroes who won the mid-ocean brutal battle." The towel aircraft 'hijacks' the younger one from the bathtub while making bombing sounds. The 'second hero' is waving his feasts in a display of victory. And thus they are extracted from the bathtub.

A few moments later I stand utterly lost as I gaze at the "ecological catastrophe" left behind in the bathroom.

PLAYING QUALITIES

Game playing encompasses deep qualities that enable the therapist to spontaneously reach hidden inner layers. This tool is extremely important when working with children, as the expressive dimension is made of both the game playing themes that characterize each age as well as the verbal language skills, which are age-dependent, and are unique to each child. (See Table 1.2 <u>Play and Development</u>, pp.248-249) Game playing allows the teaching of any theme as well as working on behavioral situations, using simulations through Game playing that contribute to behavioral learning experientially. Through game playing, the child can easily articulate what are his feelings and emotions, allowing the therapist to be exposed to the roots of what is clouding the former's psyche.

Game Playing – New, Spontaneous Responses to Routine Activities

Game playing evokes a new response each time it is utilized, enabling a different resolution (of a given challenge) every time. A game, every time it is played, summons new and different types of energy, stimulation and reaction; perspective appears to shift and turn, for instance, could change from the child's opposition, expressing his need of control, for cooperation, joy and intimacy, in the wake of such playful activity.

Example: walking with toddlers in the street can be quite a task. They might tire or, alternatively, energetically burst out running forward and be lost in a teeming crowd. An excellent way to change this routine into play is to hold both of the toddler's hands (one adult on each side), count the steps with him "one, two, three..." and on the fourth just lift it up in the air. This way, a daily walk can change into an exhilarating experience – the young ones usually respond with laughter and, more often than not, request to have the activity repeated over and over again.

Game Playing – a Departure from Reality to a Common Third Zone

Through game playing the participants are transported into an alternative zone, having agreed on making such shift, and accepting the rules that are derived from such acquiescence.

"This is a spontaneous and creative process, in which thought, feeling and action can prosper, as they are separated from fear of failure or devastating results. Play is another way to assimilate new information and make it part of us. We use this process to change ourselves and our perspective of the world. We dare making changes as our autonomy is not threatened. The process of play gives us a wonderful sense of increased and satisfying autonomy." *Play Therapy*, by Linnete McMahon.

Likewise, the German Psychologist H. Heusinger argued back in 1949 that, The dynamics of game playing occurs in a pre-marked playground, whether personal or cognitive, directed or freely chosen. All play worlds are transitory bubbles within the real world, devoted to the performance of detached activity. there is a different order in a playground the rules and customs of daily life do not apply.

Play has definite boundaries and rules, that exist in a either theoretical or actual context that is well-defined. These allow us to experience, dare, fail, create, exaggerate, compete, and express aspects and traits of our personality without judgment or criticism – which, as a rule, we do not allow ourselves in our daily life. Psychologists Robin Skynner and John Cleese said (in 1983) that play can only exist in a safe environment, which provides both time and place, so that the child knows where the game 'starts' and where it 'ends' and when the everyday rules are reinstated.

Play is a Serious Matter that enables

Adults, too, play and their games are serious: sports, social games, foreplay as part of intimate relationships, computer games and more. When adults play, they can revert to being children, for a moment, even forget duties and responsibilities of the grown-ups world, for playing is an enabling situation, where simple joy, going with the flow and the ability to tune in to the here and now comes into being.

A healthy Spirit Makes Play Possible

The ability to play is indicative of a healthy mental state. Mentally ill individuals often have difficulty understanding and implementing transitions between reality and the world of imagination and agreeing to participate in make believe activities.

A Glimpse into the Therapy Room

During my year of internship at a psychiatric hospital, I led a weekly female Psychodrama group in the closed ward. It was during the time before Jewish New Year's and the subject of the meeting was, "wishes we would like to bestow on ourselves as the High Holidays approached."

One of the participants was chosen to play the Lord blessing the women. They stood in line and approached, to be blessed by God with the wish they had for themselves. This game of "make believe" was going on nicely, with much joy and excitement, until suddenly, toward the end of the line, there came a young woman of Ethiopian descent, stood in front of "God" who put her hands on her head for a benediction, when the young woman started mumbling louder and louder: "No, this can't be... no, this can't be, God cannot be seen."

FOUR STAGES OF GAME PLAYING IN THE WATER WORLD

The Relation between Imagination, Play and Dreams

Imagination is what dreams are made of. It serves as a mental and spiritual platform for an inner perceptual world and engenders a subtle though profound awareness of the soul. Imagination's perception has an experiential dimension: we can imagine sounds, rhythm, motion, action, verbal messages and picture, as well as feelings and emotions. As in a dream, so when we engage our imagination, we can, for instance, experience the dynamics of swimming, hear a song, people talking or see an vivid picture of a given landscape. We can refer to all of these as: **The media of the imagination**. They appear mainly as we either dreaming, day-dreaming, free association or engaging in artistic expression.

In the water world processes happen at different levels, through the quality and meditative influence water has when coming in touch with a patient. The child's brain-waves change from alert to relax as a result of the feel of water. The state of relaxation, enables the utility of game playing where active imagination is actively integrated into the process.

Brain waves are electrical frequencies the brain produces for different levels of attention. The frequencies are measured in units of Hertz:

Delta – 4 Hz – typical of sleeping state
Theta – 4-8 Hz – a penumbra state between being alert and asleep
Alpha – 8-12 Hz – a state of relaxation
Beta 1– 14-16 Hz – a state of concentration
Beta 2 – 16-20 Hz – a state of concentration together with some alertness
Beta 3 & 4 – 20-30 Hz – a state of vigilance and high alert.

When the child is in an alpha state, memories and events surface from his sub-consciousness and he becomes aware of them. Playing with water enables the floating up of suppressed contents, as it is done by way of guided imagery with adults whose verbal ability is not well developed. Ideally, the brain moves to a certain frequency in accord with its needs. The ability to move from one frequency to another, as required, indicates the presence of good mental elasticity, which affords higher cognitive abilities, which is indicative of enhanced functionality in all areas of life. Therefore, the conscious state of a child, while playing with water, resembles in many ways the state of dreaming, where submerged contents surface, drafting a new narrative, designed to cleanse disruptive residue from the unconsciousness.

ACTIVE IMAGINATION ACCORDING TO CARL JUNG

Carl Jung, Freud's foremost student, is the first psychoanalyst that endowed the sub-consciousness with characteristics of both a soul and collective consciousness. He described the process of playing as, "enacting fantasies." Jung noticed that symbolic game playing enables the withdrawal of some early emotional contents that hold in them conflicts, forces, desires and dreams, and in turn activate an apparatus of internal psychic images. Jung shared: "The years I chased internal images were the most significant in my life." He called this process of finding the internal images: the "active imagination."

Active Imagination Occurs in Two Stages:

1. The sub-consciousness has to be allowed to become perceptible. When the sub-consciousness is 'out in the open,' it unleashes fantasy. When fantasy is let free, the therapist has to observe it carefully and attentively.

2. Reconciliation with the unconsciousness.

   Jung concluded that emotional states can take on a form and manifest in different ways: through imagery, dreams, a yarn of fantasy. These states are expressed by free-form playing, painting, sculpting, drama, dance, movement, writing, thoughts and verbalizing. By giving a form to unconscious substance, its meaning can be understood and conclusions drawn.

The medium of imagination appears in each of the forms of dreaming, imagination, play and art. They always appear in format of fusion, i.e., each of the forms combines some senses, not just one. For example, a scene in a dream can have sound, movement, color, music, text, etc. In dreams we are rather passive. As it takes place before our eyes it is akin to watching TV, while in daydreaming there is partial control by the brain.

Artists and other creative individuals make use of the ability to move between uncontrolled imagination, that appears in an artist's mind, and the ability to express the medium of imagination in real life, taking it out of private confines to the arena of common human experience.

During therapy sessions with children, I feel greatly obligated to understand their internal and external worlds, both at the verbal level of contents and emotions as well as at the visual, sensory level. Each person hold a repertoire of visual, sensory and emotional images, which he unfolds throughout therapy. Each person has a subconscious form, where broader association and ascription coexist with words, shapes, motion or voices. For example, the image of a house can take different forms in painting, sculpting, play, etc. When these forms are revealed, the child can be helped to form an emotional-mental wholeness, while at the same time there is a opportunity to enter with him into the unknown: chaotic, places and spaces, helping him to reorganize these.

THE FOUR STAGES OF PLAY IN WATER

The four stages of playing in water correspond to the four stages of dreams, as delineated by Carl Jung, which include: (i) Exposition (setting, place, protagonists, the initial situation); (ii) Development (action, complication of plot, tension development); (iii) Climax (culmination, change in situation, something quite different happens); (iv) Resolution (solution, outcome, the prescription of the Self).

Exposition – The Visual Place Takes Form

Building the water world, the child starts the healing process with a sink full of water dyed by a color of his choice, which serves as the focal point of the work. The child adds in more components, such as water plants, islands, rocks, etc. He should not be guided during this stage, but choose the components on his own from a 'picture' formed in his mind. Then, the child would relate to the area surrounding the sink, which may symbolize land, and incorporate it into the game playing in various ways: placing trees and plants in there, rocks, soil, grass, bench and the like. After demarcating the area, the figures participating in the enactment are chosen.

There is a lot of significance to the animals chosen to be placed in the water.

Water World – the Lizards' Pool – Oded, a six and a half year old boy.

A Glimpse into the Therapy Room

"There are no dangerous animals in my water world" I was told by a girl, who had hard time coping with aggression and fear.

No dangerous animals in the water world of this seven year old girl.

In contrast, a six and a half years old boy chose to have two alligators live in murky, muddy color water, and said: "these are two brothers who live in brown water. If they don't have food to eat, they devour each other."

Some children might put in the water animal figurines that in real life are not identified with water – since water, as would a dream, can contain whatever is placed in it. Take Yuval, for instance, a gifted eight years old boy diagnosed with ADHD and adjustment disorder, who was referred for therapy after he had thrown his beloved dog out of a second floor window. At therapy, Yuval stacked a huge pile of all the animals he could find, including mammals and insects, in water he colored turquoise, and only then started sorting them out to those who would remain in the water and those who would be placed out of it.

Note: Yuval was having difficulty separating different components of inner information. First, he placed 'everything' into his emotional system, and only then did he start emotional processing and regulating.

Itay, an eight year old boy: "Two alligators quarrel for the same place."

A Complication Arises – The Initial Setting Leads to an Event Accompanied by Suspense or Activity

After setting up the backdrop and "location," free-form playing begins, during which conflicts develop among the different characters deep in the water or among those on 'dry land.' The energy that rises and bursts out can be easily felt. The events change momentarily. Now the game moves at its fastest pace and concentration is at its peak, accompanied by much movement and vocal expression.

A Glimpse to the Therapy Room

Yuval, the same eight year old boy who, at first, placed all the animals in the water, created the following scene: After placing all animals inside the water, he placed an mother elephant and its calf outside the water on one side of the sink, and a lion attempting to attack a sheep on the other side. Two dinosaurs are added to the lion's scene, attempting to guard the sheep. The game takes a twist when the dinosaurs start to quarrel as to who is going to devour the little sheep. Then a killer whale comes out of the water and attacks the animals who are fighting each other (the lion and dinosaurs); it saves the little sheep (sigh of relief) alas, it then goes on shore and... devours the sheep himself.

Note: The above case stresses the distortion of Yuval's internal world's perception, as the rescuer of the little helpless animal then becomes its predator! Yuval expressed many times his inability to separate reality from imagination, which led to fears and anxieties as well as unpredictable behavior which, at times, endangered his well-being. He was later referred to psychiatric diagnosis.

A Climactic Stage – a Major Event Takes Place

There is a definite climactic moment occurring during the free-form play in the water world. This is when something powerful or unexpected happens, as in the above example, as when a ship sinks, a bridge buckles, a waterfall washes the entire scene away, a volcano erupts and so on. Now and then, it is one of the figures that makes a decision that utterly alters the interplay of forces involved in the scene.

A Glimpse to the Treatment Room

Seven year old Jonathan was referred to therapy for adjustment problems and separation anxiety. He created a bridge with a rail made of plants inside the water world, which he arranged carefully, insuring at all times that the figures out of the water will not fall in. During the game, at the climactic moment, part of the rail drops and the mother figurine (dressed in gray on the right side) falls into the water! After saving her from drowning, Jonathan adds a policewoman figurine on the left side, and a nurse/doctor figurine next to it.

Jonathan, a seven year old boy: "a bridge over troubled water."

Note: All the figurines in the scene are females, including the one he identifies with the most (the big sister by the woman with the suit). In real life, Jonathan's mother is a very sensitive, worrisome mother, who tends to be over-protective of her children and overly identifies with their anxieties. Since she is the dominant figure at home, Jonathan identifies with her. The way he uses multiple female supportive figures during game playing, such as a guardian (policewoman), caregiver and healer (nurse) is his way of balancing his inner world, as if saying: first my mom's anxieties have to be helped and solved. By doing so, he can handle his own anxiety.

A Glimpse to the Treatment Room

Dror, a third grade student with curly brown hair and brazen freckles on his nose, chose to color the water green; he called it "the Animals' World." He relayed: "There is an alligator and there are fishes in the water, with a woman and a tree outside. The woman falls into the water because the tree she stood on collapsed. There are dinosaurs outside, so the safest place to be at is on trees, where the mugging dinosaurs can't reach. The woman is a mother. She is a little girl, but her dad is not here. He died. There is no one is here for her. Now," says Dror, "three whales appear," as he places new figures in the water. One of the whales is a dad. He does not love the woman-mom. It's not pleasant, so....he calls the other two whales and they kills the mother and place her out of the water." Dror then summarizes the scene, saying "it's unpleasant, but that's how it is!"....

Note: Dror was referred to therapy by his mother due to deterioration in his social situation, also, he followed strong, dominant kids, who manipulated his conduct, taking advantage of his desire to be a included in the group. Water therapy unveiled turbulent, murky and problematic intra-family relationship and difficulties afflicting the parents' marriage. Dror had two older brothers, who, together with the father, are represented by the three whales. Following water therapy it became clear that Dror identifies with the loneliness and isolation experienced by his mother, being an American (in Israel), who lost her father (who lived in the USA), a couple of years earlier.

Resolution – Outcome Derived Facts in a Dream

Resolution is the situation at the end that is desired by the creator in dream state. It can be expressed as a new period, following a chaotic one: the arrival of assistance, the quiet after the storm, and the like. In water therapy, unfolding the conundrum can appear through numerous contexts where solutions are presented, which augur the beginning of a better, brighter future, such as: "And then the infant was reborn," or a more finite solutions: "Then everything was destroyed, everyone fell into the water and died." Sometimes, an external figure arrives and saves the situation, resolving the complication (deus ex machina[11]).

A Glimpse into the Therapy Room

Following the events at Dror's water world, he created an aquarium (see Chapter 5, Preservation, p.98), where the water was green. He placed the mother figurine and a black snake in one aquarium, and three whales in another. In the next week's session, he took the soft furry snake that serves as a pillow in the room, and said: "I will help

---

[11] A plot device whereby a seemingly unsolvable problem is suddenly and abruptly resolved by the unexpected intervention of some new event, character, ability or object.

you sleep. Do you want to hear a story?" And this is the story he told: "There was a snake, who wanted black stripes like everyone else, which he did not have. One day he went to bed and his mom told him: "don't worry. You needn't worry. You, too, will have black stripes. He went to sleep, grew a little, and added black stripes, and then more and more, and then he had lots and lots of friends!"

Jonathan's bridge, as built in the conservation stage after playing in the water world (See chapter 5, preservation, p.98). One can see the different choice Jonathan made, of a "strong" figure walking over the bridge, elucidating the emotional shift he went through while playing.

A Glimpse into the Therapy Room

Another example of a conclusion to a playful scene is that of Idan, 8 year old boy, who found it difficult to express his anger at his father for remarrying following a divorce from Idan's mother. He was afraid that expressing his feelings would cause him to lose his father's love. Therefore, he decided to 'drown' his stepmother, and for a few weeks she was left at the bottom of an aquarium, until he completed the process of acceptance, forgiveness and coming to terms with his feelings about the new situation in his life.

Idan – drowning his stepmother, a solution he devised at the end of a game. During the process of preservation Idan asks to use wet sand "so she would not be able to get out." (On preservation, see Chapter 5, p.98.)

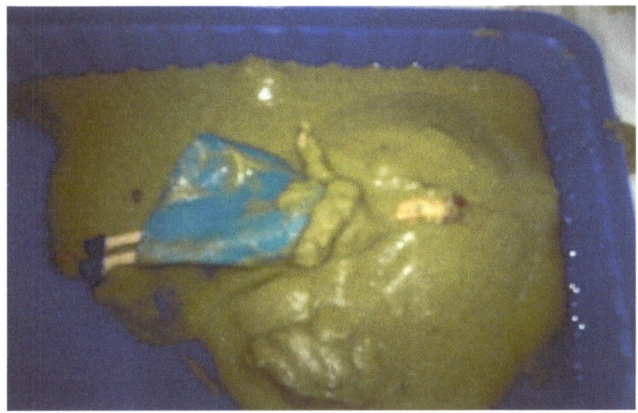

Preservation aquarium - "the stepmother."

the manner by which resolution is formed, is indicative of the patient's perception of the world and the resources he summons in order to solve a given situation. In time, one can notice the adjustment made as to the resources drawn in resolving the plot. Children who experience difficulties in resolving a scene in the water world can be helped by being asked, "How does it end?" or, "So, what's the end of the story?"

Moreover, pulling the plug and draining out the water enables the restoration of peace and order in the world; in effect, bringing about an awakening from dream state and a return to the real world.

STYLES OF GAME PLAYING

Each child arrives at the game's playing grounds with a unique energy of his own, which dictates the character and rhythm of playing. Such attitude is highly indicative of the child's levels of openness, attention, his emotional state and more, and provides the therapist much data, enabling insight into the patient's complicated world. (See, Toolbox at the end of this chapter, pp. 96-97).

Here are some common play patterns that recur at the therapy room:

Flowing Game - a game where the child propels the figures and has them interact with each other; associations flow freely and the therapist does not need to move the events along with words (such as "and then?"). In a game that flows, the plot evolves while building relationships among the different characters. It is important to indicate the age group of the patient in relation to relevant developmental stages and interests that match such age group.

Fragmented Game - a game where the energy of the play-story progression reaches a dead-end over and again, it begins taking shape then the child stops. Some of the children show resistance, using such words as, "I don't know what should be next," or, "and then everybody fell into the water and died," or, "I don't care to work with water any longer." It is crucial that the therapist would read these signs, for such resistance or blockage might imply that a significant issue has surfaced during therapy with water, and the child is, possibly, not yet ready to confront it or, it might be indicative of the surfacing of a memory from the sub-consciousness, one of an unpleasant experience. The therapist may inquire with the child as to the reason for the blockage, or she might just let him move on to another area of the therapy room.

Repetitive Game – a game that repeats itself and usually has the same figures in play. This type of game awakens in the child the need to recreate certain emotional experiences, such as a need for control or for dealing with a particular fear; occasionally, a repetitive game relates to traumatic events.

The Story Model – As the game progresses, a plot is developed in which, at times, conflicts rise to the surface. These conflicts either find resolution or reach a dead end. It is important to identify the overall story structure, which usually has a beginning, middle and end. It is important to check how the problems that rise in the story are solved: whether by the hero or by another figure in the plot, or by an external force, such as forces of nature, super hero, fairy, God, etc.

Shlomo, a five and a half year old boy created this scene of "a family at the lake." Note, the physical isolation of the child.

TO THE TOOLBOX

Diagnosis while Creating the Water World

This stage is characterized by choosing a single color and building a water world, focused inside the water in the sink and at the sink's edges by the water.

Major questions related to the process:

1. How did the patient arrange the **spaces** inside and outside the sink, regarding:

   - esthetic design

   - the placement of objects and figures

   - did he overload the space or kept it rather empty

   - anomalous elements that point to a discrepancy with the area, context, size or content.

2. Which figures were chosen to be placed in the water? Sea creatures, mammals, human beings or other objects.

3. Which figure were chosen to be placed outside the water and which at the sink's edges?

4. What defines the main characters? Is there a major hero?

Diagnosis During the Game – Integration

Main questions related to the process:

1. What is the game style? Is it a one that's flowing, fragmented, spontaneous or repetitive?

2. How does the interaction between the inner part of the sink and the events outside it take place? Or, is the activity focused at a particular area?

3. What is the story model? Has there been any development of the story?

4. How were emotions expressed throughout the game? Were there sounds made? What kind of movement, if any? What facial expressions and body language were observed?

5. What kind of emotions surfaced? Aggression, anxiety, sadness, excitement, joy, etc.

6. What kind of interaction occurred among the figures? What **relationships** had manifested during the game?

7. What contents, images and metaphors surfaced during the game?

8. How were the technical problems solved and how did the patient cope with them?

9. How did the water therapy conclude, once an end was declared?

10. What was the name chosen for the water world? Was there correlation between the name and the event?

Chapter 5

PRESERVATION

Preservation of therapeutic materials is matter of considerable significant in therapy, since preserving emotional processes at different temporal junctions in life, using creativity and art, is the remedy to the sense of oblivion, of a void, to our primal fear – the dread of death – which most human beings have in common.

From time immemorial human culture has been dealing with preservation. In ancient times mummification was used by various cultures, believing this would preserve the dead's likeness in the afterlife, thus allowing their journey to carry on. Ancient cave drawings, traditions, rituals and beliefs preserved the spirit of such customs, as well as the cultural identity in which such preservation was conducted. Nowadays, conservation is focused in any number of areas, including, historic sites, endangered plants and animals, old documents and manuscripts, art, furniture, tools, etc. People visit museums around the world to watch preserved collections which we call art. Everyone is taking pictures and document the little moments of life, as well as the big ones, commemorating the culture in which they live and themselves in it. These acts of preservation lock the moment, the spirit and the creative outcome. As a matter of fact, art reflects, even long after it was made, the non-material energy in the substance. This reflection is like a mirror of the spirit and its constituent elements.

In spite of the difficulty of defining the experience of creating art, it is such artistic creation which remains, once the numinous experience of its creation has faded away. In a therapeutic process that includes drawing out strong emotions through painting, the patient expresses himself in sweeping gestures of hands on the canvas, and he is wholly engrossed in the creative process, body and soul. At the end of the process, the painting is left to dry on the canvas, and transmits the 'spirit' of the event (of its creation) to the spectator.

I usually reserve all works of my patients at the treatment room for as long as therapy of that particular patient is in progress. This act of preservation carries with it deep and extended strata of healing.

Preservation in Art Therapy as Means for Developing Self Esteem and Self-Image

Artistic expressions are significant in therapy of children and youth, in both the esthetic context and the creative-expressive ability. Art creates a tangible product, made of one substance or another, the child can use for measuring his accomplishments. Usually, at the end of the therapy process, we exhibit all art pieces, at which time the child can see himself surrounded by his own authentic creations, including those that are not "beautiful." We walk together in the exhibition, looking, as we reminisce about the encounters we had. The child names his own exhibition. Amit, a seven year old boy, called his exhibition, "Amit – Simply I." Ron, a 10 year old boy, called his exhibition *"the Twisted Journey"* and Liat, an eight year old girl, called hers "Life Party.*"*

To build their own identity, children need concrete values: *who do I resemble? How much am I worth?* Likewise, their self-esteem builds up as they express their inner world and while reflected in their personal reality. It is important for a child to experience success, to feel empowered and to develop self-acceptance.

Observing the exhibits together, is akin to standing on stage in front of an audience. The patient makes his inner world public. By creating art on his own, it is as if he declares to the world: *I am here*! If the children wish to share with their parents the feelings and thoughts that surfaced as a result of the exhibition – these works form a significant basis for such sharing and dialogue.

A 13 year old girl's exhibition

PRESERVATION IN WATER THERAPY

Cleansing and Purifying the Psyche

Preserving the works is an extension of the therapeutic process. While the child's major secrets shall have been exposed by the time of the exhibition, manifested in concrete substances, and he no longer carries then alone, within, he would have realized by now that these can be detached and he no longer need to bear their burden, investing energy in their concealment. The message relating to the child is: *All demons, shadows and monsters can be left behind, here! You can depart to a clean, liberated world. There is someone else who will take care of these!"*

A Preservation Container – "Evils Ones who Kill" –
by Liron, a nine year old boy.

Tracking and Perspective

Preservation of patients' works allows the tracking of therapeutic development regarding information and significance, enabling further development and extension of the issues that came up as a result of the therapy, relating to them from different angles. Moreover, the preserved works allow tracking of choices, the use of different materials, manner of performance and verbal expression accompanying the work. The aquarium is a kind of a bookmark that captures the spirit of the game and the last subject the patient had dealt with, allowing the patient and therapist to go back and recall it; it also allows the therapist to follow the therapeutic progress.

For instance, Oded, a handsome, smart six and a half year old boy, a fraternal twin of Ofri and a brother of two older sisters, was delivered while suffering fetal distress, and both twins were kept for a while in a neonatal intensive care unit for follow up.

When Oded worked with water he colored blue, he created a water world where two infants struggle to survive on a raft he created from a wooden plank he had floated on the water. The main focus of his enactment was the environment where the two infants had struggled in utero. (See Chapter 12, Trauma and Birth Trauma, p.255.)

The infants then were seen each floating on a flower; evidently, he no longer felt threatened.

Oded's first preserved water world.

The next time Oded created a water world, he chose to color the water black. Once more the infants were seen on a raft, this time they were guarded by a pair of frogs. The enactment shifted from focusing on the infants to a sea turtles' family who has to cope with harrowing experiences that threaten their survival. This time an aquarium was fashioned that preserved the new theme: the family that copes.

Oded's Second water world: The twins with guardian frogs. (A close up picture taken during the enactment.)

Oded: a water world in a sink colored black.
The sea turtles' family on the floating leaf.

A preservation aquarium of the sea turtles' family.
The number of sea turtles equals the number of Oded's family members

Feedback – Reflection

Preservation of works of art allows feedback of inner contents, which may be reflected to the patient, as one would be leafing through an old photo album and a perspective of time is thus availed. Reflection enables the patient to meet himself now and then: what have I been doing in the beginning and what am I doing now? How did I feel in the beginning? How do I feel about it now?

An on-going process, the patient uses the aquarium to create a new water world.

Take, for example, Eyal, a tiny seven year old redhead boy, who arrived at therapy after experiencing adjustment difficulties as a first grader. He cried a lot and was responding helplessly to any challenge where he was required to act independently in the classroom or at home. Eyal refused to go outside and play with the other kids at the playground after school, and any separation from his parents felt ominous to him, bringing up anxiety followed with resorting to infant talk, his body going limp. During water therapy Eyal worked on the family theme while arranging families of animals, associated by groups.

A family of tigers arranged at the countertop at the edge of the sink

Eyal was dealing with the matters of separateness and independence while struggling with the question of how to place a distance between himself and his parents, both physically and emotionally, and how to remain close to them. He kept playing in the water world with the tigers' family, focusing on the father-tiger, mother-tiger and tiger cub.

In this picture a tiger family is seen crossing a bridge over orange colored water.

The aquarium he created at the end of his playing was identical to this picture (above). Eyal filled a rectangular container with orange colored water, placed a wooden bridge over it with the family of tigers on it. The aquarium was standing in the therapy room for some weeks as therapy continued and Eyal began to better cope with separation. He started to connect with other children at school and dared, occasionally, to go out to the playground at his place of residence. Then, one day, as he passed by the aquarium, he paused, looked at it, and said: "Now the little tiger can cross the bridge by himself!" As he was saying this, he removed the two parent tigers from the aquarium, smiling contentedly. In light of the process Eyal and his parents went through (the latter releasing over-protectiveness), the statement he made constituted a landmark in his therapy, which also marked his farewell from the therapy room.

THE PRESERVATION PROCESS

The process of preservation takes place a few moments after playing with the water world is done, while the energy of the game is still present at the sink, together with the figures, objects and plot.

Steps in creating the aquarium
Offer the patient to take some of the colored water of the water world and put it in a transparent container, then he choose the objects he would like to put into and preserve in the aquarium such as animals, plants, figurines, rocks ,etc.

Water is taken from the sink to fill a moderate size container, preferably a transparent on.

*

The patient then chooses different elements from his work, then places them in the aquarium.

*

He then arranges these objects into a new, reduced setting in the water inside the aquarium.

*

The patient then may name the aquarium in words (optional).

Yoav, a six year old boy building his Aquarium.
Golden colored water.

The next stage comes after creating the aquarium. You tell the patient: "Now, that we have created the aquarium, it is time to unplug the sink and part with the water world."

The water starts to drain. It is important to pay attention to the patient's reaction and document it. The figurines, the animals, the sailing fleet and all else are taken out; these will now be dried up in a separate container.

Cleaning of the sink – it is important to let the patient participate in cleaning up the sink and bringing it to the state it was in prior to commencing the water therapy. (See, Cleaning up the Sink, Chapter 3, Color, at pp. 77-78.) Emptying and cleaning up the sink serve as an emotional closure and as means of 'coming back to reality.' Also, the patient regains control over his world while engaged in cleaning the sink up.

A Glimpse into the Therapy Room

Seven year old Dalit was referred to therapy when her parents felt she suffers from inner turmoil. She had difficulties choosing and deciding for herself, and nearly every time she was asked what she likes (to have, to eat, etc.), her answer would be, "I don't know." She was described as a complex, perfectionist child, who considered it very important to have precision in anything she does or creates. On the other hand, she was portrayed as shy, introvert and lacking self-confidence. She also suffered from a hearing impairment.

Dalit was a middle child between two brothers – one three years older, the other just a infant. she entered first grade that year, there were none of the kids she knew from kindergarten there with her and her social adjustment was harrowing. Academically, despite her slow paced work, she excelled.

Dalit chosen the color blue (Chapter 1, Water in Our Lives) as she commenced her interaction with the water world. She created a triangular island, with a one tree 'forest' where a single tiger resided. The water world was empty, save for a lone turtle; the countertops at the edges of the sink were utterly bare.

Her creation reflected a great deal of loneliness. Dalit said: "There is a volcano inside the water world. When it erupts, the water turns red."

Note: The volcano by the tree does not look ominous but, as indicated by Dalit's utterances, it appears that things may be brewing beneath the surface. Dalit hinted, that what might appear quite and solitary from the outside is fraught with rage and forceful control on the inside.

The aquarium she made preserved the feeling of loneliness and looks just the same as her expression during play in the water world.

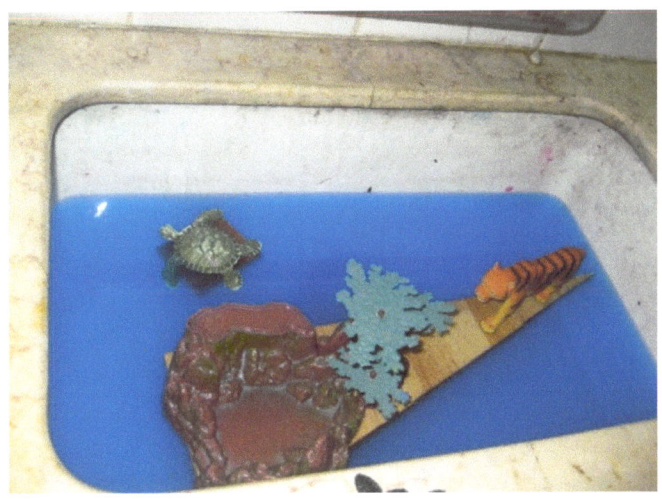

The lonesome Tiger.

In a later encounter with the water world, Dalit used the color red and new characters appeared in there. The island was visible and several water creatures were placed around it: a whale, dolphins, a sea-going cat, a lobster; now, however, no tiger was in evidence! The projective character of the tiger, who served as a guardian – there to be presented to the outside world – was gone. By then, she has given it up. Instead, she now focused on other aspects, present in her inner world.

Untitled

Toward the end of the therapeutic process, Dalit formed a light, nearly transparent, yellow water world and said: "This way you can see the animals inside. You can watch them and see if they feel pleasantly in there." Dalit created an aquarium insisting on adding to the water some gold color, explaining, "This is so that it'll shine in there!"

She devotes much attention to arranging the aquarium, adding details that she had never placed there before: rocks, water plants, coral and fish.

Note: Dalit allows herself and those around her to see her inner world, as it appears in the aquarium: harmonious, quiet, even, to a degree, sparkling. Her ability to detail the inner components of the aquarium, is indicative of the progress she has made in getting to know herself and be in touch with her feelings.

When individual therapy ended, Dalit moved on to group art therapy where she continued to grow, and develop her social skills. She took upon herself leadership roles in the children's group, was comfortable, her self-confidence increased and she began to express her ideas and feelings out in the open.

PART 2

WHAT ARE WE DIVING INTO IN WATER THERAPY?

CHAPTER 6

DEPTHS DISCOVERED IN WATER THERAPY

Through the course of our life we focus on world around us, using our five senses, relating to this reality as being central to our lives. Parallel with this known world, each person has a living, breathing inner world within himself. This world is driven by emotions, associations, scents and colors, and creates the reality which we experience within. Contents of this world surface and are animated by emotional and mental associations, which manage each and every action and thought we have.

This inner world starts to form immediately at birth and some claim that even before birth. Melanie Klein, a well-known psychoanalyst, called this internalization, a quality of the inner world, 'phantasy'.

The phantasy contains first expressions that rise in the mind of an infant as a result of two main factors: (i) his instinctive activity; (ii) his relations with the environment.

Sigmund Freud was the first to talk about unconscious processes, symbolism of mental symptoms and conflicts, but Klein stressed out that the inner world is a tangible reality in itself, not just a reflection of the reality outside, although for the most part it is unconscious. Therefore, during therapy, these two worlds have to be observed and diagnosed. One cannot deduct inner processes directly from observation of the external world. The inner world is influenced by the interaction between the external reality and the internal, developing one.

The inner world of a person requires attention and regard, at least as much as the external one. This world contains desires, dreams, wishes, hopes and aspirations, as well as fears, angers and frustrations. All these and more must receive enough time and attention in order to be released, freed and healed. Klein maintained that children give way to phantasies and unconscious experiences through play, and the characterization is symbolic – hidden just as in dreams.

D. W. Winnicot said that the individual has his whole life to manage his inner world, which includes worrying as to the vitality of internalized objects. According to him, the mother is the major factor in the developing 'mind' and this is the way experiences are internalized, becoming part of a relationship with the inner world (as opposed to our relationship in external reality).

What is this reminding us of? It is just like computer games, where one builds an imaginary world with virtual characters. One will develop a certain attitude toward them, follow them, develop and take care of them so they can exist in spite of certain conditions which may harm them.

This is also consistent with what we know of holographic memory that stores mental and emotional coding of objects, as well as positive and negative states. (See chapter 9, Memory.)

A person's inner world contains also his unique mental powers. These forces live within us even if they are not in daily use, and they serve us when necessary. They are stored so deep, that sometimes it takes a major shock to force them out. Nevertheless, when the therapist lights them up for the patient by reflection and echoing of what is radiating from him, the person can become aware of these powers, and strengthen his natural ability to use them. The ability to preserve the inner world and its elements enables one to maintain hope, love and creativity when dealing with feelings of disappointment or loss that rise as a result of events in the world around.

SUB-CONSCIENSNESS

What is the sub-consciousness? Is this a suppressed element in the depths of an ocean that is our soul? Is it a latent memory from early childhood? Is it ancient cultural associations transmitted in a DNA cast, or a collection of emotional experiences and physical feelings that were processed and cut to tiny particles whose reconstruction takes a lot of expertise so as to make logical sense? It seems that each philosophical, psychological, neurological and spiritual stream has some explanation that stresses the part of the sub-consciousness in our lives. Sub-consciousness is a hidden treasure box of behavioral science, which seems shapeless, colorless and voiceless. Although it is within us, we cannot express it directly (or it would not be *sub-consciousness.*) Nevertheless, it is with us at all times, and through symbolism, imaging, art and dreaming the soul can radiate its innermost layers.

Freud claimed that each experience registers in the sub-consciousness, forming layers upon layers of memories organized in different forms and orders, some on the axis of time, some by the different senses and some by emotional feelings. As a result, each person has a series of memories catalogued by subjects, the association of which are like spider webs. These memories flood the consciousness when there is an association leading to them, or when consciousness is quiet and they can permeate up.

Ken Wilber describes the sub-conscious as small fragments being detached from the central id (I), repressed into a dark area of awareness, where they would stay locked down in a cellar without being able to develop. Guarding the door of this cellar is a defense called "the lie," which consumes some of the mental energy, holding back on the development of the central 'I."

Some parts of the sub-conscious surface up during water therapy.

Water relaxes the child and relieves him from conscious thoughts. When entering the world of imagination, the gates of the subconscious mind open by themselves and the contents surface. Focusing on playing enables symbolization and creating a world of images, therefore the emotional barriers lose their grip when the child presents what's in his heart. The daunting emotions that sometimes attach to these memories do not influence the child while playing, as they do not apply to him but to the animal or figure that symbolizes him. This behavior is called 'projection' as the child projects his feelings on the object or figure in the game.

As progression is made in the creating the water world, the child exposes more and more of his sub-conscious. These are things that make the most influence in his inner world and affect his perception of reality. It is just like a huge chest filled with golden coins, sunk deep in the ocean for a long time, covered with algae and corals. If we want to pull it out of the water, while we are outside, it will take tremendous force to overcome the pressure of gravity. But, if a strong current of water would come, washing the chest from under the sea, it will move the chest from its place and make pulling it more simple and easy to do, uncovering its secrets.

"My life is not a series of objective events lined up like rocks and simple order. My life has deeper subjective components, and I need to understand and interpret them by myself. I can see the surface but it's the depths I need to interpret. The more I interpret correctly the more transparent my life become to me." Ken Wilber

For the therapist to know what are the concealed contents that require interpretation, they need to be expressed in some externalized manner, whether by play, symbolism or metaphor, that appear spontaneously. These externalizations, which use imagination, offer bypassing of brain filtration, easily uncovering contents of the deep sub-conscious, bringing them into the therapeutic space where clarity promotes their interpretation and cleansing.

CONTENTS SURFACING FROM THE SUB-CONSCIOUS

The mental system contains certain fixed amount of energy that serves our mental ability to conduct daily tasks and overcome crises if they come upon our way. This system of energy is akin to a fountain operating in water and circulating 'mental water.' The movement of water in the fountain creates a circular direction of water from the inside out and vice versa. This movement cannot be seen in the deep, only on the surface do these circles grow wider and wider.

Let us think of the conscious mental substance as the 'water surface.' As conscious mental substance is uncovered, floating and accessible, then respectively, the mental substance of the sub-conscious is an 'inner current' that surfaces in life via dream, play, metaphors and imagination.

During water therapy, as the patient is touching the water, contents from down below, from the sub-conscious, surface up, squeezing aside the extant conscious contents, which float above the water.

Gradually these rising contents are better expressed and can be better understood and felt. These hurtful feelings, faded memories, secret thoughts and urges, which were efficiently stored or suppressed, or less so, are revealed to the patient and therapist as the therapy commences.

This process is natural and silent, concerted with the basic need of the person. The soul within us is a smart entity, aspiring to attain balance just as does water as depicted by the law of 'communicating vessels.' Suppression is usually the default, a way to save the system's balance. But cleaning the suppressed emotion and memory is the full, efficient, desired way. When a negative emotion that occupied space in the system, causing blockage, is surfacing up, there is an immediate relief on the child's face, leading to a significant improvement in his behavior and the way he experiences life. Sometimes the change only occurs after some regression, felt immediately after water therapy and causing hypersensitivity. This is a result of pre-organization (re-adjustment), but shortly after improvement can be felt and be noticed .

The soul aims for a new order in the contents of its sub-conscious, while cleaning up needless accumulation. Some of the contents surface easily during water therapy, while others, that lay in the conscious mind, are squeezed aside to either make room or sink downward. This is an ever-repeating circular motion ,allowing for regulation, balance and order, offering inner calmness in and of itself. Torus, as this motion is known in physics, enables recurrent observation and revisiting of the surfacing contents, leading to awareness and ventilation. Even if there is an initial difficulty in identifying the bubbling energy and inner motion, the dynamic circles over the water are easily noticed. The sub-conscious contents would surface, propelled by the images the child is using, the narrative he expresses and the manner he is choosing to play. Many times the patient starts with a water world that manifests a very general statement, but later on the sub-conscious contents come up to the surface one after the other.

It is safe to say that **the process of water therapy is essentially a genesis of an inner world that starts from a simple order, progressing into a complex, two layered one: the one on top is the conscious mind and the lower one, the sub-consciousness. There are two parts to water therapy – the inner one, represented by the sink and its content, while the external one by the sink's edges**. The sink's edges represent the patient's association with reality. They present the view of life's settings, such as family, relationships, physical location and.the like. The edges represent a kind of a holding area, as they are a container where the sub-conscious contents can move to and freely float. When placing the different symbolic elements (representing the consciousness) on the edges of the sink, unconscious processes may develop, appearing not only in the sink but also at its edges.

Therefore, once the patient has defined the limits of consciousness, associations to reality may now bring up sub-conscious contents ,as the limits set are clear and safe. It is similar to working with guided imagery, consenting to set the journey on. This consent sets the limits of the process ":*I now consent to leave from here toward imagination. While doing so I understand that I will also return to reality.*" Indeed, when concluding a guided imagery journey, we say, *"We now return to this room, at such and such time, please open your eyes."*
Similarly, in water therapy the sink's edges form the boundaries of the imagination. Even if figures and elements from reality were initially placed at a given location, through the process of playing, the freedom to create and imagine is exercised, becoming part of an imaginative play. For a clear return to reality we empty the sink and wash it, an action that sends a clear signal to the brain that the previous stage has been sealed off, and now we are back in real life.

Ken Wilber stresses the importance of raising the sub-conscious contents to the consciousness, calling this inner space and action, "the Psychology of the Depth." Wilber maintains that one cannot reach higher awareness, spiritual growth or enlightenment, if some parts will remain stuck in the sub-consciousness, not coursing with self awareness. These parts will hold back the person's development, hindering him from reaching his full potential, balance of life and experiencing love.

A Glimpse to the Therapy Room

Uri, a rather serious 4.5 year old boy with brown eyes and black hair, had arrived at therapy. His parents reported that he had become introverted and were afraid he had communication problems in school. They had moved to a new neighborhood the year before, with Uri and his 7.5 year old older brother, who was diagnosed with Pervasive Developmental Disorder (PDD). They reported that Uri was not making eye contact and that he tends to hide at the entrance to the new school, where he was enrolled for the past eight months.

Shortly after session began, Uri found a figurine of a parrot in the puppets' basket, whom he called 'Shmoolik .' He built a whole world around Shmoolik the parrot. He told me that Shmoolik is a three year old and that his family was lost." We created a house for Shmoolik made of card board. It was a pleasant home and Uri added cotton wool to make it soft. Some accessories were added in time, also, to make it easier for Shmoolik to get along: a sword, binoculars, archery, walkie-talkie.

 As work developed, a mother and a father made of Play-Doh were also placed in the box.

The parrot Shmoolik and his family

Note: The first stage is creating a nurturing container for Uri's projected figure. There is in it symbolism of Uri's emotional blockage at age three. He created external defense mechanisms: sword, archery and a soft place. Uri brings his parents into the container out of a need to protect himself and to protect them. In creating a safe world, the box, Uri can enter the less known zones, as will be detailed below.

Every time he came to the treatment room, Uri would go and see how the parrot Shmoolik was doing, and then tell a different story: One time Shmoolik got lost to his parents at the gas station. On another occasion he got lost at the beach, "then he went to the parrots' life guard booth and said he lost his parents. He was very sad." On yet another occasion, his parents drowned in the shuttering waves, "they shuttered", and one time, Shmoolik's parents were lost in a book store.

Note: Uri dealt with separation anxiety, loneliness and sadness in each of the meetings. Along the way, aggression had appeared, first toward me, then toward figures during play. At the same time, there was an improvement in his life. Uri started to look me in the eye, participated in circle time in school, and became more open, happy and sociable.

About four months into therapy, Uri's parents announced their separation and got divorced. Uri then substituted the "parrot Shmoolik" for a yellow bath duck.

We moved to water therapy. Uri chose colors in this order: light blue, red, green, yellow and black.

The duck was swimming and yelling: "Help! Help!" when Uri made a safety net from plastics. At this time, a dialogue formed between the parrot Shmoolik and the yellow duck:

(Uri is relating: "Parrot Shmoolik is angry with him [the duck] 'cause he ate all his food."

Shmoolik is attacking the duck out of the water, then checking to see if he is dead. Shmoolik throws him food made of Play-Doh that was in the box from an early sessions, then says: "Serves him right! If he eats it he'd die!"

Shmoolik the parrot leaves the sink, takes the box that's the "house", takes out the cotton wool and says: "This house is ruined!" The duck is crying on and on .Shmoolik says: "I will throw you too in the water!" and throws the duck in the water. Then he dives into the water to see where the duck is at.

Shmoolik then says: "You have not listened to me. Now you are being shot with an arrow," and he kills the duck .

Uri then left the role of the parrot momentarily and explained to me: "Because the duck became a infant and doesn't know how to fight, he doesn't have a weapon!" and he then buried the duck outside the sink under the fabrics.

At this time, Smoolik's mother, she too is made of Play-Doh, appeared and said: "What have you done to the cute duck? Why did you kill it? You shouldn't have done that!"

Shmoolik the Parrot must have felt very guilty after what his mother said, as he immediately said to her, "I will eat you, too! You are dead! He then pecks the mother-bird, pulls her Play-Doh tail, and makes a lollypop of her head (the head was attached with a match). Uri then says: "The duck is still alive," and he sticks the mother's heart in his chest.

After that, Uri made an aquarium with turbid water, put the duck in, and placed Play-Doh on its eyes, saying: "Now he has new eyes."

Note: Processing and jolting can be well felt in Uri's water world work, in light of the new situation with his parent's divorce. He is describing something basic that was destroyed, where he was left little and helpless in the wake of the stormy event. It is well presented in his choice to divide himself through the projected figures. Also, his inner conflict between Shmoolik the parrot, who dealt already with the loss of his parents, and the young duck that cries for help, and is helpless to the point that Uri cannot bear his weakness and kills it. The moment Uri kills the duck he asks to "step out" of his role so he can explain. When he does so, he returns to the boundaries of reality to reduce his anxiety, as his self-aggression is heightened. The relationship with the therapist is a safe harbor embodied in the presence of an adult that contains him, strengthens the boundaries of reality, and allows him to maintain the imaginary play. At this stage, there is an emotional transformation where the aggression is redirected towards the real objective – the mother. It seems that Uri has anger in his heart toward the mother and the sense of guilt she creates in him. Therefore, he "disassembles" her both practically and symbolically. Yet, the deep connection between her and the little duck is clearly shown, when he takes her heart and puts it on the little duck, thus reviving him. It is important to see that Uri keeps finding solutions to dealing with situations of aggression, anger, guilt and "disassembly. There is a transformation when the disassembled elements help the little duck to live: the new eyes or the heart, which is received form Shmoolik's mom, who is actually his mom's, too, as the duck is a split, or a shadow of the Parrot Shmoolik. This action is as if Uri says: one needs new eyes to see life.

Later in therapy, in the encounters set for preservation (see Chapter, Preservation), Uri continued to process the change in his family, while bringing out a lot of anger, frustration and conflicts. He managed to express his anger outside the treatment room, and was openly angry with his parents and brother. This behavior demanded a change of attitude on his parents' part, as well as guidance, which ultimately contributed to the well-being of all involved. Sometimes, the process that affects the children radiates to the environment and makes the family move into a different emotional zone.

Chapter 7

THE INNER WORLD OF IMAGES

Each child has a rich inner world which is expressed through symbols, images, colors and stories. Whether the child shares this richness with his environment or keeps the "sights" and "sounds" to himself, they live within him and form his inner reality's landscape. Water therapy gives us a chance to dive into the child's inner world and traverse with him that landscape.

Metaphor and Images

The therapeutic metaphor may be considered a figurative language which enables the child to project his feelings onto objects and figures, thus experience them as less frightening.

A metaphor is arrived at in many ways. The most direct one is an emotional statement manifesting as a direct projection of the child's emotions onto a doll or some other figurine found in the therapy room. Hence, instead of saying, "I feel sad," the child would say, "My bear is sad; he doesn't have friends," which makes it possible for him not to feel overly exposed.

The emotional statement can also be conveyed as an act. For example, the child takes a toy snake, wiggles it as if moving it forward, then turns it toward the therapist and the snake bite the latter. This clearly signifies a statement of aggression and anger yet, while doing so, the child does not openly associate these harsh emotions with himself but projects them onto the snake. In other words, the metaphoric expression is an enactment of a scene, serving – by representation – as a substitute for a real life manifestation.

What metaphors and creative activity have in common, is that both are products of a sensual-perceptual "mix" that transforms into a third, even more complex whole, which often is an amalgam of disparate elements.

A therapeutic metaphor may take several forms during play: language, activity that uses the body or objects, as well as resorting to a visual metaphor. A given metaphor is unique to each person for its formation stems from a broader perceptions of the senses, memory, imagination and mental activity. Each person's makeup is different and unique. Accordingly, metaphor formation will take place in line with such complexity.

That notwithstanding, common elements may appear in different metaphors, such as: superheroes, which are typical of boys in kindergarten and the first few grades in school; the influence of TV series have on kids of different ages; or, religious and cultural contexts in certain communities of same disposition, such as children of religious families or children sharing common experiences, e.g., trauma or a natural disaster occurring in the same region. It is important to notice the individual characteristics within the collective context, as the metaphor forms.

Any specific material used in art therapy also serves as an expressive tool of this kind. When children work with different materials they give deeper expression to their hidden emotions, both in the expressive form and by way of the artistic endeavor itself, both of which are revealed during and at the end of a creative session. Take Jordan for example.

A GLIMPSE INTO THE THERAPY ROOM:

Eleven Year old Jordan arrived at therapy after his parents separated and discipline problems were reported by several teachers. Jordan was both very withdrawn and proud, and had a hard time opening up and sharing his feelings regarding his strenuous relationship of his parents. He wore a thick armor to cover his vulnerability and sensitivity.

After a while, a measure of trust was established between us, and I offered him various materials to work with. He opted for clay, which I laid on hard cardboard, as a bed, and he sculpted a muscular hero figure. As he was working on a clay figure, I saw him taking the clay cutting knife and making small slits in the hard cardboard. He was concentrated on what he was doing and did not let go until actually peeling off parts of the cardboard and scratching other areas. We put the clay creation aside, and I let him go on slitting and slashing the cardboard. This activity fascinated him – he made lesions, cut, slit, peeled, punctured and pulled off entire layers of cardboard, using different tools – knife, fork, tooth picks and other such implements and instruments.

Note: There was no need to reflect these actions to the child. The therapeutic metaphor was clear: I am angry, I am hurt, I peel off all my layers till I bleed.

At the end of the "wounding" process, I asked Jordan to choose a soft material, such as Play-Doh, clay, gouache paint, etc., and Jordan chose papier-mâché. The mixture's preparation, paste with water, was in complete contrast with the hardness of the cardboard material. I asked him to look at his cardboard creation, and choose on which areas he would want to work with the papier-mâché. Now, the process was the reverse of the previous one: Gingery, he got hold of wet paste and laid it on the 'scratches' in the cardboard. He filled up large holes with the paste, while other areas of the cardboard he circled with the paste, distinctly framing them in a way that **accentuated** *the mutilated areas. Several other parts of the defaced cardboard were privileged to be plastered, bridged over with* *miniature overpasses, had band-aids applied to them, etc.*

Note: The artistic creation with different materials served Jordan as means of healing all the emotional pain he had carried all along, which he had found difficult to express. Slitting the cardboard, for instance, voiced aggression, anger and the energy trapped within him.
Working with papier-mâché and covering the slits expressed softness, sensitivity, compassion, a need for shelter and filling up the sense of emptiness he had felt and healing the deprivation he had experienced. It is important to notice, that in this case the therapeutic metaphor appears at the periphery of the artistic creation of a clay figure on which he was consciously focused. Had I disregarded the tangential activity, the therapeutic metaphor would not have materialized, and healing of the requisite emotional would have caved in.

More than anything, Jordan formed a deep bond with himself, as he verbally mapped the different parts of his endeavors, while designating each aspect of his creative efforts with a different title. This manner of declaration as to each particular part, while focusing on it, led to the healing and acceptance of deep emotional injuries. In a subsequent discussion with Jordan, the relationship of each part of his activity to specific aspects of his actual life were brought to the fore.

Jordan started by forming a hero made of clay. Clay, the material which was meant to be the therapy's focal point; a hero – as if saying "I want you to think of me as strong and invulnerable." In reality, the artistic creativity took him to wounded and painful areas, flowing in, so to speak, below his radar screen.

Note: It is important to observe and listen to patients. They would tell the therapist, sometimes clearly and sometimes just by hinting, what they need and what would help them heal. The therapist should listen to them, as well as to her own intuition.

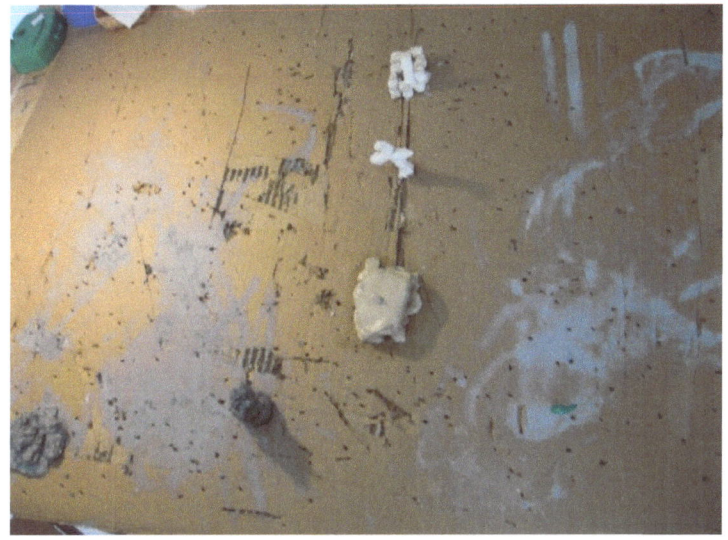

The "wounded" cardboard, viewed from above.

This picture depicts the papier-mâché covering the slits (on the right) and the clay chest, with which the creative work – that ended with the cardboard – started (top left).

Structures created on the punctured cardboard, reminiscent of monuments, totems, tombs and the like.

Metaphorical communication means are rather significant and have the potential of, literally, discovering a child's inner world, the anxieties, desires, aspirations, feelings, fears, beliefs and thoughts he harbors within. By resorting to metaphors, the child can obtain a lucid awareness of his experiences and solve problems. While playing, children construct a scene that is often derived from objects or contexts with which they are familiar from their daily life, thus shape a sense of self and relate to their trials and experiences through metaphors.

Images Can Appear as:

    1. Allegory/parable – a symbolic description by way of allegory or metaphor;

    2. Analogy – utilizing similarity in some aspects between things that are otherwise dissimilar, a form of logical inference or an instance thereof;

3. Imagination – fantasy – turning something imaginary into one that is visible and perceptible;

4. proverbs/sayings;

5. Stories or tales;

6. Art and crafts;

7. Use of objects and figures.

The Effect of Using Metaphors on the Child

Description (or hypothesis) of the inner world. Children can examine different situations and perceptions without criticism, guilt or denial, which capacity enables effective emotional management and problem solving. This capacity could come handy later on, as they cope with various challenges in life.

Experiencing control. The use of a metaphor presents the child with a sense of control, for he is the one creating the metaphor. This experience provides the child with coping tools and strategies. Above all, it makes hope and faith – in relation to his ability to adjust his life – accessible.

Raising self-awareness and re-enforcing sense of self. Use of metaphors by the child enhances his ability to get in touch with his feelings and thoughts. Such contact and expression contribute to his ability to regulate negative feelings he might harbor.

Development of creative thinking, spontaneity and emotional release contribute to the expansion of inner range, enabling release of blocked patterns and a transformation of limiting perception and thoughts.

A Glimpse into the Therapy Room

Eight year old Yaron was working at the sink, creating a blue water world. Around it, he planted trees and flowers in a garden which he fenced in, declaring: "No one may enter this place." A family, two parents and two children, stood there. He then took the two children, attached them to a Play-Doh base, and said, "This is a roller-coaster ... you don't want to know where it's going. ..." He then lifted up the two children stuck them in the Play-Doh, then lowered them down, dipping them into the water, then back up, repeating the cycle over and over. This roller coaster turned from being a fun experience to a life threatening one.

Note: The use of the term "roller coaster" conveys the visual and emotional association of a pleasantly exciting experience for children in an amusement park; however, the body language embodied in an activity where a roller coaster is immersed into water, with small figurines in it, created a incongruent context of a "deadly horror" train. This expression communicated how he experienced reality ever since his parents' divorce a couple of years earlier, where he and his little sister were being tossed in the murky relationship the parents created.

Eight year old Yaron,. Reason of referral – divorce. The roller coaster represents the effect of the divorce on his life. The "perfect garden" is visible at the edge of the sink.

Playing a roller coaster game: A free falling experience.

Using game playing and creative activity in water, as well as other forms of expressive therapy, a therapist can join the child at his inner world. These processes offer direct, immediate communication where language is but another assistive tool. Such a therapeutic attribute facilitates the reaching of sensitive and deep regions, where children have hard time conducting verbal expressions. This difficulty stems from different causes, such as limited verbal ability, communication disorder or emotional difficulty, being withdrawn, introverted, etc.

USING VERBAL LANGUAGE

"Language is the metaphor of experience. Many words can be used to describe one single experience"
NLP Counseling by Roy Bailey

As a child works on his creation, or at the end of the process, I ask, "What's the name of this place," or, "What kind of water source was just created?"

Children form a multi-sensual experience when working with water, an experience that includes tactition, olfaction, vision, audition, feelings and thoughts. They use verbal expression to describe, explain, define and the like. Use of language, aside from its vocal component, allows one to form a spoken metaphor. When children define their work by naming it, a few things happen simultaneously, which significantly advance diagnosis and therapy.

in her book, The Handbook of Gestalt Play Therapy: Practical Guidelines for Child Therapists, Dr. Rinda Blom asserts that semantic explanations contribute to reinforcement of the sense of self in children.

The Implications of Verbal Definition of Artistic Creation

Neurological integration. A link forms between the right brain hemisphere and the left one.

Information is conveyed from the sub-conscious to conscious mind, allowing the therapist to build a dictionary of terms and metaphors which help him understand the child's inner landscape.

For Example: When a child says, "The river of blood," the former knows what the child feels, what he has in mind in context of such statement. The intention behind the term he had just devised arrives with a depiction and a feeling and by articulating the metaphor, the child transfers to the therapist his feeling and intent. After all, the term 'a river of blood' can assume different meanings from one mind to another, however, when the patient creates something which he then explains, a cohesion is formed among thought, emotion, the picture mentally imagined and the experience, as it is felt by both the patient and the therapist. In other words, the way the child articulates metaphors while talking to the figures and objects in and around the water, helps him communicate with the environment and be clear both inwardly and the with those around. A **unique language evolves** in such a process, which characterizes the child and reflects his uniqueness.

Deep empathy and understanding are enabled at several layers between the conscious and sub-conscious aspects of the mind, the layers between sensible and palpable, between reality and imagination and between the left and right sides of the brain. Integration is formed between the different aspects that connect body, mind and spirit.

Entering at Once Immediate and Symbolic Emotional Experience – "I feel caught in a whirlpool" (the patient creating turbulence in the water using movement, sound and color). The metaphor in water therapy can also be physical in nature, using hands or head movement, facial expression and other gestures.

"It is all confusing, mixed up; I can't get out. The turbulence is drowning me", said an 11 year old boy whose parents divorced and battled each other in court for his custody. As a result, the child had to appear before a judge in family court. The stress and emotional blackmail he went through resulted in severe emotional distress.

Many metaphors and images will come to the fore during water therapy, rising from the child's sub-consciousness (see Chapter 6, Depths Discovered in Water Therapy). These hold internal programming by which he is managed and through which his thought patterns, emotions, fears and conduct are formed. For the therapist, these images and metaphors are the golden keys with which to facilitate the child's psychological healing. As the therapist identifies a given key and utilize it, together with the child, to unlock the image at issue, a hidden structure is librated and comes up the surface. This is when the child is freed as well. He is unchained of fears, of an obsessive, irrational thought, he becomes free to be a child.

In his book Counseling through NLP Roy Bailey asserts that our metaphors are the way we understand ourselves and our world. They are the means to synthesize our senses and code them in our language, in the belief system we have for ourselves, others and the situation in which we operate.

Chapter 8

ARCHTYPES, MYTHS AND SYMBOLS

Symbols And Myths

A myth is a narrative used by human society to tell its story; it is about its past, as we gaze into the future of the society where the myth has formed. Members of this society create and preserve the myth in the collective memory and it serves as a societal identity card. In their book, The Shaping of Israeli Identity: Myth, Memory and Trauma (Israeli History, Politics and Society) (1995), Robert Wistrich and David Ohana assert that myths shape the various thought forms and beliefs of human society. That myth and memory cross-fertilize and shape one another and together these elements, concurrently, formulate and reflect a given culture.

Myth's Characteristics

Myth is a narrative or its encoded embodiment, whose kernel is not factually established yet, it has an ancient overtone of grandeur.

Myth has either an overt or a covert theme, which is designed to instruct conduct.

Myth occurs in an alternative reality, another dimension and is at variance with familiar reality.

A myth might include super-human heroes as well as super-natural powers and entities.

The history of symbolism shows that everything can assume symbolic significance: natural objects (like stones, plants, animals, men, mountains and valleys, sun and moon, wind, water, and fire). ... Man, with his symbol-making propensity, unconsciously transforms objects or forms into symbols (thereby endowing them with great psychological importance).

Carl G. Jung, Man and his Symbols (1964).

Jung goes on to state that symbols have great psychological significance since they reflect various aspects of the human psyche it has expression in his dreams, in art he creates and in his identification with other symbols that surrounds him. See, ibid.

Archetypes

Archetypes are symbols of images of significance to human society, that enfold nearly every aspect of our lives. Carl Young discovered that symbols and images in fairy tales are expressions of the language of the subconscious. Each image or symbol is not merely a metaphor, but a handful of cryptic life in its own right. Therefore it is worthy of unwrapping, to be unveiled. Such symbol will, forever, summon something new into our awareness, of which we were not conscious before its arrival. through legends and myths we will, symbolically-experientially, encounter the other side of life, we will learn about various aspects of the human psyche and be able to cope with the demons and irrational elements found within us.

Avi Bouman, The Devil with the Three Golden Hairs.[12]

The appearance of various symbols has great significance in art therapy in general and water treatment in particular, for these are the primal fundaments in the context of the collective subconscious, through which myths, legends and the children's personal stories unfold, an amalgam that would serve them as a personal subconscious.

---

[12] Based on a Grimm Brothers' fairy tale by that name.

In effect, our essence, within, is made of our inner narrative, the one we tell ourselves. In other words, each one of us has a personal life chronicle, a type of personal and familial mythology, composed of our ancestral history as well as the wider context of our culture and religious affiliation. These elements shape our perception of the world, our deepest fears and the expectations we have of ourselves and our children.

Art therapy allows symbols and images to easily rise to the surface, since art's expressive means bypass the guard, so to speak, posted by the conscious mind at the gate of the subconscious, thus enabling hidden psychological materials to float up from the depths of the mind to a more aware plateau where it is more easily discernible.

Through water treatment or, when water is present during art therapy (e.g., where water is part of a painting, placing a pond in a sandbox or in any such activity where water is used), nearly always it is possible to identify symbols taken from an ancient, arcane repertoire of various cultures and peoples.

In all cultures it is possible to find the mythological hero who is destined to deal with the resident pain and fear dwelling in the depths of his psyche, emotions that block access to inner treasures. Eventually, courage emerges through the hero's heart, that leads him to a quest for those treasures even if, as a result, a risk of drowning looms. The hero may discover how to open invisible gates, how to let loose inner powers, summon supernatural creatures to his aid and facilitate magic, until he discovers the hidden treasures, together with a new quality of his own and, perhaps, he himself is re-born into the world.

Riva Perry, Rebirth, Modan, (Psycha Series) (2003).[13]

---

[13] Originally in Hebrew.

During water treatment many attributes may be observed, that relate to existing myths manifesting as stories and creativity.

Omer, a six year old, firstborn child, related to me, as he engages creatively in water he colored red: "Once there was a king who lived in the castle with statues, who had a treasure box he guarded. He had there diamonds, crystals and guns. The king was wicked. Now I'm going to drown him in the river. The river is toxic so he will die!"

There are several distinct elements in Omer's story relating to the world of myths. The central character is "an evil king," a blocking figure, who prevents the hero, Omer, from obtaining the treasure. Many tales and legends tell of a guarded treasure where a demon, monster, scaly dragon, cruel king, and the like, block access to its possession. Moreover, in the psychological context, Omer's tale may be looked at as being associated with the Oedipal stage where, according to the ancient myth, Oedipus kills his father and then conjugates with his mother.

Omer, as stated, feels the need to cope with a mighty threat before he can attain independence. Perforce, "the obstacle" caused by an evil king evokes antagonism and aggression in the hero and, therefore, he has a desire to throw his foe into the toxic water.

Six year old Omer is strongly bonded with his father. He spends many hours with him in the yard or at the garage, as they engage in repair work and carpentry. Spending time with his father entails coping with boundaries placed by the father, with formation of identity, separation and authenticity, and all of these while facing the need to be loved and to belong. Spending time with his father apparently brings to the fore emotional conflicts in Omer's world. Omer has a five months old infant brother. Thus, the mother devotes herself to the newborn infant and Omer seems to encounter difficulties in competing for her attention – her heart – as he is facing the new "man" in her life. Omer suffers from ADD and is involved in a number of conflicts with members of his peer group. There, the need for control is heightened.

Myths and symbols lie latent at the bottom of each and every one's subconscious mind. These are part and parcel of the collective unconscious, as human society and they may be accessed through various means of expression. Exposure of the symbols enables the convening of various aspects of the human psyche that can reinforce and heal us and alter the course of our lives.

Water Symbolism As a Creative Element

The water present during therapy stand for different forces in relation to the context with which they appear. Due to their quality and natural attributes they may symbolize any of the following: Emotions, cleansing, a threat, a flow, flooding, being filled up, cleaning, birth, healing and more. Moreover, when water make an appearance in treatment, it may be said that it may serve as the key to the psyche, in other words, each time the presence of water becomes visible during treatment we can assume that we have touched a place of deep emotions. The verse in Psalms 69:2 says, " I am come into deep waters, where the floods overflow me." This utterance emerges from precisely the same place – water seeps so deeply they reach the inner depth of a human being where his innermost self resides.

Healing Process through the Myths and Symbols of Water Treatment

The child arriving at treatment expresses himself in a manner that is convenient for him. As he works with water, his subconscious mind is freed, and figures, symbols and stories emerge. Some will receive a coherent interpretation by him while others will exhibit a commanding presence, one which, at times, he himself would be unaware of.

The role of the therapist at this juncture is to be attentive and perceptive to particular elements of the creative manifestation formed by the patient: Does it resemble a Biblical story, e.g., Infant Moses in the basket? Does the serpent have several heads? Maybe the figure has several arms and hands? What does this symbolizes? Sometimes the situation is taken out of the context of an esoteric culture that could not possibly be familiar to the child from his current reality. Hence, where does the figure belong to and what does the attire symbolizes?

The therapist is the bridge between the child's subconscious and the myth or symbol that drives him from within. Identifying such symbol can be of great assistance in the healing process of the child. Accordingly, it is essential that therapists and educators who work with children from diverse cultural backgrounds and become familiars with the myths accompanying the culture they encounter and examine the symbols and myths associated with it. Keep in mind, that the subconscious is a vast sea of memories and symbols, and it is not unusual that a child from one culture would bring up symbols and form figures related to ancient folk tale that are no longer present on planet earth.

Therapist's Role in Interpreting Symbolism in Creative Manifestation

At this stage of the treatment, the therapist undertake any number of roles, an investigator, detective, anthropologist and symbolic archaeologist. As he unearths a figure, a symbol or the tail-end of a tale that could relate to the depths of the patient's subconscious, the former begins his research work. It might be on the Internet, it might resort to the use of books on symbols and mythologies, it might even requires delving into movies' archives. Allow yourselves to reach every nook and cranny intuition and inspiration could take you. The moment you locate the source of a given symbol or figure, you will experience greater clarity about matters that, till then, were not too comprehensible about the patient.

Stage 1

The child participates in creative activity as part of the psychological water treatment.

Stage 2

Images or a figure or some kind of a hero are created, at times as a picture, story or a scene in a play.

Stage 3

The therapist looks up the myth or symbolism and its cultural context in various sources of information.

Stage 4

The therapists awakens the child's ancient memory.

Now we are presented with four possibilities of taking action:

a. **The therapist identifies the myth and its symbolic meaning, as it relates to the treatment but does not share these with the patient.** Just the fact that the therapist has become aware of the myth or symbol at issue is often sufficient to promote the therapeutic process. The therapist is mentally aware of the myth or symbol's context, which he would utilize as part of his evaluation and might opt not to share this information with the patient. In most cases, this newly acquired knowledge clarifies for the therapist many issues and previously unanswered questions; it enables him to choose means of therapy and ways of communication in concert with the narrative by which, he now knows, the child is govern.

For example, Amit, a 10 year old girl of divorced parents, whose separation process was fraught with confrontations and court hearings. Her father remarried immediately after the divorce was final. The new wife had three children of her own. The mother, on the other hand, went through a prolonged period of mourning her shattered marriage. Amit, working with clay, created a pubescent girl with no hands. Instead of legs, she sculptured a fish tail for her and called her work, "the Mermaid." The mermaid's face were given emphasis, her lips were bright red and her dress had a generous décolletage.

"The mermaid" – Amit, a 10 year old – treatment due to parents' divorce.

The mermaid's myth depicts a stage of development where a pubescent girl ponders her femininity. On the one hand, she falls in love with a sailor. On the other hand, in order to be with him, she would have to give up on her underwater world, for if she would choose love she could never go back to her family.

The psychological aspect of the story relates to the Self archetype,[14] that superior essence that hold in it all other archetypes of the psyche. Consequently, she has to undertake a protracted journey if she desires reaching individuation.[15] First, she has to develop an Ego, as she becomes integrated with the external world and with the Ego, the feminine aspect must grow and assume its mature form. The mermaid experiences an intricate psychological process till she encounters the handsome prince: She floats up from the sea floor (a place that stands for the unconscious), however, the ascent to the sunlight and the adaptation to land entails considerable torment. She has to forego a part of her physical body, her tongue and voice in order to obtain human legs. Moreover, her legs will serve as a reminder of the pain and suffering that will accompany her for the rest of her life.

In Amit's specific case, the context the mermaid's life had in it, in a concentrated form, conflicts she was coping with: the desire to win her father's love brought a great deal of heartache into her experience, since she had to compete with other contestants, including the new wife, her children and Amit's own brothers. On the other hand, she identifies with helplessness her mother projects, as the latter is shaped

---

[14] In Jungian psychology, the Self is an archetypes, signifying the unification between consciousness and unconsciousness, representing the psyche as a whole. (See, Josepf L. Henderson, "Ancient Myths and Modern Man" in C. G. Jung ed., Man and his Symbols (London 1978) p. 120.) This archetype, according to Jung, is a realized product of individuation – in Jung's view the process of integrating the personality. See, Zweig, Connie (1991). Meeting the Shadow. Los Angeles: J.P. Tarcher, p.24.

[15] Principium individuationis, i.e., the principle of individuation, describes the manner by which a thing is identified as distinguished from another thing. See, Audi, Robert, ed. (1999). As per Carl Jung's theory of psychology, individuation is a process of psychological integration. "In general, it is the process by which individual beings are formed and [become] differentiated [from others]; in particular, it is the development of the psychological individual as a being distinct from the general, collective psychology." Jung, C.G. Psychological Types. Collected Works, vol. 6, par. 757. Individuation is a process of transformation by which the personal and collective unconscious are brought into consciousness (for instance, by way of dreams, active imagination, or free association) to be assimilated into the entire personality. Jung, C.G. (1962). Symbols of Transformation: An Analysis of the Prelude to a Case of Schizophrenia (vol. 2). New York: Harper & Brothers. This is an utterly natural process, necessary for the integration of the psyche.[4] Individuation has a holistic healing effect on the person, both mentally and physically. Id.

as a mermaid with no arms. Amit perceives femininity as being seductive, thus the bright red lips and the generous décolletage, measures utilized by the new woman to "ensnare" her father. Amit is engaged in a search for her feminine identity, a search that is affected by her familial circumstances.

b. **The therapist identifies the myth and shares the patient the narrative's meaning or the significance of the symbol, while placing an emphasis on the deep qualities of the information shared.**

Let's take, for example, eight year old Miri. With her golden tresses and blue eyes she looks like a fairy who just popped in for a visit out of a tale. She was adopted when she was 18 months old and arrived at treatment due to difficulties in socializing, learning and power struggles within the family. her mother related that Miri tends to sit at the computer, conducting searches for her original family. In contrast with the fairy appearance, she actually creates an unpleasant feeling around her. One day, during a therapy session, Miri asked to sculpt in Play-Doh. This was just before Passover and she and her classmates were being taught about Moses in the papyrus basket.[16] Miri made a basket in which she placed a baby girl. She even made a tiny blanket with which she covered the infant. She also created a lake, representing the Nile, where the basket floated.

We observed her creation together and she told me the Biblical story while expressing empathy for the newborn baby who, she said, had "to manage all alone in the world." I asked her whether she knows the rest of the story, how Moses was saved and where he grew up. Needless to say, she knew it all. I then had an idea. I said: "Miri, did you know that Moses was also adopted?" Her eyes brightened up, "Really?" she retorted. "And," I asked, "did you know that the Lord chose him, of all the Children of Israel to free his people from slavery in Egypt?" Miri lifted her head toward me, her eyes opened wide,

---

[16] See, Exodus 2:1-3.

expressing great pride and with a sense of much satisfaction she smiled at me a toothy smile abounding with joy and exhilaration. Following that session Miri would repeat, time and again, to all who would hear her that Moses was adopted, just like her, and she, too, she declared, would do something important in life.

c. The therapist identifies the myth or symbol and the figures or additional relevant context and presents them to the patient, using focused intervention, e.g., by introducing another figure into the play.

For example, a boy named Sharon was a first-grader when he was entrusted into my hands for therapy. Sharon and his parents returned to Israel after a four years' stay in the U.S. They settled in a house in a little town. At the start of the school year, having little knowledge of Hebrew, he began attending a new school where he had no friends. Sharon's parents were busy most of the time with arrangements having to do with re-absorption in the country.

Sharon was both shy and introverted and had difficulties socializing. He began speaking in the name of an imaginary named Chips for whom he either acted as a translator or spoke in her stead. His anxious parents indicated that he failed to exhibit social skills in the States, but they tied it to the fact that they were "aliens" in the land.

during his treatment, Sharon repeatedly, endlessly, would return to a theme he had created: the lonely island. He painted the island, sculpted it in the sandbox and formed it in his water world. After reiterating a few times the matter in our discussions, where he talked about his experiences of loneliness and isolation, he wanted to build the lonely island in the therapy room. using pillows, we formed the lonely island. He placed the refreshments basket on it, together with a puppet parrot made of a hand glove. He traversed the island, swam in the "ocean water" surrounding it and ate "a coconut that grew on the island." I related to him an abridged version of Robinson Crusoe's story, about the man who lived on a lonely island and learned to get along with nature.

Sharon listen and identified with the tale. I then proceeded to tell him about that special day, when Robinson Crusoe met Friday, the local man whom he never saw before. I suggested that I would play Friday while he would step into the shoes of the man who lives on the island. The result, was a fascinating role-playing game, where Sharon met me and, using a form of sign language, was able to communicate with me and describe what resources are available on the island and how I could assist him in building a shelter.

The game became rather intricate and Sharon and 'his man Friday' became close buddies. At that juncture, I determined to expand the story beyond its original plot. I invented new friends. Friday introduced to the protagonist other individuals who lived on a nearby island. There was Bomba, the corals' guardian and Gogo the oysters' fisherman. Sharon hosted them all and sought to adapt his approach to each of them, with element he liked, individually. Each time they met he was delighted with the new encounter.

In his reality outside the therapy room, Sharon began opening up to other children, he started playing in close proximity to, and slowly embark on conversations with, them. His self-confidence grew and he expressed interest in other children. At this stage, Sharon announced that the imaginary figure Chips had to travel abroad, having been sent on a mission to a faraway country. I asked him if he misses Chips and he said, "I miss him a lot, I'll write him a letter; surely, Chips has by now some new friends."

Sharon – a lonely island build in the sandbox

A bottle for the potion, "the Island."

d. Inquiry into the symbol by expanding its context, using arts in order to receive additional information about it and its either broad or personal context in the child's memory.

For example, five years old Yoel, as a infant, ate hair as he crawled about. He collected the dog's hair found on the floor and put them in his mouth. When he could not find dog's hair he settled for his three years older sister hairs. At present, each time he found himself under stress or frustrated, as a result of a given event, he would eat hair. His parents mentioned that he tends to have unstable moods, that he wakes up at night due to fears and that he is too afraid to stay home by himself, because he suffers from abandonment anxiety.

After a psychiatric evaluation, followed by a yearlong family therapy, he arrived at my clinic. He was preoccupied with issues having to do with aggression, control, good and bad figures, winners and losers, in the context of the children in his kindergarten and his family relationships. Additionally, also came up for discussion were matters relating to the wholeness of one's body and imaginary figures he invented and drew, ones that gave expression to experiences of violence and the notion of death.

One day, after a couple of months of work, he discovered an iron chain on a wooden shelf in the therapy room. He started moving in the room wielding the chain. Later, he connected the chain to a thin iron rod and cuffed his leg with it, saying: "Iron chains were used in Jerusalem to capture and kill."

I asked Yoel, "Who is cuffed in iron chains? Do you know him?" He replied, "Yes." I suggested we sculpt that person in clay, thus I would get to know the person . During four sessions Yoel sculpted figures and their surroundings. It included a father and mother figures and the pole to which the person in chains was tied, and related: "It's child who's between 3-5 years old. He has holes in his legs and his mother takes him to be operated on, to patch up the holes in his legs. They put him under but he is afraid of being asleep for he'll have nightmares. Then, they wake him up without patching up his legs and, as a result, during night, he becomes a monster. His mother could not be present during the operation – they would not allow her in, they put some sleeping medication on her eyelids." I asked him, "What are these whole in the legs?" Yoel explained: "These are like a monster's features. He feels that he is not liked, that he is seen as a monster then he was taken to another place, 'The Medical House of Little Children',[17] this was in Spain and there is this pole where they tie the monsters. [He now shapes the tying pole in clay.] There, they did like him, because every day he became nicer and nicer; he wasn't reasonable, yet – still devoured human beings all the time, had sharp fangs and was swathed in long hair that covered his face. There was this physician who tied him up and was the person who liked him the most. His mother had visited three times a week, till he devoured her and she did not come any more. The physician said that it wasn't a good thing that the child became more and more of a monster. The child said, "I really want to see Mom." There were other ordinary children there in need of healing, however, he was a child who'd remain there for the rest of his life.

Notice how seeing the chain in the room enabled Yoel's recollection of a deep, ciphered memory not present at the "here and now." Art work with clay allowed him to relate, in detail, to the experience secreted in memory and recount it to me.

Historically, mentally ill patients were often tied up and were treated like prison inmates. The iron chain ignited the memory and the work with clay facilitated the recall of details. The relation between Yoel's story and his current difficulties, including the consumption of hair, had to do with the child who was tied to an iron pole and, apparently, suffered from mental retardation or mental disease and yearned for human contact. The one thing he could touch, in that previous experience, was the hair of his head that touched and caressed his face and which, most likely, came in his mouth. Likewise, it was possible to sense from his story the experience of social rejection and longing for love. The other issue his story brings to the fore is the relation to a mother and the sense of loss engendered when her visits ceased. At present this manifests in abandonment anxiety.

It should be noted, that Yoel was never at a psychiatric institution nor was he ever treated psychiatrically with psychotropic medication. His

---

[17] This is apparently reference to a children ward in a medical facility.

birth was uneventful and he was a child who functioned within the bounds of what is considered normal mentally; he attended normal kindergarten and his family may be defined as normative. He never suffered any abuse and was not punished either at home or at his kindergarten. After constructing the story and telling it in detail, he stopped eating hair.

Stage 5
Providing Space for Creative Expression and Emotional Release of the Patient

At this stage the therapist will await further developments or see what art creation or new scene, in some form of play, would emerge. It is possible that the image being created will evolve and expand and it might not. At any event, there is great significance to giving expression to the ancient contents that have floated up. The images and myths are built-in links in a chain of the child's personal mythology and they may have been a dam that had hindered emotional processes. When these images acquired emotional and visual expression, the patient met them and had the opportunity to gaze at them. The process of unhinging them from depths of consciousness, causes them to evaporate. Now, the river of emotions can freely flow and grow changes and emotional processes.

If images are sources of strength and support, when they are unearthed they ignite processes of growth and empowerment quickly and in a liberating manner.

How Does Water Contributes to Raising the Ancient Memory and to the Appearance of Myths?

Water treatment is integrative, i.e., it enables use of various art forms and playing in the context of water. Forming such a space of activity facilitates the scrutiny and construction of any number of symbols, appearing during treatment.

For example, a child who constructs a water world and says, "I need a submarine!" It is possible, in such a setting, to build a submarine in minute detail, in juxtaposition to a readymade submarine picked out of a toys' box. As we do so, we expand the symbolic value of the submarine for now we can examine the appearance of the submarine, what's in it, how does it work, who is in it, who operates it and so on. As the submarine meets the water, play therapy is engaged, the tie between the symbol at issue and the deep symbolic context of a submarine submerged in water, is assembled. In other words, the submarine stands for an inner urn, a kind of a womb. When the patient creates the submarine he can ascertain its structure, i.e., what symbolic parts does it have: Its wheel, for instance, represents control; the sonar is a symbol of reception while the alarm claxons speak of vigilance. Moreover, the submarine -- created here by the patient -- may be seen as a soft place that has in it clothes, beds, even an armchair, hence, a place for rest and relaxation. All those symbols may be brought back to the patient in a subsequent conversation that would serve to enhance inner qualities hidden within him.

When the patient places a submarine in water that he perceives as "stormy," he forms a correlation between two inner terms he has created in his inner world. These terms are deeply connected to the patient's inner ability to cope. The patient "solves" the difficulty through the imaginary game, hence he creates inner tools for coping with reality.

Fears, by 12 year old Nimrod

"What I like about water treatment is that it feels so real." The aforementioned Nimrod.

Once the therapist has completed the water treatment, the emotional experience, in the context of the ancient memory, will fuse together and affect healing and change.

How Could an Image Affect a Sub-Conscious Shift?

A glimpse into the Therapy Room...

Six year old Naor, a kindergarten student, arrived at therapy as a result of complaints about aggressive behavior, resistance to authority and difficulties in sensory regulation. Naor is the middle child, between a nine year old sister and a three year old brother. His father was just diagnosed with cancer and, at the time, was undergoing radiation therapy.

During one of the session he asked to prepare a potion. We took a bottle and filled it up with water and added sparkling colors and pieces of Play-Doh. When we were done and sealed the bottle Naor said: "That's the healing potion that restores life, it can heal any disease."

"What diseases," I asked.

"Fever, allergies, even cancer," he replied.
We talked about the subject of illness and Naor told me he is really mad at God for causing his father to contract a disease called, "cancer" and, even though he is furious with God, he keeps on praying to Him so that He would protect his entire family.

"Healing potion that restores life."

Naor asked me to preserve the potion and each time he arrived at the therapy room he would make sure it was there. After the potion was created, the parents reported a major improvement in Naor's everyday behavior at the kindergarten; they no longer received complaints from his teachers. Whoever knew the child asked 'what medication they have been administering to him?' for he had totally calmed down.

Potion is an element of myth found in children's stories, folk legends and in various cultures' narrative. It is usually made of water and additions made of either herbs or some other liquids. Different potions have different qualities and serve different purposes. On occasion, it is charged with evil intentions of death and disease; on other occasions it is used to generate romantic love, awareness and healing diseases.

Mention can be had of certain well-known potions: Shakespeare wrote in Midsummer Dream about a love potion that is spread on those who are asleep who, in turn, fall in love with the first person they see as they open their eyes. Similarly, magicians have any number of potions, such as those mentioned in the Harry Potter books

Alchemists concocted potions of an assortment of ingredients, designed to make the user have "eternal life."

Mythologies are filled with stories were potions either kill or resurrect heroes. Even these days, homeopathy makes use of potions, concocted of minute portions of herbs, mixed with some water and alcohol and poured into bottles.

As a therapist, over the years my shelves have become loaded with potions concocted by children, that have helped them cope with challenging situations such as diseases, loss of loved ones, divorce, and certain chaotic situations. The potion contains the child's emotional energy and those contents the child desires it would have. It is kept in the therapy room and the children can come back and link up with it and its meaning. Accordingly, it works and can help them bear some of the burdens and lift up some of the prayers poured into it.

Common Myths and Water Treatment

Birth and Creation Myths

Chaos prevails in most myths telling about the creation of the world in different cultures, chaos that is, necessarily, accompanied with lack of clarity and lack of definition. Creation means bringing order into the world by separating the elements. As it is written in the book of Genesis: " In the beginning God created the heaven and the earth. And the earth was without form and void and darkness was upon the face of the deep and the Spirit of God moved upon the face of the waters." Id., 1:1-2.

In most myths the initial element is water, at times appearing as "the Infinite Sea" and sometimes as "the Ancient Waters." In most myths the Divine is tied to the water and mostly described as a feminine entity. The water is the womb whence the world emerges. Some tie these correlations to human birth, out of water.

One of the known forms of birth, is that of an egg and the notion that the world was born out of an egg is found in a number of cultures in the world.

Five and a half year old Uri talked about his creation, made of Play-Doh: "Once there was a tsunami, a whirlwind, sea cucumbers and the ghost of the sea. Then the wind made magic, the whirlwind disappeared with the ghost that throws money about, then the sea calmed and there was neither tsunami nor whirlwind anymore, and there was stillness.

The Egg

A Creation myth from Finland tells of the goddess Ilmatar, a nature goddess who became tired of the loneliness in heaven and dropped down to the sea, where she floated on the waves. The sea fertilized her and she kept on floating till a bird in search for a place to nest appeared. It landed on the goddess and laid a few eggs on her. The goddess bent her knee and the eggs rolled down to the void below. However, some of them were not lost, and the world was created of them.

In another Finnish myth it is said that the earth was made of the lower portion of the eggs and the sky of their upper one. The sun was made of their yolk and the egg's white formed the moon.

A Pelagasian Myth tells of a nature goddess who landed in the form of a dove and laid the egg of the world. "All that is ... the sun, moon, planets and comets, earth, its mountains, rivers, trees, grasslands and all living creatures."

The Homeric-Orphic version speaks of the night goddess who mated with wind then laid the world egg in the lap of darkness of which Eros was born, which is the force that powers the world.

Seven and a half year old Roni, "the egg of Bluey."

A Glimpse into the Therapy Room...

A five year old, likable and energetic first born boy named Yam ("sea" in Hebrew) arrived for therapy. He had a two year old sister. Yam was referred for treatment following various regulating difficulties, including regulation of external stimuli perceived by the senses that undergo sorting and processing in the brain and are then translated into reactions.

He was often disciplined at his daycare center due to wild behavior and he often conducted a range of experiments at home involving breaking or destroying things. These experiment did not make his parents happy and on many occasions he was at the receiving end of yelling and punishments at home, as well.

He encountered difficulties enduring in a game or a creative exercise for any length of time. One day, while he was searching the toys' shelves at the therapy room for something to play with, he ran into large plastic egg, originally depicting a dinosaur's egg. He took it and declared: "This is a treasure egg!"

Yam placed all kinds of thing in it – which I was not allowed to see – then closed it and asked me to wrap it tightly. We took scotch tape and wrapped the egg with it. The items inside rustled. Yam, joyously, held the treasure egg while rattling it in order to hear the sounds from the inside. It rested for a few weeks on a shelf in the therapy room. One day we attended a treatment session at the sink. At its conclusion Yam created an aquarium were three frogs resided. "The frogs are a family," he said, "and they all came out of the treasure egg."

I told Yam a mythological story about an egg after he created the aquarium and he simply said: "The world was not created of my treasure egg, only a family of frogs who ate all the treasures that were in the egg, they even ate the egg itself."

The egg symbolizes for Yam the realm of family, a "melting pot" where his primordial life was formed, from where he is nourished and grows. The challenges in raising Yam burdened his parents with challenges both in their relationship as a couple and as parents of a child with regulation problems. The egg was filled up with "invisible" items, things he put in it which he did not want me to see. His senses told him that certain processes occur which he cannot identify.

The water treatment "gave birth" to the frogs which are, apparently, the unresolved issues in need of handling. Then the appropriate foundation was laid, that fits the treatment of the issue of family – as Yam perceived it – and at a time of his own choosing.

The Frog

The ancient water were often the source of earth's formation. In Asian myths the frog plays in the water and raises the landmass up of which it creates earth.

Likewise, for the Native Americans it stands for change and renewal. They maintain that when frogs laud their voices, they are actually summoning abundance of rain that brings forth life. Because they exist both in water and on land, they represent a bridge between the inner realm and the un-conscious and external reality.

A Glimpse into the Therapy Room...

Alon, an eight year old, was hard at work at the water world he had created. The protagonists in the game he imagined were two frogs that struggled to survive, not to drown in that watery realm. They managed to survive because of a waterfall (water flowing from the faucet). A waterfall, which stands for renewal and cleansing, came to the frogs' rescue and they floated on the sink's strainer till they could come to rest at the fall's point of origin.

Alon is an only child of a financially challenged family. His mother works hard in order to provide for the family. His alcoholic father was removed, by a court order, from the home. The frogs are a

projection of him and his mother. The choice of two figures of the same size demonstrated Alon's sense of joint destiny and identification with his mother, as well as the role reversal between the two. Alon is depicted there as a mate in those situations where his mother feels helpless. The frog also symbolize survival: Even such a small animal can survive and succeed. The story elucidates Alon's strength in the areas of healing and coping, which help him overcome the hardships in his life.

The frogs in Alon's Aquarium

Myths of Change and Renewal

The mythological hero is not afraid to be engulfed by the horrors of the maternal deep – that of the beginning, of genesis = the sea – the water, indeed, he even brings himself, purposefully, into such danger. Jung explains that the treasure the hero finds in a dark cave is life itself. He is re-born out of the maternal, dark cave of the unknown, where he was helpless as a result of directing the libido inwardly though the libido is the force of life and the engine of growth.

The theme of the mythological hero who is thrown into the water and who finds himself inside a sealed container, 'as if he were buried within himself' is echoed in Biblical tales:

Noah – He is saved from the flood by an ark floating on water. The flood kills all living beings, only Noah and those gathered in the ark are saved. They experience a new genesis and the formation of a new world.

Moses in the Basket – Moses was secreted in a basket left to float on the Nile, instead of being cast into the water as was decreed by the Pharaoh. He is rescued from the water by Pharaoh's daughter.

The Prophet Jonah – Jonah finds himself in a life and death struggle in the middle of the sea. He ends up in the belly of a fish and only after he prays to God does the fish throw him up on land. A modern version of Jonah's travails in the belly of the fish is found in Pinocchio's story.[18]

In cultures were sun worship prevailed there are heroes locked in container of different kinds, a barrel, a closet, a basket, etc., during a night journey in the sea. These heroes were condemned to death or near death till they are either rescued of are awakened back to life.

The ark, closet, basket, ship, submarine, etc., are all symbols of the womb, as is the sea.

---

[18] *The Adventures of Pinocchio* (1883) by the Italian writer Carlo Collodi.

Noya, 10 year old – the boat; hammock. Notice the resemblance between the two forms drawn, both symbolizing both a womb and holding.

A Floating Coffin

A Glimpse into the Therapy Room...

Eight year old Or is a brother to 10 year old Lihi. During his brief childhood the family had lived in several countries. Or was diagnosed as a gifted child, suffering from a severe case of ADD.[19] He is very creative and has a number of artistic talents, such as painting, sculpting and playing the violin. At the same time, he is impulsive, and suffers from a number of anxieties that have been affecting his life. His mother reported that he has deep fear of water and is not willing to get in, even though they have a pool at home and he is used to swimming. He still wet his bed when he arrived for therapy. Or

---

[19] Attention deficit disorder (ADD), also called Attention deficit Hyperactivity Disorder Predominantly Inattentive (ADHD-PI), is one of the two types of attention deficit hyperactivity disorder (ADHD). The term was formally changed in 1994 in the new Diagnostic and Statistical Manual of Mental Disorders, fourth edition (DSM-IV) to "ADHD predominantly inattentive" (ADHD-PI or ADHD-I) though the term Attention Deficit Disorder is still widely used. 'Predominantly Inattentive' is similar to the other subtypes of ADHD except that it is characterized primarily by inattentive concentration or a deficit of sustained attention, such as procrastination, hesitation, and forgetfulness.

was born following a difficult pregnancy. However, his birth, according to his mother, was uneventful and calm.

Or's therapy was long and rather fascinating. His rapport with me was outstanding and he trusted my presence in the room. During the encounters he opened to me his deep unconscious world, where his nightmarish existence and unfathomable fears were revealed. These included, among others, aggressive tendencies aimed at himself. He would, for instance, draw self-portraits, which he would then tear to shreds or "abuse." One theme appeared again and again in different forms in his creative endeavors: A womb and fetus. Once he sculpted with a knife in wet sand and wood a head (a circle) to which he then added a torso, then stubby legs, followed by sidewalls on both sides of the body. The knife was used to create an outline in the sand. Every once in a while he would stab the fetus them mend the injured figure making it whole again. Once he was done sculpting, he asked to preserve the fetus as he covered it in dry sand and placed a piece of green cloth on it.

In a related conversation with Or's mother, regarding the pregnancy and birth, she did not remember any particular event that could have been experienced as traumatic by Or while in utero. However, a while later she recalled that on the day her contractions commenced, she

experienced heavy bleeding, which greatly frightened her, for there was a an apprehension as to the life of the fetus and she was taken by ambulance to the hospital to give birth.

During the first few sessions, Or worked with animals (see, e.g., Chapter 2, pp. 45-47 on building space in the sink).

In subsequent sessions he built a detailed house model and created a figure that lived in it. It was a child he called, "the child with the violin." After the house was built he informed me: "Now we need to construct a grave for the child with the violin." I offered him various materials, then he said, "I need materials that would float on water, the grave must float. We built a coffin and he placed the child with the violin in it. We then filled the sink with water and the grave indeed floated, though he first sealed it with an apparatus made of threats and said: "When he'd want to come out, he'd be able to unwrap the threats by himself."

The floating grave – eight year old Or

This story ties directly with ancient Egyptian myths where the hero, trapped in a sealed container of some sort is cast into the sea. He then awakens and manages to overcome his predicament; he is saved and then re-born, as a result of the change he had affected.

The therapy in this particular case, is the healing process that occurred the moment the grave was floated on the water. The patient "revived" the dead child when he said that when he will be on the water, i.e., in the emotional space, he'll be able to open the container, come out and live! It is possible to observe in this process how, despite the perception of this projected image, that comes with a harsh and pathological meaning – "the dead child who plays the violin" – the patient has the ability to build a container that will contain the distress, and may have worked to remove it from the child's psyche.

The "dead child with a violin" in the floating grave

A Ship

A ship is symbolic of an inner container that allows floating and arrival at a new destination, often indicative of coping and renewal. In very many folk tales, especially in those regions where fishing is a means of making a living or places by the sea, myths were born about heroes that depart on ships for a journey during which the ocean tests them in different ways, e.g., encounters with sea-monsters, storms, demons, mermaids who tempt and then kill them in the depth, a flood – as in the case of Noah – and more.

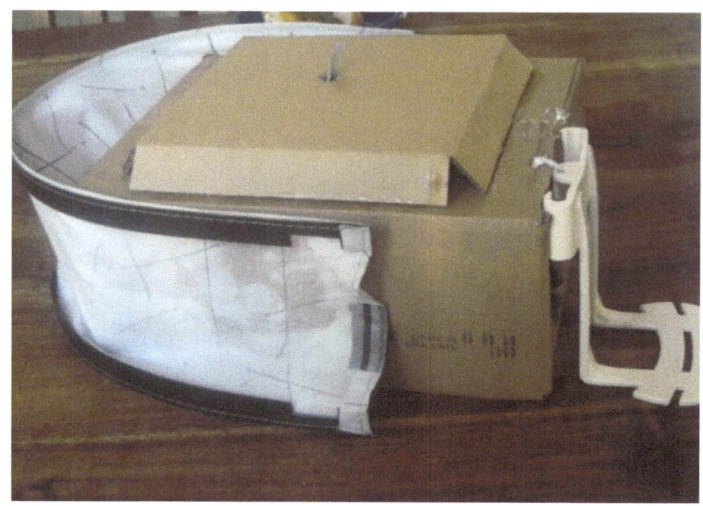

Emry, a seven year old – a ship

A glimpse into the Therapy Room...

Noam was seven when he arrived for treatment with his mother. As he entered I saw before me a pale, blue-eyed child. He was brought for therapy due to his difficulties in communicating with other children at school. He did not form social relationship and he threw tantrums at home. His mother warned me that he does not express himself verbally and talks sparingly. She said that he is pedantic, meticulous and acting rather childishly in situations that require coping. He cries a lot and looked helpless whenever he is faced with a new challenges.

Noam's treatment lasted for quite a while. It was with great difficulty that he opened even a little and, indeed, he conversed almost not at all. Because of his need to control any situation he was in, I began his therapy with pencil drawings, an excellent means of control because the product can be mended by deleting and re-sketching.

Noam drew a ship in an outline form. After a few sessions, during which we got closer, I asked him whether he wanted to build something. He gladly agreed and told me he wanted to use Lego bricks and that he builds special things, a ship for example. He then added, "Only if it can really sail."

"Of course," I replied and added, "I can also show you where it could sail."

I knew then that I found a bunch of keys to Noam's psyche: the obvious place for such endeavor would be a sink filled with water.

Just as the treatment took quite a while, wrighting the ship, also, took a long time to fully materialize. We draw a work plan at the start of every meeting dedicated to building the ship. At first there was only the ship's hull then an engine was added. Noam then completed its superstructure. This was followed by the addition of an entire floor on top and exit from the main floor. Benches and four beds were placed inside, corresponding to the number of his household members, and the finishing touch included a steering wheel, an anchor and, lastly, life preservers.

With a great deal of dignity the luxurious ship sailed the blue water of the sink, even had several voyages, accompanied by great excitement as Noam had realized his plan.

Noam then determined: "There is a problem, the ship needs to dock at the shore." Again, the whole process started, this time dedicated to building a pier with wires, a crane and complex bridges.

The whole process was fascinating: Noam opened up and readily interacted with me. He spoke about his life and experiences in the world as he glued things, assembled and constructed the ship and pier.

Once the ship (symbolizing his home and his sense of security) sailed out to sea, he immediately felt the need for bond with earth, reality and the world.

A positive change began to occur in Noam's everyday reality, and it appeared that the dock he constructed served as a bridge for him, manifesting not only in the creative work itself, but also in his life. He began to connect with children, express his needs without crying and without feeling a sense of helplessness. By the end of summer that year classmates were inviting him to their homes, he even attended a summer camp dedicated to ... Robotics!

An example of another vessel, representing coping with social conflicts:

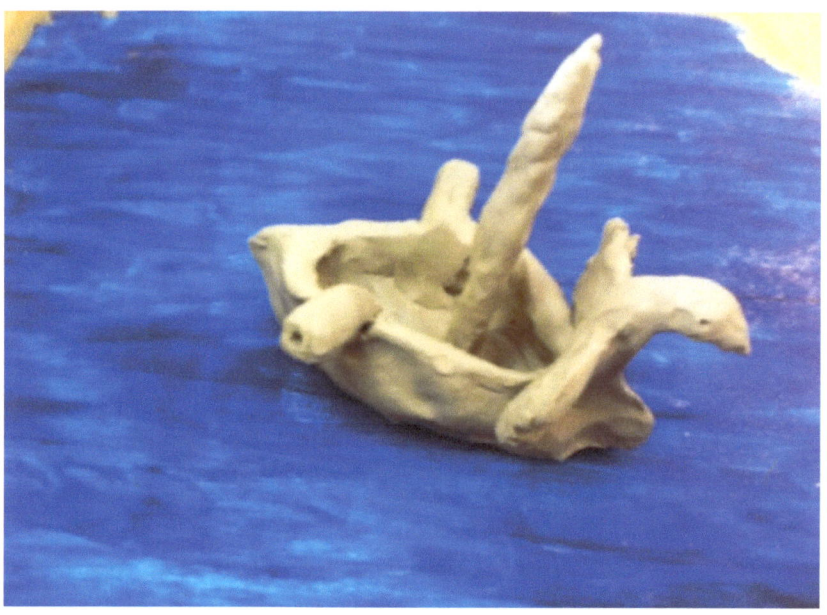

Eight year old Dan – battleship

Chapter 9

Memory

This method of water treatment is a doorway into the heart and mind of the child. There are vast treasures in his interior world, some both crucial for, and play a constructive role in, the process of personality formation, while others disrupt his personal development and the making of a love-filled joyous life. Each and every one of the child's experiences is preserved and cataloged in his memory, charting his perception and conduct. The fluid, elastic motion of water allows penetration of these veiled regions and washing blockages out of the depths of memory into the sink. There, these memories will be clearly reflected as stories, circumstances, colors and voices, allowing us to examine them and remove any excess.

What is Memory?

Memory, is usable data an aware human being can accumulate in his nervous system. Memory serves as the central foundation stone for building the private and collective human identity, since we are who we are thanks to, and sometimes despite, the contents and experiences that have accumulated in our memory, whether we are conscious of such contents or not. During our lives, our system of memory catalogues our life story within ourselves, thus, shaping our sense of identity, self-image, familial models, our relationships and so on. Our myriad memories are both positive and negative in tone, some empower us while others block our path; there are numerous memories in countless shades and degrees of vigor. Negative memories, naturally enough, cause delays in personal growth, however, there are those who cope and function by moving right through such memories. In many cases, memories of traumatic and negative events cause people to undergo protracted internal crises that manage their lives from the inside and affect their emotions and conduct on regular basis.

Human beings are unique in that we are the only creatures on earth who possess autographic memory, i.e., human consciousness could and is able to move forward and backwards in channels of memory thus re-experience past events. Events that have been etched in memory allow the mind to form future models, based on such memories.

The data cumulated in memory in the human brain allow its owner to formulate future plans from the same stored materials; after all, if we could not remember anything, we would not be able to foresee how things could look in the future.

When do we Start Remembering?

Most people have no recollection of their birth or their early years, nonetheless, they remember how to walk, hold objects and talk. This phenomenon is called "childhood amnesia." Memory of that early period is selective, that is to say, we remember acquired skills however human relations and other emotional memories cannot be quickly drawn from the layer holding our narrative (at its current version) in the conscious tier. Instead, it is secreted away into the subconscious. These unconscious memories constitute a major factor (though there are others) in the dynamic forming our social interaction in adulthood (e.g., in our intimate relationship with mates) and are part and parcel of the bundle of fears that often administer our lives.

Most individuals report having first conscious memories from two and a half to three years of age. It is at that age that the part of the brain responsible for spatial orientation and long term memory start developing, which explains the onset of conscious memory. It is the long term memory that creates the subjective, autobiographical human memory, with which a human being narrates his life story and manages his existence, whether consciously or unconsciously.

Another significant event occurring at that juncture, is that at about age three the child begins to identify himself. If we take a child who is between two-three years of age and place him in front of a mirror, he will notice that the figure reflecting is him, i.e., he will identify himself. Thus actually commences the construction of personal identity. Research on the subject, conducted on children in this range of ages, determined that the better children were able to identify themselves the better they could recollect toys that were first scattered in a room then removed; being able to indicate with precision the exact location of such toys as well as describe any that were missing.

The child's environment contributes much to the construction of his autobiographical memory. The process can be reinforced by asking the child questions and discussing events that had just taken place. From the moment language is acquired, we can use words to bring memories up to the conscious level of the child's mind and the child can then describe the experience in words so as to preserve it in memory at several levels: sensual, emotional and verbal.

What is Memory Made of ?

Memory is a vast weave of nerve cells, about 100 billion. These cells are connected through a vast system operated by an electrical signals that are conveyed from transmitters to receptors, utilizing secretions of chemical materials called neuromodulators. These cells operate as a coordinated teams called neural networks.

These days it is theorized that memory is stored in an activity format of neural networks, which are spread out throughout the brain. The process of memory formation and retention may be divided into two main stages:

1. **Short term memory** - also called 'working memory' and it is of limited capacity, lasting only a few hours. It is very vulnerable and any number of interferences may bring about loss of such memory.

2. **Long term memory** - has unlimited capacity and data can be preserved in it for a lifetime. It is resilient and erasure is difficult even when it has a detrimental effect on the quality of its carrier's life. Means of removal are the employment of imagination and creativity that are capable of entering through backdoors (so to speak).

There are three main feats performed in the processes of memory operation:

Coding - receiving data, for instance, verbal data that is coded according to its importance;

Storage - in particular in relation to long term memory, storage of information that is emotional in nature causes more intensive secretion of hormones that enhance the function of storage.

Retrieval - shift from long term memory to short term memory.

Where in the Brain are Memories Stored?

Naturally, researchers have sought to discover the 'memories' room', the place where all the pieces of our experiences – from the time we are still fetuses till the present – are stored. Just like a personal museum, where all items are arranged by subject, either chronologically or in some other order, possibly, according to their importance. This picturesque anticipation notwithstanding, no one specific location where memories are stored was ever found, indeed, it turns out that they are spread out through numerous locales in the brain.

Neuroscientist Karl Pribram, in collaboration with physicist David Bohm, who have jointly and engaged in brain investigation and its ability to remember, have posited the holonomic brain theory. The significance of this model has to do with the possible understanding of how the brain stores data and, consequently, how stored data may be unleashed thus enabling disentanglement of repressed emotional distress which may cause various psychological symptoms, even pathology. One of the more significant findings of this model is the opportunity to swap a "bad memory" for a "good one," or alternatively to delete traumas that are etched in memory, a means to reaching the ultimate psychological healing.

The Holonomic Model

In the 1960's physicist David Bohm was engaged in the study of quantum physics. During his research on the subject of the order of the universe, Bohm found that there are different levels of order in the universe. He ascertained that, where everything we see from our angle as a lack of order is actually at a very high level of order.

To demonstrate, Bohm took a jar, placed a rotating cylinder in it and filled the space between the cylindrical motion and the jar with glycerin. A drop of ink floated motionless in the glycerin. When the cylinder was rotated by an external lever in one direction, the ink drop dispersed and disappeared. However, when the handle was then turned in the opposite direction, the ink drop was recreated. Bohm called this phenomenon, of things that seemed to disappear, "the implicate (or enfolded) order."

The Hologram Model

This is a more familiar model of the phenomenon. A hologram is a three-dimensional projection that gives the viewer the sensation he is looking at a real object. It is well known from the use it has in the world of entertainment and as an aid in lecture halls, presentations, exhibitions and museums. Lately, holograms began functioning as substitute for certain service personnel in airports.

The picture below shows a clear and "real" depiction of planet Earth, however, one could actually pass his hand through the image as if it were nothing but transparent air, and the moment the machine is turned off it would just vanish.

How is a Hologram Constructed?

A hologram is based on a physical phenomenon known as "interference" (wave propagation). Interference is a form composed of two or more superimposed waves to form a resultant wave of greater or lower amplitude. Interference usually refers to the interaction of waves that are correlated or coherent with each other, either because they come from the same source or because they have the same or nearly the same frequency. For instance, by throwing two stones into nearly the same spot in a pool of water, we create interference as the wave action expand, and when the two meet we get a pattern made of depressions and protrusions formed due to the collision of these waves movement. The waves' collision is what is termed "interference."

A hologram is created from a split of a single laser beam into two separate ones. One returns from the object being captured, while the other returns from the light of the first beam. When this occurs, the phenomenon of interference takes place and it is then recorded on a recording medium, much in the same way a photograph is made.

Now to the eye, the recording medium would contain a pattern of rings akin to those observed in the pool of water where we dropped the two stones; however, if we illuminate the recording media with a laser beam, a three-dimensional image would appear, one that looks absolutely real but if we try to touch it we will see our hand going right through it and that it is just an illusion, in fact, there is nothing there but air. A phenomenon no less remarkable than the hologram occurs when we cut a film (serving as the recording media), on which the hologram is imprinted and illuminate the part we just cut off. The image recorded would appear in its entirety. In other words, all the information of the entire image is preserved in any part of the film, as opposed to a plain film which, if cut, will show only the portion of the image imprinted on that part of the film.

How does the Holographic Phenomenon Relates to Human memory?

In the 1940s, neuroscientist Karl Pribram began to research – corresponding with Bohm's effort – the subject of human memory. He sought to determine the location of memory in the human brain. When he read about the hologram phenomenon Pribram understood, that if the recording media (then there was only film) could be cut up and still each portion would contain all of the data recorded on the uncut film, it might be that different brain particle could hold the necessary information for restoring a complete memory. This is how Pribram discovered that human vision is holographic and ascertained that the visual centers of the brain are surprisingly difficult to remove with surgery; it turned out that even after 90% of the visual cortex in a rat's brain were removed, it could still perform complex visual feats.[20]

In 1966 Pribram published his research, demonstrating the electrical communication in the brain, taking place between brain cells through neurons, is not the only task they perform. Neurons branch out and when an electric message reaches the edge of such a branch, it is projected out like a ripple in a pool of water, and since neurons are densely packed these electrical waves, as they spread out, cross each other's path, forming a kaleidoscopic pattern of endless interference which is probably what gives the brain its holographic properties.

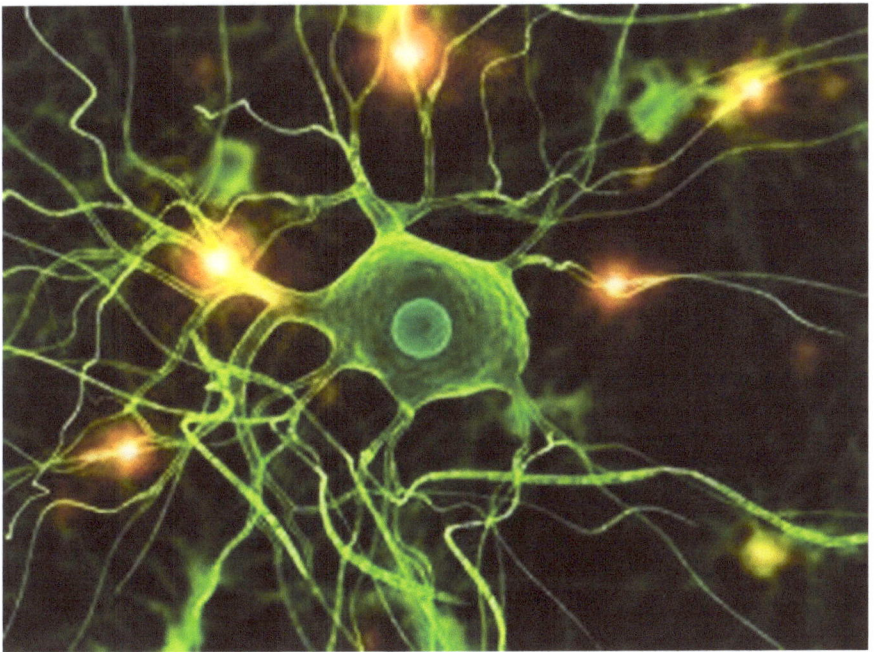

---

[20] Karl Pribram had worked with psychologist Karl Lashley on Lashley's engram experiments, which used lesions to determine the exact location of specific memories in primate brains. Lashley made small lesions in the brains and found that these had little effect on memory. On the other hand, Pribram removed large areas of cortex, leading to multiple serious deficits in memory and cognitive function.
Pribram, H.H. (2011). Recollections. Neuroquantology, 9(3), 370–374.

How Could the Brain Hold such Vast Stores of Data?

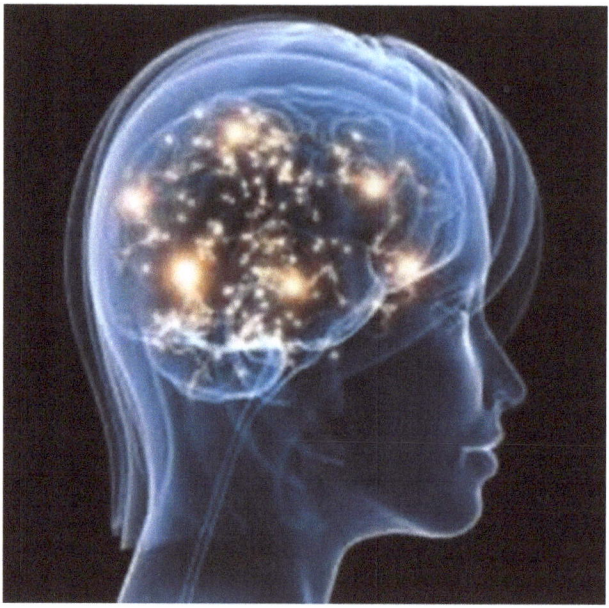

The quantum of information the brain stores equates to that held by all the personal computers in the world *times one billion*.

A hologram can also store vast amounts of data. By shifting (on multiple occasion) the angle of the laser, as it meet the recording media, numerous images can be embedded on the same media and each can be retrieved by illuminating it with a specific laser beam at the appropriate angle in relation to its location. Scientists have calculated each square centimeter on a holographic recording media can hold as much data as ten Bibles.

The shards of recording media on which our memories are imprinted explains our ability to recall and forget, just as the angle of the beam of light projected onto the media does not hit the correct angle and therefore cannot illuminate a given image imprinted on the media.

Other phenomena, related the way images are imprinted on recording media, may be explained by the process. These include:

Associative memory, that occur when we encounter a scent or an object that evokes a chain of past memories; it is akin to the manner by which the various images are recorded on the recording media in the holographic process.

The ability to identify familiar objects, for instance, when an individual ambles at a fairground in a crowd of hundreds and unmistakably recognizes the countenance of a familiar person, his neighbor for example; similarly, this relates the ability to recognize a face irrespective of the angle from which we are looking at it.

Eidetic memory,[21] is a capacity owned by individuals with access to vast areas of their memory's hologram, wherefrom they project the data precisely and clearly.

"The Whole World in a Grain of Sand"

The encounter between Bohn and Pribram in 1970 brought them to develop the theory that not only does the brain work holographically, but that the whole universe is a hologram. The theory could, therefore, account for the effect of consciousness on matter at the subatomic level. Bohm believes that consciousness is a more subtle form of matter, located at a "veiled" dimension. Consciousness is present at different levels of visible and invisible spectrum in every substance. It is also, according to Bohm's theory, present in space, time and the whole universe.

We saw already, that each particle of a hologram contains the whole, looking at the same model on a macro level it may be said that every portion of the universe enfolds the whole in it. Unbound energy is held at the implicate order level, which accords life to all that is in the universe, it contains at least one sub-atomic particle that either was or

---

[21] Commonly referred to as photographic memory or total recall, eidetic memory is the ability to recall images, sounds or objects with great precision; it is innate, not acquired through mnemonics.

will be in any possible form of matter, energy, life and consciousness.

This concept enables various schools of thoughts in psychology, originated by Jung and represented these days by the trans-personal school – a school that regards consciousness to be holding all of natural history, all religions and the entire collective human memory.

Bohm contends that that consciousness is a ceaseless stream of motion at various levels of consciousness. Consciousness exists at a deeper level and is the source of our thoughts. He equates our ideas to ripples and whirls on the surface, some steady while others are eliminated the moment they appear.

The Tie between the Holographic Model and Therapeutic Avenues

During therapy the therapist provide the patient with a self-reflection either directly or indirectly. She would project to her patient an aspect of himself, that would be lodged in his conscious awareness. Such aspect stirs an image or some other memory out of his deep consciousness that will float up and be present in the therapy process. Levinson (1975) believes that the cause for such therapeutic occurrence is resonance. He asserts that a therapist always knows when treatment succeeds: there is this deep sensation that pieces of a hidden form start to fall into place. The therapist does not tell his patient anything new, instead, he resound something the patient knows already in his sub-consciousness. Levinson adopted the believe that three dimensional representations of the patient's experience are holograms embedded deeply in his subconscious, and that emotional reverberation between therapist and patient cause such representations to rise, in a similar manner to how laser light invokes a particular holographic image.

What is Emotion

Emotions from a psychological perception are a key to putting into motion human behavior, formed by neuro-biological activity. Emotions are responsible for organizing and operating one's awareness and the various levels of consciousness. Such emotional forms from a cognitive perspective, are affected by personal differences and learning in social and cultural contexts. Ariel Shlomo, Ph.D., refers to such emotion-forms this way: <u>E motive = emotion motive = emotion-forms</u>.

How do Emotions get Activated?

We are driven by "basic emotion-forms" (Izard 2007)[22] that includes positive feelings such as, joy, affection, and negative emotions, including, anger, sadness, fear. These two basic emotion-forms function through the senses and constitute our reaction to stimuli of the senses. Our ability to recall various levels of awareness, emotions that we felt as a result of sensual stimuli, enables us to develop a system of selecting that help us survive. For instance, a child climbs a tall ladder and feels fear. The fear registers in his memory and, for example, causes him an avoidance reaction When the child, once more, will experience fear, though in context of different circumstances, e.g., when lifted up on a chair during a birthday party (a common custom in Israel), the avoidance reaction may be triggered. In this manner, emotional forms develop that, originating as survival and adjustment mechanisms but tend to create behavioral patterns that

---

[22] Carroll Ellis Izard (1924), an American psychologist known for his contributions to Differential Emotions Theory (DET), a theory that maintains that universally recognizable innate, basic emotions emerge within the first 2 to 7 months of birth "without facial movement precursors" (Izard, et al., 1995). He also proposed the facial feedback hypothesis, according to which emotions that have different functions also cause facial expression that, in turn, provide cues about what emotion one is feeling.

do not, necessarily, correspond to the actual situation or experience. The reaction created by the embedded fear is to a past experience, not the one occurring at the present.

There are children with emotional experiences that are so etched in memory, they affect difficulties in their ability to function. For example, feelings of social rejection, fear of abandonment, a feeling of shame before an audience, etc.

Children craft effective devices as they cope with such feelings. Often, however, they make their parents' life – and their own – rather miserable when, on the surface, it is unclear whence the fear originated. Other children internalize various feelings related to social and family relationships and drag them to their adolescence and beyond, hence, they have to cope for many years with the consequences of such emotional forms that were buried even at an early age.

The significance of emotion-forms is in their effect on our lives, on our ability to adjust to new situations or different events, our ability to regulate our emotional state of being in situation where we feel emotionally flooded and confused; and, indeed, emotion-forms affect, foremost, our perception of reality. Our emotional memory directly affects our way of thinking, which has an impact on the way we operate in every area of our lives. (Izard 2008).

The Effect of the Emotional Context on Memory

Memory is affected by any number of things. The deeper we have inquired into it, the more we have discovered the complexity and sophistication of this indexing and retention system. One of the factor that significantly impinge on the intensity of remembering a given event, as well as on the retrieval of information to the conscious level, is the emotional milieu of the individual during the event being recalled. Studies have shown that a person's mood at a given moment affects the type of memories that come to mind. Accordingly, a person who is in a bad mood, recalls negative events that were coded into his memory during times he was in a similar mood in the past. This notion could assist a therapist during therapy and guide her patient to remember a particular event by bringing him to the emotional state of being he had experienced, as he coded that particular event.

Na'ama, a 13 year old girl,
"the relationship between emotion and memory."

Memories that rise during therapy bring with them deep emotions (associated with the memory that came to the surface), that till then were locked in the individual's inner reservoirs. The harsher and more momentous is the memory that is rising, the stronger would the associated emotion, buried with it, be. The relationship between emotion and memory is consistent and rather potent. In fact, an emotion that locks in with a companion memory creates a very real emotional block that prevents a full expression of that particular locale (in one's inner landscape) or of the emotions associated with it one way or the other, all of which in order to avoid the sense of pain carved deeply and powerfully as an emotional memory.

Numerous studies have attempted to examine the effect of emotion on memory. It turns out that autobiographical memories are the strongest and most distinct when they are emotionally significant. It was learned that we tend to recall more quickly events with an emotional context in our life as opposed to events that lack such context. Such emotional memories are more detailed and may be retrieved faster, even if they are lodged deeper in the temporal dimension.

Emotional experiences may be measured in one of two indexes:

The Arousal Index - that ranges between relaxing and thrilling/exciting.

The Value Index - ranging from very positive to highly negative.

When we experience stimulation that is emotionally significant, the level of arousal rises, attention to details intensifies and likewise the duration of observing details. Accordingly, powerful and precise coding of the experience occurs in the individual's memory, which makes it more sustained and more intense. Conversely, neutral emotional stimulation tends to ebb over time. Consequently, individuals who tend to suppress emotions and give more thought to their behavior – and a perceived need to control their emotions when conversing with others – would be less likely to recall what was said during such a conversation.

One proposed explanation of this phenomenon, is that physiological systems involved in the release of hormones, that affect the coalescence of memory, are activated during the presentation of arousing stimuli as well as at the end of it. This explains the singeing effect of trauma, strong negative emotional events that are coded and stored with the same intensity as positive events.

During water treatment this process takes place as play therapy where the characters interact, as part of a relationship enacted by the patient: the figures in the sink, those 'on land' in its vicinity, and the therapist. For instance, the patient, as part of role-playing, may enact a fictional angry figure. As he vents anger under the guise of the figure, he fashions the emotional context to those memories charged with anger and allows the mind to draw an emotional memory coded with anger-filled experience from his past. In this manner, he is able to disentangle unresolved historical predicaments that have already been managing his life for many years, bring them out to light and discharge the loaded emotion trapped and hidden therein.

The establishment of an emotion-complementary environment, adjusted to the type of memories caged in, is also typical of healing processes associated with intentional regression, which brings the patient to where he can draw memories buried in the far past. Water therapy, art therapy and other expressive types of treatment, accord great importance to repressed emotions and the process of their extraction. By releasing such emotion, a corresponding release from mental and emotional impasse and a return to psychological and mental balance are thus facilitated.

Relation between Memory and Emotional Patterns

All of our motor, cognitive, and emotional learning skills are an outcome of the relation between emotion and cognition.

To illustrate: a small child is climbing a ladder at a playground, where he put into action a large number of motor skills. Likewise, he feels excitement due to the effort he must exert as a result of the physical challenge. Naturally, he must first overcome his fear of the new experience and the fear of disengagement from the ground and ascending upward. However, the moment he reached the apex (of both the tree and the experience), he would feel a sensation of satisfaction and accomplishment: "I have reached the place I sought to arrive at!" All the while, his mother is cheering him on, praising him for the effort and the achievement: "Lovely son; more power to you!" The positive reinforcement, directed verbally, enters the sorting apparatus of the mind and is registered as "positive." The child feels that he did had accomplish something worthy, something positive. As he descends, after the exerted climbing journey he had just been through, his mother hugs him, thus according him with a physical acknowledgement for his trial. His memory records the following impressions:

Self-exercise = success

Overcoming fear = a positive feeling

An activity I engaged in = positive reaction from mom = pleasant

the ladder climbing is now coded in memory as a positive experience that forms positive thoughts and a positive reaction toward the environment. When another such experience will occur, the young child will draw the emotional pattern experienced this time and will apply it. This is the source of the saying that success brings success, while negative experiences become embedded in the schemas of emotion and often affect one's motivation to undergo an experience or, alternatively, the quality of performance of other task in life. Since life is not without a share of negative experiences, action that would, emotionally, produce creativity and spontaneity, as in games, art, dance, etc., would assist in transforming negative emotion-forms to positive ones. Such activities may be undertaken at any stage in a person's life and would enable release of any emotional gridlock and facilitate the formation of emotionally positive alternatives.

Value of Language in Emotional Definition

Words and language clearly and distinctly can express more insubstantial elements, such as feelings and the spirit's inner voice. Such speech, whether by a child or adult, constitutes the pouring the spirit into matter in a way that someone on the outside could hear and notice its contents. Hidden emotions would thus be expressed, in the words chosen, the sentences composed, the subjects brought up in a conversation, in stories told and in the tone of voice used for such expression.

During therapy, language will have considerable import in the process of creating emotional patterns, both as a reflection the therapist provides the patient and in the ability to implement emotional processes/emotional expression during treatment.

Through the various linguistic expressions by children, by way of activities and play, it is possible to evaluate emotion-forms engraved in their memory. For instance, when a child who is about to paint or draw says: "Surely this will fail ..." he actually gives expression to his negative emotional perception about such activity as painting. During therapy we will meet the child with his various perceptions regarding emotions, that seize up his activity processes and we will seek to lift, to a higher level of awareness, the blocking emotions in order to replace them with different emotions. For example, the child who is anticipating a failure with painting could be guided to verbally delineate his apprehension of failure by (the therapist) saying, "You never know till you try," or, "Sometime you succeed sometimes you don't, it happened to everybody."

The Relationship between Non-verbal Processes and Art

We are all familiar with the feeling that we know what we are experiencing yet are unable to identify or describe what we feel. The inability to put into words such a feeling does not annul its impression in one's consciousness, nor the ability to draw it from memory; it may be accomplished through alternative avenues, since the emotion schema is stored in the brain though not "filed" under linguistic or intellectual categories. Consequently, other processes would be necessary in order to elevate the sense of the experience so that it could be expressed and not just conventionally, e.g., verbally.

Water therapy facilitates the raising of non-verbal emotions. As a result of contact with water, a fluid, calm ambience imbues the process, which allows information to percolate outwardly with little if any friction. Such information may manifest in the choice of colors, in the artwork, the specific preferences in the use of imagination or play, as well as the verbal definitions that in fact create a verbal mapping of non-verbal and emotional aspects of a given expression.

As a result of such activity, emotions float up from deep layers of consciousness to a more surface level of awareness and a "clean-up" can occur, ventilation of emotions that were log-jammed deep in the mind. Once these emotions rise to the surface, the child experience them at a new, safe locale, while being treated and in the company of a mediator and while he is able to convert them, with the therapist's assistance, to more positive emotions, by reorganizing, regulating and releasing them.

The Relationship between Emotions, Play and Learning.

Through evolution the brain has developed its complex ability to acquire tools of learning by way of imitation. This development has served the purpose of creating means of adjustment and social endurance.

Mirror neurons (Rizzolati 1998) are cells in the brain that allow us to sense what another feels and act like him. The allow us to synthesize visual input with kinesthetic sensing.[23] It is presumed that their function relates to the ability to feel empathy, i.e., to perceive the mind-set of another and ascertain his intentions, learning by imitation and, perhaps, even to the ability to learn a language and create a culture – to be **human**, in other words.

These cells in fact are engaged in communication, in transmitting information between transmitter and receiver, in identifying activity undertaken by another. This is the basis of and condition for communication in general and, eventually, for the development of human language that has no equivalent among other living things in nature. We often hear a teacher tells a child who heart the feelings of another, "Think how you'd feel if anyone said that to you ...." Our capacity to ascertain or imagine the feelings of another comes from these mirror cells, that can "read" fellow human being's thoughts, perceive how he feels, thinks and plans. A deficiency in this ability is a form of "psychic blindness," and in an extreme situation it is a severe handicap characterized as autism. Mirror cells contributes to the marked social abilities of the human race; are valuable to the learning ability of a human being, to his sophistication and to the existence of human culture.

Moreover, these cells are responsible for the phenomenon of self-conversation, which include translation of emotions to words, first to oneself then externally, to the whole world. Their importance is in the formation of communication with another, however, it is no less significant in creating self-communication as part of the individual's construction of his own world within and his ability to sort out his emotions.

In therapy, during part of the time, the therapist unconsciously activates the mirror cells thus creating an empathetic reaction toward the patient, as well as an emotional reaction by the patient, which

---

[23] This process is absent among autistic children, whose mirror neurons malfunction. See, Ramachandran 2004.)

reaction is fed to the therapist in order to create therapeutic context and communication in order to generate healing. Likewise, water therapy enables empathy through the use of game playing as a means for expression and enhancement of emotional mechanisms created in the mirror cells.

The Relationship between Emotions, the Conscious and Unconscious Mind

Emotional experiences become etched in us continuously, starting while we are in utero. A newborn infant feels and stores emotional data in memory, as does a two year old. The more unpleasant it is the deeper and further he would secrete it, a mechanism that allows us to keep on growing and developing despite the objectionable event.

Infants that undergo invasive procedures, such as circumcision, probing examinations, being poked by needles, operations and the like, exhibit pain facially. As they grow older their reaction to such invasive procedures become anger. Infants experience basic emotions but lack the ability to report them verbally; those emotions occur at one level of awareness or another. The same emotions that form a neuro-biological process and become registered at deep levels of consciousness – are called, at times, the unconscious. That is to say, emotional activity takes place distinctively in the body and brain systems but also is registered at different levels and is accessible to the formation of expression in various ways. After the acquisition of language they may, occasionally, be reported symbolically (as in the case of play), behaviorally, bodily, facially and verbally.

As the level of the child's development grows, his ability to create more complex emotion-forms grows as well. Hence, language becomes a tool of emotional management, self-regulation and other functions that execute inter-personal communication, e.g., affecting empathy toward and identifying with another.

What is Therapy and What is it Needed for?

Both children and adults reach therapy for any number of reasons. Some have to do with the effect of daily reality on the quality of one's life or it could be a result of a momentous event that had visited their lives. Other reasons could also be the manifestation of repetitious behavioral patterns that bring about negative experiences or difficulties in relationships; and, lack of emotional fulfillment.

When a person turns to therapy, he expects to receive assistance that would alleviate his anguish and improve the quality of his life. Every once in a while, there is an expectation of a shift in one's life and the achievement of goals and objectives. Observing the components of the challenge, one can notice a common denominator composed of three elements:

1. **Emotions** – stored in the individual's memory;

2. **Memory** – a complex system of emotional and cognitive information that is stored and coded.

3. **Thinking** – historical thought patterns, a system designed to reach conclusions, a system that processes information out of memory which creates a worldview.

These factors encounter some form of reality to which they react and by which they are operated, akin to a relationship between a person's interior and the external world.

The aim of emotional therapy is to bring relief and better balance to the individual and, ideally, to cause a change and bring about an improvement in his life. In order to accomplish these, there is a need to be in touch with those factors that significantly affect the interior, i.e., emotions, memories and thoughts, the ones that form the requisite dialogue with the exterior world.

This is called a therapeutic process. Generally speaking, its aim is to raise the patient's level of self-awareness as well as his external awareness to emotional patterns, using processes of events thoughts and emotions' recall from memory, that sustain inner balance and serenity.

Emotions can be accorded expression through either verbal or non-verbal manifestation, for instance, through art. Inner flow of unconscious emotions, formerly confined for a very long time in a low awareness level, may be facilitated as the emotional patterns are provided means of expression. Treatment through art in general and water in particular allows access to these regions where awareness' level is low and in part pre-verbal.

The use of art and creativity constitutes an open forum for material that exists in a secreted place, i.e., imagination for example has a strong tie with deep contents at a low awareness level; the contexts that arise in imagination-driven, creative processes hold both the expression of the hardship and the opportunity for a solution. It is analogous to a person coping with a problem in external reality who dreams a dream a t night that presents an allegory of a challenge from the dreamer's life in the outer world. Such dream is where the person dreaming finds a solution to the problem by coping with the challenge presented in the dream. As he wakes up he may recall the dream and distills from it the solution to the real problem. In other words, the substance of the problem also holds in it the solution, since everything, including our imagination and subjective reality, is within us.

Accordingly, if we take the sentence: Thought creates reality, we would understand that as we get in touch with our emotions and memories, craft a deep shift in our perception of our world and the way we look at reality, we could change, for ourselves, the reality in which we live.

How Does Water Treatment Give Expression to the Inner World?

Water is an effective stimuli for unlocking the inner world and floating up memories stored there. They are perceived in consciousness as a "place" of the inner world. This reaction is a consequence of (i) the neuro-biological tie between water and the human body; (ii) the qualities of water that are detailed elsewhere in this book; (iii) the fact that when we are born, we emerge from a liquid environment to a gaseous one, and the watery world we emerged from remains in the "cellular memory" as a historical world where processes had taken place, an impression was recorded and memories of growing in the mother's womb had registered. (See, Chapter 12, Trauma and Birth Trauma.)

Water treatment, therefore, is based on human beings' natural affinity with water. As the patient encounter water during emotions' focused therapy, he sees the water, touches and hears it through a system of senses that engages immediately and which transmits a stimuli to the brain that releases at once a holographic memory containing emotion-forms stored in a very deep level of awareness.

The internal reverberation created in the patient by the water allows materials from the hidden layer to appear in the form of color, movement, sound and play. The release of these emotion-forms is made possible when the method of expression is visual and sensory. That is to say, emotion-forms can be expressed only through the internal world's codes which appear in the "language of imagination" as symbols, pictures, sounds and short motion picture clips. Little wonder that such representations often appear in dreams – as these representations, emerging from the inner world are raw and primary, it is not surprising that they mostly appear illogical and hazy, just as the inner world processes of representation are raw and primary, which constitute in fact what we have defined as the hidden layer.

Otherwise, we would have been aware of them and they would not be "unconscious."

Since water easily releases contents and materials from the hidden order to the open one, such contents and materials float up and rise as the encounter with the water evolves. We could therefore observe, discern and understand the materials of which the inner world was formed. A similar process also happens with the use of other types of art therapy, however, these water processes produce rapid results, since water serves as an " memory agent" of the human body and the human psyche.

How does Emotion-Oriented Water Treatment Help Maintain and Organize the Mental inner world?

Emotional treatment in general, and water treatment with a creative bent in particular, allows a child to express his inner world, introverted within him, and bring certain aspects of it out into the therapy room. Since internalization of characters that are primary objects is done at very early stages, during childhood, starting with birth and through the first few months of the child's life, which continue to evolve as the child's personality grows and develops, these events are usually stored at very deep levels when the verbal aspect does not yet exist as a mental function. For this reason, water treatment is not based only on the verbal aspect of the person but also allows the use of colors; creativity and imagination play key roles in the processes.

In addition, the inner world has life of its own and it collects holographic memories which are stored in the memory located in the brain. The ability to access these memories traverses the inner world, that serves as a kind of a virtual location, through which once can be in contact with the objects residing therein. One "communicates" with these objects in 'their own' language, the language of imagination, which includes, vision, sound and motion. We can communicated with those sequestered representations. A example, borrowed from science fiction is where one is able to enter another's dream as a character who functions in there In such situation, the character can co-exist with inner representations and certainly be able to affect the plot of the dream.

Water therapy that is combined with art (water-art therapy) allows us to respond to imagination's inquiries thus: Water-art therapy facilitates the use of imagination by the patient, by allowing inner representations, that "live" within him, their expression. Moreover, creativity and art are composed of the same media that form the inner world and which are stored in the holographic memory. Thanks to the visual, vocal and motion qualities of art, these media have the same resident "language" that is present in the inner world, which significantly contributes to communication with those internalized representations.

The use of water as a substance the patient comes into contact with, the sounds of water and those produced by interaction with it; the appearance and movement of water affect sensory resonance in the brain, releasing memories trapped in the depths of consciousness since early infancy. Thus, a permitted entry into an inner, internalized world is facilitated, at least partially.

Game playing is another factor that enables motion and change in the inner world. When a kind of a game, one that can set the problematic media in motion, is combined with art therapy, a natural movement is created that causes the inner world to move, open and raise up inner contents to conscious awareness and then deliver them, literally, to the therapy room.

Inner materials, in accord with the holography principle, have a tendency to locomote from a hidden order to an open one. Hence, such "materials" as emotions, memories and thoughts can float up from levels of lesser awareness and surface at a higher level. Eventually, such passage manifests as an overt expression through play and art, and in relationships. Such process allows the therapist to reflect to, and elucidate for, the child the contents he gives expression to and assist him in preserving, organizing and regulating his inner world.

As therapy comes along, the patient would be able, due to such favorable conditions as holding (emotionally), sensitivity to his emotional and mental needs, acceptance and faith in him and in the healing process – through such a dynamic process that works – to achieve growing degree of balance between his inner and outer worlds.

Water Therapy – the Process

The patient gets in touch with water through the senses

The senses convey to the brain electrical signals through the nervous system.

The electrical signal awakens holographic memories, stored at various locations in the brain, as well as through reverberations that water forms in a tangible medium that is related to the human body

Memories containing emotion-forms of past experiences = "inner world"

Emotion-forms float up & surface from a lower (deeper) levels of awareness to a higher (more conscious) one

The inner world – it receives expression through symbolic expressive forms such as simile, symbolism, metaphors through the likes of art, voice, movement and play

Materials lodged at hidden layers are released and surface at an open level of awareness

Inner world's creativity and contents join together into a picture, occurrence, relationship and plot

The inner world is projected outwardly, reaching the patient and through him the therapist

The patient reorganizes inner contents thus improves his inner representations' array. The therapist provides the process room, she contains it, witnesses it and affords positive feedback without any judgment

The patient can now reverse direction, bringing his inner world back in and re-internalizing it differently

This process affects a deep change in emotion-forms, memory and thought. The inner world continues to exist and is now charged with renewed vitality in a renewed weave of emotion-forms.

Chapter 10

The Role of the Therapist

Taking a joint journey at a sink in the therapy room does not start then and there, it commences by building a relationship with and forming a bond with the child and delineating a space where he feels secure enough to express himself and be creative; the establishment of open, flowing communication that allows the child to express what he holds within and a link with the therapist that facilitates the interpretation of symbols and signs that will be revealed as he "plays" with water are also needed. I never know in advance what will be the right timing for commencing the "wet journey," however, when the moment is at hand, it reveals itself and usually at the exact right instant. Be that as it may, there are signals that denote its arrival.

Indicative Signals of Readiness for Water Treatment

1. Direct Request from or a tendency by the Child to play with water

The request by the child for engaging with water will usually appear when he will be handling "wet" materials, such as hand paints, water colors, gouache, a wet sandbox and the like. The child might provide hints during therapy, when materials that contain water are in use (such as wet clay). There, energy is vested in water though the focus is on the primary substance being used (e.g., clay or sand). Some children exhibit a tendency to create "mud" from clay and, again and again, add water or engage in placing clay in water and then taking it out, not really focusing on sculpting anything in particular.

(See, Chapter 12, Water Treatment in the event of a Trauma -- a Case Study, pp.255.)

2. Failure to Achieve Progress in Therapy

A shift to water therapy is effective in many cases where lack of progress is evident and the child's behavioral patterns repeat, e.g., he plays the same games over and over again or, a defense mechanism is apparent, manifesting in a fixed choices of art work that do not change, such as a drawing the same model time and again.

3. Contents that Relate to Water

When contents rise to the child conscious awareness that relate directly to water, for example, drawing a ship or a lake, sculpting a distinct lake or a sea in the sandbox and that is where events occur, a puppet show that has, for instance a marine mammal, e.g., a whale, as well as stories about water that arise from observing a painting, playing in a "small world" and/or any other therapeutic medium.

During a discussion with parents at the therapy room, a father who was a law school professor, repeatedly inquired: "I don't understand how the therapy works, how is it that my five year old son arrives at this room, plays with you, paints and talks and then his social skills at the kindergarten improve?"

This question constituted a noteworthy lesson in my attempt to actually define what the therapy does for the child and what is it that I do 'that makes the difference' and contributes to the formation of such a significant shift. The various therapeutic theories, schools of thoughts, styles and numerous blessed influences are akin to an ocean of ideas, that for years have been my fishing grounds. I identify with some; with others, less. The insight that came up and reverberated in my mind as a result of that question is that play therapy, just like art therapy, gives the child an opportunity to express his emotions both verbally and non-verbally. Using play, the child expresses his difficulties symbolically and learns to channel them more effectively. This, in turn, allows him to form a relationship based on trust with another person, the therapist, and, consequently, behavioral patterns that were caught up in a loop/jammed (a conduct that is defined as "abnormal") is released, becomes open and flowing, i.e., "normal."

The psychotherapist Violet S. Oaklander (1994) spoke about therapy through play according to gestalt[24] where emphasis is placed building a therapeutic relationship (between therapist and patient) as a necessary condition for the formation of a treatment process that enables validation of the sense of self and a self expression of the child. This is followed by the stage of self nurturing, then the completion stage. (See Chapter 5, Preservation, p.106.)

My reply to the father was as follows: The healing occurs as a bond forms between the child and therapist and, as is the case in every relationship with others, we encounter different aspects of ourselves that observe the other and are reflected in her. In this, as in any other relations, it is impossible to ascertain, before the bond is formed, what we might discover about ourselves and what kind of persons we would become. One thing is certain, however, the relationship between you and I will significantly look different when we part ways.

The function of the therapist who resorts to water therapy is not different than his function throughout the therapeutic process. The difference is that water therapy is a **focused technique**, a technique that serves as a therapeutic tool designed to focus the process, enhance it and converge energies on a particular matter.

---

[24] Oaklander is known for having developed therapy methods to treat children and adolescents using a wealth of therapeutic techniques such as expression through art, clay, poetry, storytelling, the sand tray, music and puppets – all associated with the Gestalt Therapy theory, practice and technique as the underlying framework.

Reasons for Opting for a Focused Technique, i.e., the Water Therapy Method:

1. Continued Process of Regressive Experience

Work with water relates to a situation where there were previous sessions during which there was some use of water and a regression occurred. These would include work with wet sand, finger painting, clay, liquefying Play-Doe under hot water, and the like.

2. Concentrating on a Specific Subject

Referring a patient to work with water is a zoom-in on an emotional subject that began rising at the therapy room and demands further attention.

3. Disentangling Situations that did not Find an Expressive Outlet

Situation where therapy is stuck, water therapy may be a key to a locked gate.

A Glance into the Therapy Room ...

Five year old Nadav arrive at therapy as a result of bursts of aggression and anger in kindergarten and at home. He is the third child in a family of four children. He has a brother and a sister who are older and an 18 months infant sister. Nadav is a gifted child with an impressive intellectual ability, yet there was a large gap between his intellectual and cognitive ability and his capacity for expressing emotions; he also had a need for control that he conveyed through aggression and anger. Nadav's treatment included different types of expression such as game-story, drama, puppet show, painting, sculpting and more. In all the different means of expression he utilized there were two main characters: the first an authority figure, such as a king, a cop or a father, the second figure is one that is always crushed, killed or attacked, a monkey for instance or any other animal he chose to undergo such an ordeal.

During the eighth session he wrote a song while drumming: "I'm the king at home, I like to destroy all the animals, it makes me feel cozy! In the kindergarten I demolish Nathaniel for he beats me up, I tell the teacher, but she does not do anything! I love getting punished and sit in the corner, since participation is punishment!"

Note: At this stage Nadav has opened up to the notion of sharing and voicing his feelings as to situations he creates and becomes caught in. But despite the fact that Nadav's capacity for expression improved greatly, the internal reason for his loaded anger was yet to be discovered.

During the ninth session we worked with water, till then the treatment mostly involved the use of materials that require control. Nadav's choice was to color the water orange. He placed four crocodiles, a whale, a starfish, an octopus, an elephant and four sharks in the water. There were two leopards, a lamb, a horse, a donkey, a dinosaur, a teddy-bear and a lion out of the water.

Nadav describes the water world this way: "There are carnivores in the water. Outside, the lion is quarreling with the animals there. The bear may not enter the water because he'll get wet and die! If anyone falls into the water, the animals would devour it in there. The bear is not afraid to jump into the water because there is no other place with water around here. The bear got into the water and, oh no, he didn't die!!! The animals outside are waiting, wondering when their pray might emerge." He then places his hands in the water and says: "Help! Help! The shark almost devoured me!"

Notice: One can observe that Nadav is recapitulating the matter of aggression in two dimensions: The first within his inner world and the other in his outer world. In both there are carnivores laying in wait for prey. Note, that he has chosen the figure of the bear to represent the one who is in danger. The bear may not enter the water, to avoid getting wet. In other words, Nadav is identifying with a childish, infant-like figure. In his pessimistic outlook, if the figure would enter the water it will surely die. When he places his own hand in the water, he actually wants to experience the danger with his own physical body. At that juncture he succeed in "getting wet," i.e., be in touch with his own emotions and fears, by being at the place that is the most frightening for him – where he is utterly helpless.

Another point worth noting, is what he says about the water: "There is no other water!" So that is all that is! Once more, his pessimistic approach to his emotional life's qualities.

The encounter at the sink enabled a subsequent series of therapy sessions were the subject of sibling's jealousy. During these sessions Nadav described his infant sister and created a series of acts expressing anger and annihilation aimed at her. He took a infant doll and fried it in a frying pen, poked her eyes out and said: "All girls should be whacked." I then ask: "Mom, too?" "No," he responds, "neither mom nor dad," he replies fearfully. "But my older brother and sister, yes!"

During one of the encounters he colored the water blue, which indicates the need for expression. This time, instead of the bear, the figure that was immersed in the water was a diver: "He isn't afraid of the snakes in the water."

Note: In effect he says: 'I'm willing to dive into the depth where the unresolved issues are and encounter them. Nadav, in fact, began expressing and getting in touch with his real fears, that were wrapped by violent and aggressive behavior. He created a superb process through which he released the anger he felt toward his parents, caused by the birth of his sister, where he was too afraid to be mad at them for he feared losing them.

During our last session he opted for the color red and said: "Red is my entire life." He took a doll house and placed it at the edge of the sink. There were no carnivores in the water this time. Instead, dolphins, turtles and horses were placed in there. I was told that he began participating socially at his kindergarten, that violent events no longer took place and, at home, he exhibited much empathy toward his infant sister; he also sought touch and warmth from his parents.

The Role of the Therapist During Water Therapy (I)

The therapist performs a variety of tasks throughout treatment, which enable gradual progress and healing.

A Catalyst who Furthers the Process

In an integrative therapy such as this (water therapy), the therapist's initial task is to be a catalyst who foster the process by providing focus. The focal aspect of the treatment is the very experience, the course traversed by the child. Focusing is on what the child does and how he does it; what he feels and what he wants to express.

A Mirror that Reflects

Children have a natural ability and tendency to be immediately focused on the moment itself and the therapist accompanying a child being treated reflects to the latter his own self. Accordingly, the therapist does not advise the child what to do but lets him become aware of the process itself.

The Therapist's Role During the Initial Part of therapy:

At the start of water treatment, therapist and patient stand side by side, the child, usually, standing on a small chair with an apron and his sleeves rolled up. Together, they are looking at the sink and it is now time to pick colors and mix them into the water in the sink.

Therapist and patient stand side by side at the sink at the initial stage of the water treatment

During this initial part of the experience, the therapist assists the patient with technical matters while also participating in carrying on the new "experiment," containing, and expressing enthusiasm about, it and expressing surprise as the color of the water changes and excitement regarding contact with paints. She also would assist in printing the colors on paper.

While the therapist functions side by side with the patient, she would closely observes the latter's body movement, his communicating through eye-contact, noticing verbal and non-verbal reactions, the modulation of tone of speech and the energy in general that accompanies the process, going through its varying phases such as apprehension, joy, hesitation, impulsiveness and more. The child's body provides rich and detailed data about his emotions and will provide the therapist with signals about the emotional process he is undergoing.

The Non-Verbal Messages provide rich information in real time about the emotions the patient is experiencing. This is especially noticeable in those cases where children (as well as adults) have suffered a trauma, where the body experience was severed from the emotional aspect of the person. In such cases we can observe children and adults have a "frozen" physical expression in those areas where they are supposed to be limber, flowing and physically coordinated.

Note: Children have, build-in, associations and contexts in their way of thinking. At times, associations that are tied to contexts rooted in reality, while on other occasions they are not. At this stage (of adding color to the water), associations will surface in the child's mind. This is a tool that is useful in discovering elements that are suppressed away from the conscious mind, that are not expressed in normal behavior, at least not in a direct fashion. The therapist can navigate these associations to the right location and/or relate them to the expansion of the emotional picture that comes to the fore as a result of the treatment.

A Glimpse into the Therapy Room

Danny, a 33 years old adult patient, is the youngest of three brothers. He still resides at home with his parents. His father is mentally ill and his mother is a diabetic whose limbs have been amputated. Danny sought treatment because he greatly desired to leave home and build himself an independent life: get married, work and depart the sickness and inertia he felt he was mired in. Working with water, he picked three colors: orange, violet and brown. With each color, a different association came to his mind, however, when he mixed all three and a murky brown resulted he said: "That's the sewage color that oozes out of the clogged sink at home – I also have to deal with that at home – and then all this yucky stuff comes out and it reeks!" He had hard time putting his hands into the sewage color and when he finally did he said sadly: "My life really stinks and I'm the only one at home that deals with all this repugnant stuff, no one else would bother to lift a finger."

Creating Conditions for Communication

Creating conditions for communication sets the foundation for the whole treatment. If the conditions become optimal, the child will communicate all that he has accumulated inside. Conversely, lack of optimal conditions would impede such communication. Therefore, an emphasis should be placed on those elements that affect children, in general, and the child character, in particular. After getting to know the patient, such optimal condition could encompass the following:

a. Formation of a therapeutic relationship that includes: Attentiveness, creation of a therapeutic area that honors the patient rhythm of doing things, a non-judgmental atmosphere of acceptance, building, in the patient, a feeling of trust and a sense of security that would allow him to feel relaxed and comfortable, free to utter anything that comes to his mind and to express his emotions. Encouragement and support of his sense of self and the establishment of conditions that will facilitate the various trials and experiences he will undergo during treatment.

b. The therapist's faith in the patient's healing process, fine perceptive, sensitivity to verbal and non-verbal messages, shaping a message of hope and love.

Formation of a Transition Area
At this stage of therapy, formation of a transition area is made possible in which therapist and patient become partners. At this area the therapist creates a neutral zone where communication is indirect. In other words, they jointly participate in events, however, there is a measure of separation between them, since play in water does not involve direct interaction. The psychologist Linnete McMahon calls such relationships "personal yet structured."

In each and every kind of art and play treatment, the "third thing," the in-between area – the sink – forms the place of encounter where the therapist and patient meet, since the relationship is projected onto the third object and is not a direct encounter between the two.

During the first part of the treatment the therapist's role occurs at the joint area. During the second stage, the joint area turns into a "private domain" as the sink becomes the exclusive territory of the patient and his playing ground, where he gets the opportunity to play unsupervised and construct the water world any which way he desires.

The Therapist's Role During of Water Treatment Part II

At this stage the therapist comes to stand behind the playing child, close enough that her presence is felt but she is not on a horizontal line with the child and no eye contact is had. She can, however, see the child's body movements and hear his tone of voice.

The therapist standing behind the patient at an angle that allows observation of the patient's body language and facial expressions.

Note: The purpose of the shift in position is to enable holding, a term borrowed from various treatment methods that resort to physical holding of the patient's body as a means to regulate particularly stormy feelings and behaviors that may be accompanied with loss of control by the child or patient. Such holding require the therapist to hold the patient from behind while the child sits in her lap. It's a "hug" that in effect controls the child's movement, not allowing him to move much till he slowly relaxes. In this manner the therapist becomes an external, present container for the child.

However, the therapist's posture during water treatment is done without physical contact. Likewise, the shift of location brings about the expansion of the space available to the patient for movement and play, so that he can assume autonomy during the symbolic game. The therapist serves as a witness and observes what is occurring; the child is aware of the therapist's presence but can opt to ignore her.

It is akin to the principles of the world of theater, where there is an unstated agreement between the audience and those on stage: both parties are aware of the fact that the theatrical production is not real yet readily ignore it and make believe that the occurrences performed on stage are genuinely real.

In a theater there is also a separation between the playing area – the stage – and the audience, that provides the actors with some latitude. They accept the situation that the audience is watching them from a distance. The therapist's presence during the patient's interaction with water legitimizes the experience and, in fact, tells the child, "I, too, am aware of what is transpiring and of the emotions that surface here."

A Glimpse from the Therapy Room

A second-grader name Ro'ee arrived at therapy following an episodic eruption of uncontrolled rage, aimed mainly at his mother. By then, his parents were divorced for three years and he had a brother who was two years younger. His parents also reported about apprehensions and low self-image though he excelled at everything he dealt with.

During treatment Ro'ee related to the notion of "home" in several different ways. He built his father's place out of cardboard and even formed a man's figure in his forties, in effect telling me about a rigid, punishing and humiliating personality who lives alone. He also created a woman's figure whom he buried in a sand formation, saying, "She ought to remain there; she's worthless!" He also drew their old home, where they lived as a family before the divorce; then he built an amusement park, saying that he loved it the most and declared that he is not afraid of even the most dangerous facilities.

While undergoing water treatment, Ro'ee created on the edge of the sink a magnificent garden with a fence – "The area where no one may enter." In the garden he placed figures of a father, mother and a young son. there were various creatures in the water, some carnivorous. He commenced a symbolic game with the figures, ignoring my presence. After a while he took a piece of Play-Doh and fused the oldest child's legs to a wooden board, then started raising and lowering it as if it were an airplane, diving with it toward the water than lifting it up, over and over again. He then turned to me and asked: "Do you know what this is?" I did not respond and he then said, "You don't want to know ... it's a roller coaster! Whoever get aboard knows what to expect."

Note: Addressing me amid the game was an emotional anchor for him; it was as if he asked: Do you understand what I'm going through? Come be my partner in this experience, watch and see how a perfect family world can turn into a nightmare. Immediately after that, the entire family boarded the roller coaster and went through the frightening experience of diving toward the water, which stand for a stormy sea of emotions.

Water Therapy

The child commences building the water world as he arranges different pieces of small items inside and around the water in the sink those building a whole world.

Then, the child starts playing an imaginary game, using the figures of animals, people and all other items he had arranged there.

This kind of a game is therapeutic in nature, where the child's protagonists (and antagonists), the conflicts he struggles with, the alignment of forces in his immediate environment, his difficulties, strengths and defenses are all laid bare.

Occasionally, the game contains recapitulation of experiences from the child's reality, such as: pain, struggle, excitement, joy, aggression, anger, and the like.

At this stage the therapist does not intervene on makes suggestions. As was said by Clare Winnicott, "A brief acknowledgement of a painful or frightening experience may touch deeply and there is no need to wallow."

The therapist allows the game to occur spontaneously. If the child should ask her to participate and become one of the characters, he should be told: "You tell me what to do and how to say my lines – teach me." The moment he shows her what to do, he actually does it himself and the therapist should repeat his performance exactly, including voice and intonation as well as the movement of the character as it acts.

Listening and Reverberation

At this stage it is vital that the therapist would listen attentively to the child, since he needs to identify, during the game, those places where there might be a reverberation of various voices and contents that may be significant. The therapist repeats or strengthen (though she may also weaken) the reactions of the characters thus giving them life and enhancing the experience. For instance, a lion is devouring animals emerging out of the water, whose voice is weak, the therapist would then amplify it (possibly gradually while evaluating the child's reaction). This enables the child to repeat the action himself, using the strength called for by the situation. This would facilitate the release of aggressive, belligerent emotions and in fact bypasses the marking action undertaken by the child, from the intellect to an emotional channel and the path of imagination that is tied to the child and his world. A child who roars a lion emerging from the water, forms control over the emotions symbolized by the lion.

At this stage, the therapist is both a witness of the events taking place and one who echoes the occurrence and voices, while placing an emphasis on vigor. In the example where the therapist reverberated the lion's roar, release of aggression, vital for emotional expression occurs. According to Oaklander, proactive actions and gratification require aggressive energy that is more than a sense of inner strength, it requires action. The term refers to the energy needed, for example, in order to take a bite out of an apple or express a strong emotion, one that would provide a child with self support and enable initiating activity.

Oaklander also asserts that expression of aggressive energy is a necessary condition for a healthy emotional expression! I have often encountered children who found it difficult to direct aggressive energy outwardly. They were introverted and shut, and avoided initiating social relationships; they kept everything inside, which created a considerable emotional burden, at times even manifesting psychosomatic phenomena such as stomach pains, headaches, sore throats, constipation and the like.

The principle of reverberation and repeat of sentences uttered by the patient, ties in with a therapeutic technique from the field of psychodrama where a "double," who is an expanded self, is used: The purpose of the double is to assist the protagonist express hidden emotions and thoughts, move him to encounter repressed conflicts and discover his spontaneity, provide support and sympathy so that he may feel secure and open. The double follows every motion, sound and sentence uttered by the protagonist (patient) and when the latter acts, he imitates him and, as much as possible, he becomes a mirror and an echo of the protagonist.

The double technique relates to the initial development stage where the mother speaks for her infant child: "We're hungry now ... we're tired...." Her capacity for verbalizing the infant's emotional reaction serves, on one hand, as a communication extension for it, and on the other, as a mirror. Consequently, the infant feels that its emotions, desires and experience have validity – someone understands it! speaks loudly with it! Similarly, the reverberation technique used during water treatment allows the therapist to serve as both a witness as one who echoes what is transpiring; she can sound her voice and amplify what is being said and done during the spontaneous game being played.

Projective Identification[25]

The term, "projection," was coined by Freud. It relates to attributing qualities, thoughts or beliefs to another or representation of that person (the one projecting) through a figure, e.g., a doll, animal, etc., that assumes a personality (or elements thereof).

On the other hand, Melanie Klein (1946) coined the term 'projective identification,' which refers to those negative urges and images a child feels toward himself, the child "deposits" with others those anxiety aspects of the self and then he identifies with the other in order to feel renewed ownership of that which was split of the self. This is an inner process.

Use is made in therapy of not-characterized, indirect stimulation, in order to create projective identification. For example, having the

---

[25] Projective identification is a term introduced by Melanie Klein, describing a process in which a close relationship – as between mother and child or therapist and patient – parts of the self may, in unconscious fantasy, are seemingly forced into the other person. See, Patrick Casement, Further Learning from the Patient (London 1990) p. 177

patient look at pictures of two different individuals, in relation to whom with he is asked to describe a relationship.

According to Bion, infant's screams during times of stress may indicate its attempt to split out of such dire experiences by using projection. The mother's presence and her mental activities, combined with her ability to respond, alter the situation in that she becomes a vessel for containing the unpleasant experiences and enables the formation of primitive projective communication-identification. Through such vessel, the infant relates to the mother as a container-object with space (capacity) for undergoing stress. When the infant is unable to tolerate suffering, the mother provides it with an opportunity to internalize through her, with her ability to tolerate the stress at issue. The mother grows familiar with her child as he becomes familiar with itself, through what the mother reflects to him about himself; the child becomes familiar with his emotional experiences and those of others. (See, the website for professional who deal with early age children in Israel, gilrach.co.il.)

the manner by which the therapist reverberates the child's expressions, and by voice enhancement of the child's emotional assertions, she creates projective identification that returns to the child and is internalized in his emotional array. By so doing, the therapist can contains the threatening and negative aspects and re-organizes them in her internal space. Likewise, the projective identification with figures, who in actual reality are in a relationship with the patient, will taper.

The Therapist's Role During Water Treatment Part II

Following the undirected game, when it seems that the game's energy starts dissipating, the therapist would ask the child being treated to talk about the water world. "The level of timing and interpretation are crucial. Winnicott noticed that a game could reach a saturation point,

where the child could not get arrive at another experience."
(Winnicott 1971, p. 57)

The therapist now goes back to stand side by side with the child by the sink, as a partner and one who actively listens to what is being said.

At this stage, the therapist's role becomes more intricate than just verbal translation of the emotional play experience. Now she begins to expand the context of what is being played, by asking questions that relate to the actual scene being enacted such as describing the place – I often ask the children: "What do you call this place?" "Who lives in the water?" Who lives out of the water?" I also ask a general question about what is transpiring, e.g., "Please tell me what is going on here?" If I notice a form of identification with a given figure I might ask a question related to that particular character. For instance, "How did the little turtle feel when he was left all alone on the island?"

It is not easy for children to get across experiences to the plateau of conscious awareness, without the help of a therapist that would link the experience felt with its significance. Therefore, many experiences remain unstated. The ability to report experiences with clarity is difficult for them. Despite the difficulty there is a degree of introspection in children. The therapist should use, if the patient would allow it, and form for him and with him a affiliation between the cognitive aspect (understanding, intellectual perception of what has transpired) and experience itself, one that is emotional-visual. See, Copolillo, H.P. (1987) Psychodynamic psychotherapy of children.

In the event that emotional issues come up, they may be gently expanded. For example, young children tend to convey considerable amount of emotional data about themselves through projection on the game's characters, so that the questions asked may be directed at the figures themselves instead of the children that created them. As a rule,

I prefer indirect communication. It has been my experience that children are more cooperative when discussion is indirect, since what had happened to the little turtle happened to him, not to me ... !

A Sample of Indirect Communication:

Mor, a seven year old girl, constructed a magnificent water world. On the edge of the lake (i.e., the water in the sink) stood a dog. As she moved it around the periphery, it suddenly fell into the water. She moved it up and down and it looked that it was about to drown. The dog remained silent, it did not bark or yelp and it appeared that Mor opted for this kind of playing as a reaction to her situation, which involved both violence and freezing. Finally, she lifted the drowning dog up and placed it on a small bush at the sink's perimeter. When asked to describe the water world in general and her playing in particular, she said nothing about the drowning dog. I asked her, "How does the dog feel now, after finding a safe place? She answered: "He's fine now. Before, when he fell into the water, he was really frightened as he swallowed a lot of water." I told Mor, "What a brave dog. I was really worried about him when he couldn't call for help. Mor responded with a knowing smile.

A Example of Direct Communication:

Nimrod was a sensitive boy with black eyes and hair, whose social situation was dismal. He was rejected by his peers, who claimed he was a "geek." As a result, he had no friends among his classmates. He tended to be withdrawn, ensconced in his home, where he read books and played various musical instruments. His dog was his closest companion. In his water world, the water was white and he placed just a few animals such as sea algae. He also built a small island there. The space around the water world was devoid of any life!

The quiet water world of 11 year old Nimrod

I asked him: "You've described the water world as a place of silence; there are no carnivores, its color is white and water animals mostly consume plankton and plants ... does it resemble any part of the world you live at?"

This was his reply: "This water world is similar to how I feel when I'm by myself, or when I create world with plastic building blocks (Lego). At such moments, no one enters the space I'm at, no one bothers me, attacks me , criticize me or tells me what to do! That is when I feel the best, I have tranquility!"

"And in your everyday life, at home, school, is there also white water?" "it's not at all like that," he retorted. "There, there is noise all the time, I constantly feel a need to defend myself there, to be on guard to avoid being hurt by others! There, the animals are not herbivores, they devour!"

Nimrod was able to describe the great dissonance in which his life is conducted: a dichotomy between his gentle idyllic inner life, where there is neither aggression nor censure of any kind, and the reality where he is afraid of and has to defend himself from the "carnivorous" animals who might enter the white lake and destroy the harmony reigning there. Little wonder he found refuge in his inner world.

" We try, together with the child, to look at him and help him understand his feelings about this world, to cope with painful things and discover the good things. Next, we would try to merge the positive things in the child and his world, and help him make the most of his life." (Winnicott 1964 pp. 45, 57.)

The return of the therapist to the "line of occurrence" with the child, asking the child questions designed to sum up the experience at the water edge, the preservation in an aquarium (see Chapter 5, Preservation, p.106), draining the water at the end of a session, all these in effect give the adult present at the scene control over the experience taking place. It provides the child a sense of relief, in that he would no longer have to bear on his shoulders the burden of emotions that rose to the surface – he is sharing them with an empathetic individual who is a partner to the event. Now he can go back and be a child, and there is someone in this world who can safeguard his secrets, who knows how he feels. The burden has greatly lightened up.

When the plug is lifted up and the water drains down at the bottom of the sink, both therapist and patient return from a watery journey back to the therapy room, an event that contains a code that says: we are coming back to reality now, to our former roles. Jung describes it as an awakening from a dream.

Summing up the Therapist's Role During of Water Treatment:

1. Building communication up and creating a focal point.

2. An experience of sharing – a shared joint experience around the sink involving colors, discovery, and creativity.

3. Building a water world – creating a personal space for the patient, observing, listening, reverberating.

4. Documentation stage – Active listening and summarizing the story of the water world; asking questions and answers, an aspect that is verbal in nature.

5. Conservation – building an aquarium, returning control and responsibility to the adult therapist, and a return to the real world.

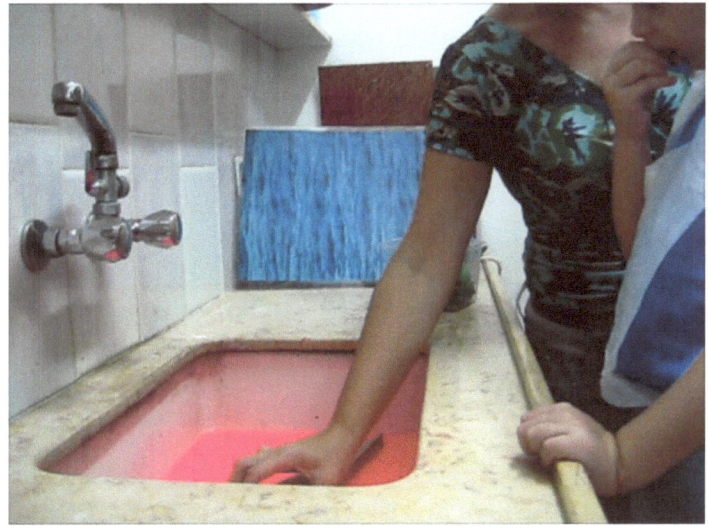

An example of an aspect of the therapist's role during the second stage. Note the patient's expression and the movement of the hand at the mouth: "I can't make up my mind."

Chapter 11

Water Treatment: Diagnosis and evaluation

During water treatment several components join together into a focused healing effort. One can look at the processes occurring during treatment through three key indicators by which therapy transpires. These metrics allow the therapist to ascertain noticeable precursors of the emotional and developmental state of the patient in relation to his chronological age. The indicators refer to the way the child thinks and feels, how he functions by himself and in his environment, and the way relationships are reflected in his world.

Thus, a scenario where an 11 year old boy opts to play a regressive game that corresponds to behavior typical of children at the very early age of 2-3, will reflect the existence of feelings of deprivation; or that the child had experienced a significant event during that period in his life, which had left a mark or a void that needs to be attended to. These gaps, as correlated with chronological age, are important keys in understanding the healing process in general and during water treatment in particular.

The indicators at issue are divided into three main axes that allow the clinician to determine where the patient is at on each axis. Hence, in addition to assessing the developmental and emotional state of the patient, the therapist is able to ascertain the dynamic of change along these axes and see developmental leaps, as they appear, in the course of the water treatment. For example, a patient who chooses to repeat the first step in the process again and again (a step that serves as an initial point for sensory involvement and which is optimized for early stages of child development) and after a while begins to play a symbolic game at the sink. In parallel with the change in the manner the game is conducted, the therapist will notice a difference in the kind of choices the patient makes at the sink and could conclude that a developmental leap, affecting that particular patient, had occurred.

In addition to assessing the child according to the three listed axes of development, there are other developmental theories that may serve to refine and highlight other aspects of the child's developmental stages, which can be taken into account when assessing the patient's status. Multiplicity of tools, for assessment of the healing process, that are also substantively assistive in promoting the healing itself, will help the therapist to (i) distinguish more precisely the condition of the child; (ii) assess his stage of development; (iii) ascertain the best means for improving his state of emotional wellbeing; (iv) identify the child's progress and his state of healing.

(See Table 1.1, the Child's Development Phases Table, & Table 1.2, Play and Development, pp.247-249.)

Axes of Development for Diagnosis and Assessment

1. **The Child Psychological Development Axis** - Relates to the classical distribution, according to Freud, from birth to age 18. Correspondence or inconsistency between the developmental/psychological axis and the chronological age of the patient may be determined through the phases depicted by this axis. In water treatment these indices will relate to psychological issues that arise from the game's plot or context and associations related to the encounter with the water. Here is an example of a discrepancy on the developmental axis: When a 13-year-old who works with water will display a desire to taste the colored water, or try to put in his mouth wet objects pulled out of the water.

2. **Development Axis In relation to Object** - Deals with indicators of distance between the child and his caregiver-parent. In water

treatment indicators of proximity and remoteness measure the distance between therapist and patient, and assess the relationship between dependence and independence, as these are expressed by the patient.

3. **<u>Play Development Axis</u>** - Relates to the developmental stages that are expressed in the manner of playing by the children. Through the phases along this axis, the cognitive and emotional conditions of the patient can be extrapolated, as well as their location on the chronological age development curve. As part of water treatment these indicators will relate to game-playing selection, such as the type game chosen, use of objects, plot development, avoiding playing spontaneously, playing a regressive-sensory game, or playing an experiential game that includes filling and emptying, examination of objects that either sink or float and more; all game types will be evaluated in relation to the patient's chronological age.

The Child Psychological Development Axis

Freud relates to the child's psychological development in 5 stages:

1. **The Oral Phase - from Birth to Age of One Year and Six Months.**

At this stage the world is examined mainly through the mouth; the array of investigation and tactile contact is done through that oral cavity. Moreover, the infant is completely dependent on the mother: it is experiencing a lack of separation, and complete identity, between himself and the mother.

Water Treatment. At this stage it is practically irrelevant, since this is a very early phase. Nevertheless, often children exhibit strong desire to taste the colored water in the sink or lick wet figures and we could relate this conduct to the oral phase.

An example of this phase can also be seen in the symbolization that manifest in the case of Yoni, an eight year-old, rather shy and not very talkative boy, who took a particularly large fish and placed it into the water in the water world -- but no other figure or object. He filled the mouth of the fish with water then pressed is belly and water sprayed out, while making audible tooting sound akin to a howling or crying. This operation was repeated again and again. Beyond that, there was no "plot," however, the same child who, before commencing the water treatment, was quiet and introverted, started now speaking freely; he seemed more relaxed and smiled more and was able to make contact with others in his immediate surroundings well.

2. The Anal Phase - from the Age of One Year and Six Months to Age Three.

At this stage the infant's erogenous zone is concentrated in the area of the buttocks. The infant begins to experience and express some independence and can avoid incontinence. It feels pleasure due to his ability to create something of its own and it begins to form a separate identity from the mother, as a result of experiencing such independence. This sense of independence could lead to various states, ranging between anal fixation and building self-identity.

Negative results of anal fixation are generated either by excessive restraint or by excessive permissiveness. Excessive restraint will be reflected in struggles by parents around such matters as continence, compulsively cleaning after the child, preventing the enjoyment of nascent independence and a sense, by the child, that his evolving identity goes unacknowledged. Consequently, he will start to jealously guard his independence while conducting a power struggle with his parents and, in that process, opting to defecate and urinate clandestinely. Conversely, an optimal passage through this phase will occur through an understanding by the parents that eliminating is not a proper object for a power struggle, instead, it is part of exploration of the child's path toward independence, on the way to building a self-identity.

Water Treatment. Children who get stuck at this stage will invest a great deal of energy in cleaning up the sink or, conversely, in messing it up with paints. Such activities will be accompanied by various statements that describe their experience at this stage. For instance, Ro'i, a cute six year old who mixed the paints' sediments in the sink while observing my reaction defiantly saying, "I poo poo this colors and the poo is smeared ... hahaha." Alternatively, seven year old Mika, a second grader, who often cleaned the sink and while scrubbing it with a sponge, sang these words, "It'd be so much fun to clean, everything must be clean, so very clean, not a mark or a spot shall remain."

3. **The Oedipal Phase - between Ages Three and Six.**

By now, the erogenous zone of the infant has converged in the genitals. At this point sexual sensations have awakened, usually focused on the parent of the opposite gender. The tot feels competition and a threat emanating from the same-sex parent. Eventually, it would solve the problem by identifying with its perceived rival. This conduct is termed, correspondingly, the Oedipus and Electra complex.

Possible consequences of this phase are, on the one hand, the manifestation of an Oedipal fixation created when parents threaten or behave rigidly and see the child as object, someone to seriously compete with. In this situation the child will develop communicating problems with members of the opposite sex and, at times, sexual identity problems. On the other hand, sensitive conduct by the parents will enable the child to traverse the stage well and conclude it feeling a sense of trust in regard to relationships, knowing to conduct them with an open heart while developing one's self- identity.

Water Treatment. It appears to be a symbolic game that is relevant to a relationship among primary characters. Often, we will be able to observe play choices as in the case of the sea turtle and its pup, i.e., a mother and a daughter, inside a small pool of water outside the sink. At this stage, a division distinctly manifests on both sides of the sink. Masculine figures, such as soldiers, heroes, carnivores, while on the other side appear feminine ones: domestic animals, non-carnivorous animals and female figurines. At this stage, the children conduct the play drama unaided, independent of the therapist.

4. The Latency Phase - between Ages Six and 12

This stage is characterized by involvement with social activities and with forming relationships with same-sex peers. Progress in learning, hobbies and social games are now apparent. This is when children develop many cognitive aspects of the mind.

A child who has failed to resolve a previous stage will have less available energy to invest in the main areas of his current development. Positively, investing energy in the environment creates satisfying social relationships, development of various pursuits and well-adapted learning.

Water Treatment. Often, socio-dramatic scenes will form, which reflect aspects of a coping social and/or familial process the child undergoes in regard to socialization, assistance 'in times of need, competitiveness among figures in the water, power struggles, conflicts in relationships, relational structures, as is the case with the sea turtles and crocodiles' families and the like. At this stage, as in the case of the former one, the children conduct the play drama autonomously and independent of the therapist.

The Genital Phase - between Ages 12 and 18

This stage is characterized by tremendous physical and hormonal changes and an attraction to members of the opposite sex comes about. It is a complex development phase and most individuals carry with them unresolved anxieties from the Oedipal phase. In case a block develops at this stage, the patient will experience extreme anxieties in forming relations with members of the opposite sex, and will tend to direct his energies into academic pursuits and other avenues. Likewise, he might form a divide between social relationships sexual interactions. In the event that the adolescent healthily copes with challenges at this phase, he would form positive relationship with members of the opposite sex to whom he is attracted.

Water Treatment. We will see much consideration being given to construction of the water world, not the least its aesthetic components. During playing we will hear declarations and statements related to the symbolic and aesthetic choices; we will not see as much symbolic imaginary play, as we did by children experiencing previous stages. Statements heard from a 14 year old, for example, were: "I picked pink because I get the feeling it's soft and enveloping," or, "I placed a boat at the lake's edge so that, just in case, I could escape the place." Another description by an adolescent boy went like this: "The water is white in color, this lake is serene, there are hardly any people on the shore, it's an isolated place."

The Child's Psychological Development Axis – Summation

Rather often it is possible to identify the phase the patient is at, along the axis, during water treatment. Some children only provide hints as to the phase they are at while others convey the information very clearly. In most cases, only some of the phases would be seen during treatment. Familiarity with the various phases and with their attributes assist therapists to better understand the symbolism embedded in the child's play, thus promote the healing process.

Development Axis in Relation to Object[26]

The development axis in relation to an object allows an assessment of the level of individuation, which is the constant objective through which individual's potential materializes. These processes of separation-individuation are long term processes we engage in, for many years, in different fashions. Water treatment allows us a peek into very early stages of these processes.

Through observation of the water treatment process, we are able to relate to the proximity/distance between therapist and patient through an analogy of the development states, according to Margaret Mahler.[27] Since water treatment has several phases, the initial ones containing concrete, physical involvement of therapist with patient (such as joint activities like filling up the sink), while in latter ones the patient is more self-directed, at which time it becomes possible to see how patients transit from one phase to the next and what each phase summons as far as the therapist's figure is concerned (e.g., during free play where the therapist assumes a passive stance).

This axis apportion the psychological development into three main aspects, while placing an emphasis on the mother-infant's, as a system of distance- proximity.

a. Normal Autistic Phase – Occurs during the first few weeks of the infant's life; it is detached from its external environment and is self-absorbed. There is no distinction, in its perception, between the within and without and the mother provides it its initial and immediate necessities.

---

[26] Reference to a familiar person, often the mother.
[27] Margaret S. Mahler (1897–1985) developed the Separation-Individuation theory of child development. In Mahler's theory, child development takes place in phases (each with several sub phases). The main phases are: Normal Autistic Phase (during the first few weeks of life – Mahler later abandoned this phase, based on new findings from her infant research); Normal Symbiotic Phase (which lasts until about 5 months of age); Separation-Individuation Phase (between 5-24 months of age).

Water Treatment. At this stage we would find it difficult to notice any expression of the phase during water treatment, since the treatment involves memory and internalization of data supplied by the senses. Sensual memory will only surface during recollection of traumatic events that were physically etched in memory at that period of time; we could also identify birth trauma internalized by consciousness, however, their expression will only be metaphorical and their representation solely symbolic. For example, Lihi, a seven year old, described a family on an island in the middle of a body of water. The infant girl falls to the water and goes up to Heaven. Her mother falls after she does and the family is sad. Following an inquiry with the mother, it turned out, in this case, that there was an experience of danger during birth.

(More about birth traumas in Chapter 12, Trauma and Birth Trauma.)

b. Normal Symbiotic Phase – Starting at the second month of the infant's life, the child becomes of an object that provides its needs but does not distinguish between its own activities and those of the mother. According to Winnicott, a symbiosis takes place at this stage comprising of the mother unit + the infant. The infant experiences omnipotence and the mother develops special adaptation and empathy in relation to her infant, that assist it in understanding its needs. It also learns about her needs and adapts itself to her. In consequence, mutual dependence occurs.

Water Treatment. Apparently, children insist on involving the therapist at these stages, even when there is no need for it. These children will avoid moving on to the next phase of water treatment, one that is symbolic in nature. Instead, they opt to remain engaged in the joint creative experience, use of paints, placing their hands in the sink, filling it up and emptying it out. The therapist will feel that the patient is not "letting her go" and the patient will express a desire to repeat the initial stages over and over again.

c. Separation-Individuation Phase – during this phase the infant develops an inner sensation that it is differentiated from the mother, it develops a distinction between itself and another object.

Individuation is a protracted process where the child acquires certain traits that will eventually render him an individual. He develops anatomy, memory and perception, and awareness of an independent functioning ability, separate and apart from the mother. This process is accompanied with the gratification entailed in the acquisition of self-confidence, self-identity and awareness of autonomy. It is a vital stage for the course of the infant's life.

Water Treatment. This is a meaningful phase in the child's treatment, since that is where a significant leap would take place in his development. Also, during this phase contents from various phases rise up and float. At this stage the therapist can stand behind the patient and just observe the process, thus releasing the dependency and foregoing the provision of assistance in the construction of the water world. The patient would have autonomy and full control of the elements of construction and play. Reaching this phase enables emotional release, empowerment of the "self" as well as the building of identity and self-confidence out of awareness and acceptance. Implementation of this phase is both the core and the goal of treatment of both children and adults.

A Glance into the Therapy Room ...

Yuval, a blue-eyed freckled six year old, arrived at therapy because of social challenges in kindergarten. He had no friends, refused to leave the house to meet with potential friends and peers from his kindergarten or the neighborhood did not come to visit him. After a few weeks of therapy Yuval constructed a blue lake on which, with great precision, he had built a bridge, spanning from one end of the sink to the other. He placed several figures on the bridge, representing himself, his sister and his mother.

Following completion of his activity in the water world (after all figures had safely crossed the bridge) he constructed an aquarium (see Chapter 4, Game Playing). He took a low rectangular box and a wooden plank (which previously served as the bridge) and placed a tiger on it. A week later he asked for the "aquarium," placed it on the ground, went to the nearby shelves then added an extension to the bridge that went beyond the box holding the water toward the floor. He placed a band of turtles on the modified bridge in a certain order. He liked this and thus kept adding planks rather passionately till the bridge was long enough to cover the entire length of the room's floor. He then took one turtle after the other and had them cross the entire length of the bridge. At that terminus he let them rest, following their protracted journey.

During the two-three weeks when the process of the bridge-building, first at the water world and then when "the world's longest bridge" was constructed, Yuval began forming social ties, he expressed a desire to meet peers, first at his place and later he even started going to their homes. His mother was amazed by the change in him and has encouraged him to go on.

Yuval's bridge

Note: The bridge served as a metaphor, assisting Yuval in overcoming fear and difficulties found in his inner world, which previously have prevented him from "undertaking the journey" of individuation. The bridge construction past the boundaries of the preservation container (the aquarium), constitutes an expression of Yuval's capacity and desire to come out to the world and dare walk in it in his own path.

1. The turtles' aquarium

2. Yuval extends the bridge, exceeding the aquarium boundaries

3. The turtles journey outside the water

4. The bridge becomes longer during play and the turtles are in motion on it toward a target which is land at the end of the path (It is possible to see the alpha turtle at the far end of the bridge)

a. Explanations about the Relevant Psychological Phases

During the first phase patient therapist are full partners in creating the experience, the therapist stands side by side with the patient and assists him in filling the sink up, guiding him and participating with him physically and emotionally, exhibiting curiosity, excitement and making contact with the water. Then, when the patient creates a water world and an active and creative play is conducted by the patient, the therapist moves behind the patient and no longer intervenes. Instead, she is watching and serving as an echo. (See, See, Chapter 10, The Role of the Therapist, Listening and Reverberation, p.223.)

The distance created corresponds to the phase of development in the proximity relationship of mother and infant when the latter starts to crawl, walk and goes out to discover the world, in fact, distancing itself from the mother, transferring from a phase of dependency to one of independence, which will be experienced distinctly around the age of two.

A Glance into the Therapy Room ...

Five and a half year old Ronny arrived at treatment when he was at kindergarten. His dark brown hair was closely cropped, which accentuated his narrow eyes. When he smiled his gapped-toothed smile, the eyes turned into narrow slits. His cuteness notwithstanding, his parents reported about difficulties in parting, wariness and cringing in new places. Likewise, when he found himself in conflicts either with peers and with the parents themselves he would withdraw inwardly, often becoming silent and introverted. He was described as a vulnerable child who is easily hurt, who lacks confidence in the company of children, yet usually cheerful and likes to help at home.

After several encounters, during which he experienced water therapy, he fell in love with this therapeutic medium and at the start of each meeting he went back to work with water. At one encounter he went to the sink, chose earth colors in shades of brown and orange, placed soldiers and tanks in the mix, which he called 'poo,' saying: "They're all sinking in mud," then he drowned them all. He then drained the water and, as he always did, rigorously cleaned the sink till it was restored to its original white color.

Note: First messing up the sink with paints then scrubbing it up became a sort of a ritual, following which Ronny could develop issues with a greater degree of awareness.

During the following session Ronny reversed the order of things – he first cleaned the sink up and only then worked at the water world. This time he opted for pink: "It's a lovely color," he said and added, "The death monster has different colors – black, green, red, yellow. This is the blood of the death monster who lives in a whirl, and it kills!" He then dripped some 'blood' outside the sink. He unplugged the sink and mixed the residual paints in the sink, added water and cleaned it up, repeating this again and again. He was speaking with infantile annunciation and made baby-like sounds. In the ensuing conversation, he confessed, "At times I feel caught in a whirlpool and I'm afraid the monster will kill me."

Note: Ronny is coping with fears and feelings of aggression that swamp him from the inside = whirlpool, the murderous monster. Present, is an allusion to the anal phase of development (terms such as, "poo") and he channels the need to control those emotions and urges into the process of cleaning up the sink; each time an emotion comes up to the surface, he "wipes it out" with his rigorous cleaning activity at the sink. The moment he cleans these emotions (aggression for instance) at the sink, he frees himself of the need to act on them in his external reality.

Table 1.1 The Child's Development Phases Table

Estimated Age	Freud	Erickson	Feller	Klein	Winnicott	Dockar-Drysdale	Brunner	Piaget
0-12 months of age	Oral	Basic trust & distrust	narcissism (the infant alone; with the mother)	paranoid-schizoid	age of illusion the infant's is focused on the mother	initial experiencing	Enactive thought	motor-Sensual
1-2 years of age	Anal	independence facing shame & doubt	pre-Oedipal (child with parents)	prone to depression	Transi-tional experience	Integration		
4-13 years of age	Phallic	initiative vs. guilt	Oedipal crown (a child with others)		age of worry	secondary experiencing (symboliz-ation)	iconic thinking (with figures)	pre-cognitive thinking
5-12 of age	Latency	diligence vs. inferiority				(insight & conceptu-alization)	symbolic thinking	intuitive thinking (Fireberg's "Magical thinking")
Over 12 years of age	Genital	distinct identity vs. role confusion						concrete-opportunistic thinking
								abstract thinking

Table 1.2 Play and Development

Estimated Age	Sensual/creative play	Physical Play	investigative play	social play	symbolic play
0-12 months of age	Uses his entire body and senses – sight, hearing, taste, smell and touch; uses all all his senses to experience the world around	Motor-sensual, exercise play manipulative play repetitive & ritualistic play	Plays with his and his mother's body; enjoys being a "factor" – What is this object?	Games where mother and child take turns (pick-a-boo, hands' games imitating the mother's	Initial words; transitional object
1-2 years of age	Plays with his food and secretions, plays with sounds & words secretions, made by the mother	Plays related to Gross motor skills – walking & climbing; fine motor skills: construction	Exploring his physical world: inside/outside push/pull hide/seek up/down	Plays alone mother & infant play hide & seek father & infant play unruly infant & others: it plays alone, it observes a parallel game played its peers	Actively naming, Imitation, plays make belief with dolls, plays roles, plays make belief related to situations & continuity
3-4 years of age	Plays with sand, water and dough, coloring, words and stories, stories & music	Runs, jumps rides a tricycle, dances, skills with a ball, paints & cuts with seizures	Games related to problem solving, construction & jigsaw puzzles	Associative games or joint parallel playing	Expansive, symbolic & solitary playing: complex and set themes enhance symbolic aspect while using items in a "make belief" playing, imaginary friends, masquerading, talismans. Joint social-drama playing: coordination of activities and roles (wedding ceremonies, school activity, camping, plays, hunter-hunted, that continue day after day); expansive solitary playing in a "small world," books, stories, TV

5-12 years of age	Creative art-work, music books & stories, pets	Games with rules, physical exercise & sports, bicycle riding, sawing, construction & writing	create things: utilizes domestic technical & scientific skills	Joint games - domestic themes and games of chase. coopera--tive @ competa--tive activities, large social organizing	
12 years old & older; adults	creative art--work, music, writing, & books, sex & love, cooking & eating, children & pets	Sports & games, hobbies & skills	Science & technology	Official games with rules	Games with ideas, thinking, day-dreaming, role-playing & writing in life

The Child's Development According to Phases of Play

This axis has five aspects, including: social, investigative, sensual and regressive phases.

Sensual-Creative Play

The regressive phase occurs during the first two years of life. During this time period toddlers play and study the world through the different senses and, also, develop a sense of self (see Table 1.1 above: The Child's Development Phases Table). This stage develops throughout childhood and receives a different expression at each age. In later ages and in maturity it manifests as engagement in art, cooking and similar type of activities.

Water Treatment. Play occurs as children encounter water as a substance: They touch the water, fill up and empty the sink, splash it, etc. This stage is considered regressive since it is typical of very young children during development phases which is mostly a sensual experience.

Physical Play

Sensual play continues when children proceed with the use of their entire physical body in experiencing the world around them: heat, cold, water in a bathtub or a pool, splashing through mud, sensing sand flowing between fingers and toes, the wonder of gouache and finger paints, scents, etc. They begin to greatly enjoy fun-practicing new skills that entail physical movement; self-esteem and confidence are augmented as the children demonstrate capacity for self-control and control of their surroundings, a source of particular satisfaction in light of the fact that their physical bodies are tiny in juxtaposing to the gigantic world around them.

Water Treatment. It appears that children enjoy tactile contact with paint mixture residue at the bottom of the sink, demonstrating a desire, through body movement, to go into the sink. When the same paint residue is printed, expressive finger work occurs while the entire body is put into work, directing motion.

Investigative Play

This is characterized by play themes related to contact and autonomy, expressed, for example, by laying objects in dishes or other such containers and taking them our again and again, moving them up and down, a process of filling up and emptying. Often, they will verbalize as they engage in these activities.

Water Treatment. It appears that children who are engaged in examining the nature and qualities of water, sink items and float others up, fill up and empty containers of different types and undertake other such activities.

Social Play

At this stage, the child maintains the type of play in which life situations are recapitulated, however, it would include relating to other individuals and objects. He combs a doll's hair which represents his mother; he uses a spoon to make believe that he is feeding the teddy bear. The transition from focusing, during play, on himself to another, playing make belief games, facilitates departure from the self, starts relating to others and the commencement of construction of "life screenplays."

Water Treatment. It appears that children relate, at this stage, to the therapist as a playmate. In addition, the stage of associations related to the colors that go into the water serve as a kind of social play between therapist and patient. The water activity will be accompanied with a verbal description, which will be borrowed from "real" life situations, e.g., dish washing, cooking, bathing, etc. We can also observe the patient's involvement in the construction of the water world during the concrete part of shaping boundaries and creating symbolism of the place (sink) and the space around it.

Symbolic Play

This is characterized by the use of imagination and linguistic skill that serve to support the symbolic play. The child takes a real object and charges it with attributes imported from his inner world. This form of play allows the child to comprehend the world he is in and helps him to acquire control using model situations (simulations), conducting experiments and planning. Likewise great significance is accorded the symbolic play involving self-assistance as the player copes with difficult situations, such as fear, anxiety and anger. The symbolic play affects emotional self-healing. Children at this stage play imagination games, create personification of inanimate figures and also develop emotional images and symbols that assume forms in creative endeavors, art, planning and construction, and in emotional topics of inter-personal relationships and self-image.

Water Treatment. The symbolic phase will manifest in the "water world" stage of the therapy. Here, the children create an imaginary world composed of miniature items that replicate a whole world. Usually, the items are "charged" with contents and contexts taken from the child's inner world. Various emotions assume expression through imagery and symbolism of such figures as a central hero and items operated in a plot (in the play) of one kind or another.

How does Water Treatment During Regressive Stages Contribute to Emotional Healing among Children

Each child needs sense-oriented experience in order to form a meaningful relation to himself and with the world around him, one which bolsters the basic senses and facilitates an approach to inner emotions and the ability to express them outwardly toward himself, the therapist and the world.

Regressive play brings the child back to childhood experiences and sense infantile emotions and recollection, thus enabling expression of repressed emotions -- since that time -- by the child. Such repressed emotions are the ones that have created the current impasse and disrupt optimal emotional and social functioning. With the aid of play and the consequent disclosure of these repressed emotions, re-processing of the events leading to their formation becomes possible and, hence, their release.

The psychologist Linnette McMahon explains that regressive play constitutes a substantive aspect of the initial experience and may assist in the formation of missing sensual experiences. These children, she asserts, are in need of 'nesting substances' such as sand and water, soap and bubbles, finger paints, animals, puppets and stories.

It is possible to bring back to life a child's senses experientially and the play programs. Prescott and Joyce suggest a softness index (the softer the environment the more it would include dough-like substances for playing, water, finger paints, mud-clay, sand, comfortable furniture, music, painting facilities and materials, all of which serve to assist children get in touch with their senses, enabling them to feel life more authentically.

The use of water make possible a whole panoply of sensual, emotional and psychological experiences that are adapted to various age groups and which bring to the surface emotional issues that got 'stuck' in early development phases. It serves both as a complement of that which is lacking as well as the correction of an emotional injury.

In her book, A Gestalt Therapy Approach to Children and Adolescents (1988), Violet Oaklandr indicates how momentous is the sensual-regressive game as means for development of bonding, which would include: observation, speech, touching, listening, movement, smelling and tasting. The sensual play and the aggressive play may aid children who had suffered severe lack and loss; likewise, it could be helpful for children in hospitals and those with learning difficulties. Sensual work with emotionally handicap children is based on the belief that the child's senses were dimmed by the trauma.

She also points out that often these children have closeted and shut themselves away from any contact with their environment, or, especially in cases of abuse, they have suppressed their self so as to adapt to adults' expectations of them. They have locked the part that feels and therefore they lack the means to know what they feel and the tools to express these feelings.

In short, it is possible to find, in the art therapy room, a vast variety of soft and regressive materials. Their employment is vital for the healing process of children and they facilitate a 'familiar encounter' with substances taken from their known environment, be it at home or kindergarten thus serving as means of communication with the therapist, which, in turn, fosters trust and enables containing and nourishing.

Water treatment, of its own accord, utilizes a "soft" substance that holds in it an array of psychological experiences, play and sensual activity, which, accordingly, is a perfect model for regressive processes that support emotional healing processes.

Chapter 12

Trauma and Birth Trauma

What is Trauma?

Trauma is an event that occurs in human reality at that juncture where one meets violence or death, which poses a threat to his life or bodily integrity. At such events, one is faced with extreme situations of helplessness and terror. The common feeling of psychological traumas is stark fear, being startled, loss of control. Such experiences have a factor of surprise, feeling trapped and/or debilitating exposure to nature's hazards.

The traumatic event brings in its wake deep and permanent changes to the body, making it excited emotionally, in memory and in awareness. This excited state causes certain individuals to hold on to a powerful emotional state but they do not remember the event, while others remember the event but become utterly detached from their emotions, and feel nothing at all.

Symptoms of posttraumatic stress disorder (PTSD) may be divide into three main components:

1. **Over-excitation**: the constant anticipation of danger, and the inability to filter stimuli. In such mode even constant stimuli are experienced as a surprise that repeats time and again, while the subject is both asleep and awake.

2. **Invasiveness**: The signature of the moment of trauma, an abnormal coding of its memory, which bursts out uncontrollably at any given moment.

3. **Abstention and Reduction**: The reaction that blunts submission. Events continue to register in consciousness, however, it feels as if they are detached from their usual denotation. Perception is dulled or distorted, accompanied with a sense of having been partly anesthetized or a loss of certain feelings. The sense of time changes, felt as if one is moving in slow motion; there those who feel that they are not participating in a given event, as if they are watching their body from the outside or being in a nightmare.

How do Children and Adolescents React to Stress and Trauma

Rony Berger, Ph.D., a clinical psychologist and a world renown expert on stress, crisis and trauma lists those aspects that develop as a result of trauma, as well as emotional and physiological reactions:

Developed Aspects -- When we seek to assess and examine children's reactions and the ways they use to cope, we ought to consider the developing dimension, so formative in the child's life. Here are a few developmental characteristics that affect the child's coping when he is under pressure

Sense of Confidence/Lack of Confidence -- children and adolescents acquire a sense of confidence and a basic sense of trust in a gradual process that lasts almost until the end of adolescence. A significant injury to their envelope of confidence could bring about a developmental regression and severe reactions.

Ambient and Imaginary Fears -- children and adolescents react not only to external threats, assaults or death but also to their parents' fears, ambient anxieties and imaginary dreads. In this respect, it is possible to see them as the "pressure gouge" of family and society.

Coping Resources -- most children, especially during early age, have relatively little experience in coping with pressure situations. Therefore, they do not always have at their disposal those coping resources already acquired by adults. It is our role to provide them with support and enrich them with our experience.

Cognitive Ability -- children, especially young ones, have a limited cognitive capacity, thus, they struggle in understanding and interpreting crisis situations. They tend to think concretely, egocentrically, rigidly and, at times, magically. Their ability to comprehend things abstractly is limited and perception of cause and effect is partial; their sense of time is narrow and comprehension of morality is dichotomous -- "good" vs. "bad." Such limitations belabor children and adolescents' ability to properly interpret reality, create a sense of incoherence about what is transpiring and result in incorrect explanations, at times catastrophic.

Emotional Development -- even emotionally, children and adolescents' is limited. They tend to flood emotionally, thus, often use, more than adults, extensive defense mechanisms such as reality denial, "This is not really happening," and disengagement, "I'm busy with other things." Sometime, it seems that they lack interest in what is occurring outside of them, however, this is often their only means of coping with the force of events.

Sense of Control/Helplessness -- children and adolescents are highly curious and a tendency for exploration and discovery. Correspondingly, they have a great need to maintain constancy and daily routine. Extreme, persistent pressure situations discontinues routine and create in them a sense of helplessness and loss of control.

Emotional Expression Space -- some children have the need as well, as the ability, to express themselves emotionally when they are under severe emotional pressure, however, their ways of expression are not necessarily verbal. Hence, it would behoove adults to form an "emotional expression space," that will enable the former to express themselves emotionally.

Physical Activity -- the difference in physical reaction between children and adolescents notwithstanding, pressure situations usually intensify their physiological tension and many of them would need methods of dissipating of physical stress. Moreover, many children and even more so adolescents, have a need for active participation pursuits which give them a sense of control of the situation they are in.

Observed Reactions in Children under Stress

Emotional Reactions

Fears and Anxieties -- children and adolescents occasionally express such emotions in crying outbursts, excessive activity and physiological symptoms such as trembling, diarrhea and body pains; also, verbally. Fears could be concrete, e.g., fear of death or physical trauma, as a reaction to parents' anxieties, or imaginary fears, for instance, fear of darkness, of going to kindergarten or school or fear of strangers. Children who have been through traumatic experiences may be afraid of recapitulating such experiences. Fears and anxieties are typical of children of all ages but are more acute among young children.

Melancholy and sadness -- expressions of such emotional reactions are slowed down activity, emotional dullness ("the turned off kid"), social withdrawal and gradual retreat from various activities. Such reactions may appear at any age, however, they are typical of children who have lost their loved ones or older children.

Frustration and Anger -- these kind of emotions find outlet in nervous behavior, impatience and violet expressions toward the immediate environment. Among adults such expressions may appear in an acute form and be directed at themselves as suicidal ideas.

Physiological Reactions

Autonomous Reactions -- such reactions appear mostly among those who are directly exposed to traumatic events. They include accelerated heartbeat, rapid breathing, sweating, muscle tension, body tremors, diarrhea, frequent urination, and the like. It is important to stress the need for a check-up in order to exclude physiological causes.

Psychosomatic Reactions -- headaches, bodily pains, loss of appetite, indigestion, visual or auditory sensual disorder, compulsive scratching, allergies, rashes, excessive fatigue and insomnia.

Cognitive Reactions -- ongoing stress impairs mental capacity and thinking of children and adolescents and affect their ability to function normatively in an educational framework. Typical cognitive reactions include: inattention, lack of concentration, difficulty in making decisions and solving problems.

Behavioral/Social Reactions -- children and adolescents who were exposed to stressful situations react by acutely intensifying or diminishing behavioral patterns. Likewise, regressive behavior patterns appear, especially in young children.

Intensification of Social Patterns -- excessive activity, incessant verbalization, need for physical contact and nervous conduct. Similarly, at times obsessive behavioral patterns appear, such as excessive cleaning or compulsive repetition of a particular action.

Reductive Behavioral Patterns -- apathetic conduct, withdrawal from engaging in hobbies, lack of interest in recreation, social activity and pastime and disengagement from the social environment.

Aggressive Patterns -- difficulties in making decisions, recurring silence, withdrawal from engaging in hobbies, lack of interest in recreation, social activity and pastime and disengagement from the social environment.

At the therapy room we would be able to notice, during play by children who went through stressful situations, the following: Gloomy, monotonous play activity, most of which is constant, repeating and obsessively over and over. Traumatic play activity is visible and can be understood only from looking at it, so if it can really identify guess the trauma.

In cases of trauma caused by abuse, children feel isolated and reach the conclusion that adults responsible for their well-being do not provide them requisite protection, which they perceive as a type of betrayal, as if their parents participated in committing the abuse.

Therapeutic Stages of Trauma Treatment

Building Confidence -- gradual shift from a sense of lurking danger that might strike unexpectedly, to a feeling of trustworthy security.

Recouping Control -- Trauma victims feel bodily unsafe and imagine that their feelings and thoughts are out of control. There is a need to move from bodily control to control of one's immediate environment.

Memory -- the traumatic memory is both dynamic but pragmatic and the related emotional sensation is powerful, akin to camera's flash. The choice to encounter the painful memory is the patient's while the therapist serves as a witness, an ally in whose ears the victim may describe the indescribable.

Recollection of the Event -- the reconstruction of the event's narrative should be done gradually and in a controlled manner, while relating broadly to the patient's world, his environment and those who are close to him. As the strenuous moment nears, the patient finds it harder and harder to express himself in words and tends to shift to non-verbal communication. Due to the oceanic experience, stemming from the word "ocean," of the visual memory, the use of a facially expressive mode is most effective. The psychiatrist Bessel A. van der Kolk[28] came up with the supposition that this occurs because the verbal memory encoding is disabled when the sympathetic nervous system is immersed in a highly excited state, the central nervous system returns to the forms and icons of sensory memory that controlled during early childhood.

Water Treatment in Trauma Situations

Water as Memory Reservoir

It is customarily said in trauma therapy that, "The body remembers trauma." What is exactly meant by that assertion? Can the body remember what the mind refuses to? Does the body remember experiences before the coding system of the relevant memory forms? These questions and many others come to the fore when it comes to such painful and jarring human experiences, that have clobbered the individual at various stages in its development and have left a mark on his functioning and personality.

The body-mind-spirit array is a complex system where the three elements are connected, potently and directly impinging on each other. This triune relationship is affected by external events and the elements' reciprocal effect. For example, when a physical illness occurs, the physical condition immediately affects the mental one, on one's ability to regulate himself emotionally, on one's mood and, sometimes, there is an impact on one's faith in his sense of power to live, his existence and sense of hope. Various studies have measured the effect a person's faith has on his capacity to heal and his belief in his therapist. Indeed, such spiritual aspect is estimated to have a 30%

---

[28] Bessel A. van der Kolk, M.D., an active clinician, researcher and teacher in the area of post-traumatic stress and related phenomena since the 1970s. His work integrates developmental, biological, psychodynamic and interpersonal aspects of trauma, its impact and treatment. His book Psychological Trauma is the first integrative text on the subject, painting the far ranging impact of trauma on the whole person and the range of therapeutic issues to be addressed for recovery.

effect of the results of recovery in mental illnesses and disorders.

The physical body is a fascinating system that receives stimuli from its environment and translates them to vital information needed for human functioning. Since it contains more 70% water, a large part of the information received by it is coded within the molecular structure of water. In other words, we may assume that the body has a capacity to remember, using the liquids in it.

(See, Water Remembers, Chapter 1 Water in Our Lives, p.19.)

Traumatic experiences and memories affect water's molecular structure in the body. A significant number of trauma treatment include measures designed to achieve stress release, such as: breathing, physical release and movement. These activities allow water to be in motion inside the physical body and "flood" the coded unconscious memory in there, moving such memory toward elements of physical and mental consciousness. During water treatment, where water serves as a substance to generate stress release, thus alter brain waves to a state of relaxation, inspiration is formed and energetic and mental blocks are dissolved due to the association between the water in the body and that which is outside it, serving as such substance.

Water Treatment in the event of a Trauma -- a Case Study

Oren, a nine year old fourth grader is a success story. He is a leader among his classmates, an athlete, an A-student, who is loved by his teachers. He has a sister who is three years older and a brother who is three years old.

Reason for Referral:

Oren's mother referred him to art therapy because, about eight months earlier, he fractured his elbow and missed four months of school during the previous year.

Following the incident, he started blinking heavily, he was also "turned off" and "frozen." He did not say much right after the incident nor did he smile. He had to undergo several surgeries. His mother turned to a psychologist for treatment. It ended after about three months, however, since it had no visible effect on the blinking tick. The mother pointed out, that the blinking started at age four but shortly thereafter it disappeared. The parents describe the child as a perfectionist, for whom it is crucial to do well in every endeavor in his life. Any pressure he encounter causes him to responds tensely; he is rather impatient and tends to quickly lose interest. He has certain fears, e.g., while watching news, large dogs. While at home he is tense most of the time and exhibits exaggerated sense of responsibility toward his little brother. In school he is described as an excellent student, one who has a leadership ability, however among his classmates he is considered overbearing. extracurricularly, he take English (as a second language), practices martial arts and is very careful with his injured hand.

Developmental History: He was delivered by an urgent cesarean. His motor and emotional development were uneventful, transitional object till age Five. He did not experience separation difficulties nor did he have any problems becoming potty trained. At age Four the family had to move unexpectedly and Oren found it difficult to cope with the change in his life. At Five a tree branch poked his eye, which was highly frightening but essentially uneventful.

First Encounter

Oren arrived at treatment and formed good rapport; he was a little reserved at first, and refrains from telling me about his feelings. We started playing usual communication games (cards, drawings games that include name writing, one line drawings, etc.) -- games that are supposed to create bonding. Slowly he warms up, loosens up and tells me a little about school and the things he likes to do, his home, his family and more.

Second Encounter

Oren arrives at the second encounter much more relaxed. We start with a game of checkers and then he wants to work with clay. He tells me that once he attended an extra-curricular class learning to work with clay and that he is really good with clay.

Notice, Oren chose a medium of expression with which he has control and experience, this reveals that it matters to him to be good at the medium he works with and appreciated at what he is doing.

We start a game of throwing a big lump of clay in an attempt to hit a small lump on the table. This game is excellent preparation for working with clay, it raises the level of readiness for such activity, releases aggression and creates spontaneity and laughter.

He sculpts a figure he calls "Gamadi" (*gamad* means a dwarf) and another he call "Kelev" (dog in Hebrew), who is tasked with guarding over Gamadi. (See picture.)

Notice, the figures he makes are projections. The dwarf is a childhood figure -- a small person -- thus, Oren identifies with the archetype of a small adult. Also, dwarfs are considered to be "good" and, as we pointed out already, it is important for Oren to be considered "good." The guardian dog: in the context of actual reality, Oren has a beloved dog, about who he is very anxious whenever he escapes from the yard; likewise, it is a guard dog.

The inner world encounter with clay open areas of which the guard is unaware so that he will come to no harm, so that he will be protected. Essentially, he tells me: 'I'm ready to go in, when I'm in the form of a dwarf and have a guard.' The need for control creates here the opportunity for expression.

While working on the dog figure, Oren is provided with a bowl of water, used to soften the clay and smooth it out before it hardens. <u>Here starts the work with water</u>: Oren dips his hands in water and enjoys it. He then takes small, leftover pieces of hardened clay and dissolves it in water. I offer him a larger piece as I transfer the water to a larger and more suitable container, for I clearly know already that he is drawn to water -- the energy he is invest in using the water is focused. The larger piece is beginning to develop thin cracks. He takes sharp instruments, such as a fork, a ice pick, and notches and nicks it, then says: "It's cut, it's broken, it's bleeding." I then suggest to Oren to add blood. We add red paint to the clay water and the merriment begins. the "blood" surrounds the lump of clay in the water, then the lump comes out and the water splashes all over the place. Oren is very pleased, repeating the words, "cut, broken, bleeding." We create an <u>aquarium</u> with the red water and the lump but not before Oren adds readymade eyes to the partially submerged lump. (See picture.)

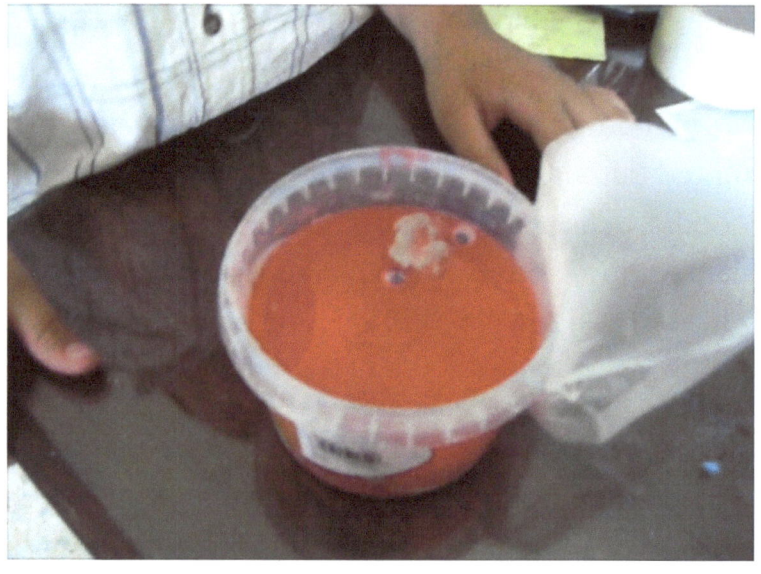

The red water bowl with the floating eyes.

Third Encounter

Oren takes the aquarium with the lump and eyes and I transfer the lump to a larger container. Oren is very excited: "Cool, the clay has turned red, it's all red!!!" He examines the red colored lump (to me it looks like an internal organ in the human body, rather disgusting...)

Yael: "How does the lump feels?"

Oren: "Red" (he expresses loathing and pleasure in tandem). "I'd like to put all the pieces together" (he then takes all the pieces and begins to join them together), "one can make a monster out of this."

Yael: "What monster?"

Oren: "Dwarfs devouring one. This is not a sensitive monster, it eats dwarfs and their dogs."

Yael: "Sounds to me like a scary monster, what powers does it have?"

Oren: "It not only devours ... it destroys! She turns good things into evil ones."

Yael: "Then, the dwarfs turn from good into evil ones?" (I am inquiring.)

Oren: "No, it's not possible to turn the dwarfs; it's necessary to kill this monster!" (While we are having this discussion Oren is pressing the clay in his fingers, trying to put the monster together.)

"I have no idea how to make the monster" -- he turns to me for help.

Yael: "How do you imagine it?

Oren: ""I don't know how to imagine."

Yael: "It it were real, how would it look?"

Oren: The monster eats dwarfs, so its mouth is supposed to have an angry expression on it, and its body is huge. Actually, it's a ghost, it has no legs and then it flies ... how do I make it's head?"

Oren begins forming the monster and then it is complete.

"I'll call it the Blood Monster -- it consumes blood and destroys things for the dwarfs, it has frontal teeth and an evil face."

Yael: "Do you think it likes blood?"

Oren: "Of course, why else would it be called 'Blood Monster'?" He now adds red paint to the work in clay, as he does that, he adds, "I'll create an evil dwarf. When the monster attacks a boy or a girl they turn into blood vampires, serving the blood monster. They have to bring it a lot of blood. I'll make her a vampire servant."

the blood monster on the right and its servant on the left.

Water Treatment--

First Step: Choice of paint colors to be placed in the water: orange, white, red.

Oren then mixes the paints in a jar. The sink is filled with water and he now picks orange and white, mixes them up and says: "A body color -- not mine, someone else's." He now adds red to the mix poured into the water and says: "What happens to body color with blood?"

We empty the sink, according to the first stage of the process, and the water drains, only paint remains on the sink's periphery. Oren says: "Blood is left."

We print the paint residue and he says, "Disgusting blood!" he wipes out the remaining paint still smeared on the sink's periphery, lifts his hands and looks at them, his eyes twist.

Second Step: Water world. Color, red.

At first, the water is clear and transparent. He then mixes the red paint outside the water then takes a bit with his hands and drips it into the clear water, "Blood drops." Then he pours all of it, his shoulders moving disquietly, his tongue extending out of his mouth like a baby's. He informs me that he wants to place the dwarf and dog in the water. The clay might be damaged I suggest. We think of a potential solution proper for the dwarf. Oren suggests that the dwarf will dwell in the Garden of Eden outside the water. He selects trees and other plants for the Garden. he adds a snake on the faucet in the sink -- "blood cancer" -- and a crocodile.

<u>Third Step</u>: Looking at the water world and Oren explains what he had created: "The blood monster and its assistant (who created me) live inside the blood lake, invisible to the outside world. However, inside there is a cave and there is blood in it and the monster and its assistant hide in there and sometimes blood there glows like red light. They have winter food supply that is blood and during the winter they remain in the cave. During the other seasons they go out and hunt."

Oren said, "The Blood Kingdom has been abandoned," the monster and its assistant went hunting, the dwarf and his dog insure that the blood monster will not return!"

Yael: "Do you think that the monster will be frightened by all the stuff in the water?

Oren: "They will not return, they went hunting."

Yael: "How does the dwarf feel up here, in the Garden of Eden?"

Oren: " Jolly, and so does his dog." (I offer to Oren to freely play with the figurines he had placed there but he refuses.)

Yael: "Please describe for me this place which you called, Garden of Eden

Oren: "The dwarf came from Garden of Eden, it's a good place to live at."

Yael: "Were you ever at such a beautiful like the Garden of Eden?"

Oren: "No."

Yael: "Did you ever see such a red lake?"

Oren: "Yes, I've seen a brown one."

Yael: "Where?"

Oren: "Let's drain the water" (he is twisting his face).

Yael: "You have hard time with this lake?"

Oren: "Yes. I don't want the blood monster to ever return!!!"

Yael: "Okay, than let's prepare a curse or some other thing that will block its return forever."

Oren: "If she ever comes back and jumps into the water, then everybody outside the water would jump her!"

Yael: "An excellent idea, let's do that! Let's decide that when it returns, everybody will jump her."

Oren: "The monster will jump into the water there will be a whirlpool ('cause I'll take the water out) 1, 2, 3 ... (he's counting) " Oren then throws a plastic animal representing the blood monster into the water. He immediately throws all the other animals on top of her. He is very pleased.

That is how the water world came to an end. We clean up the sink and go play a box game.

> During a conversation with Oren's mother I ask her whether there was a lot of bleeding when Oren broke his hand. She says that there was no bleeding at all. I relate to her that he is rather preoccupied with blood. I ask her when did he encounter blood, and she answers, "When he was a five year old a tree branch poked him in the eye and it was at that event that he bled profusely." There was a major panic, both on her part and his and, in fact, there was fear that would lose his eye. The mother reports that, rather surprisingly, during the last few days he stopped blinking his eyes.

After the Water Treatment Oren Stopped Blinking!!!

During the next sessions Oren worked with water in different ways, forming the blood monster in the water as a mask made of plaster. The encounter with plaster enable Oren to reconstruct the event where he broke his hand and the attendant operations. The plaster, as material, evokes a clear association to the cast that set his hand after the accident.

Working with plaster is a multi-step and gradual process. Whenever Oren takes a strip of plaster bandages makes it wet with water and cover a layout in the form of a mask, so that the story of the event unfolds slowly, under control, and during moments that memory causes pain or discomfort Oren becomes silent for moment but continues to dip the strips of plaster in water then goes back to narrating the story.

At the end of the process a face-figure is formed from the story and, in contrast with the fracture in his hand -- that had formed fissures in his body and psyche -- it is whole.

The water, in such a case, is a key to the effectiveness of the therapy, since already at the third session Oren brought up the trauma. To my mind, a different kind of intervention would require many more sessions, in order to solidify the patient's trust and to set up optimal conditions for floating up such a trauma to the surface of the conscious mind. The traumatic event included bleeding. Concrete exemplification, using liquid water combined with paint, created context in the mind of the encodes memory. This enabled Oren to remember the blood, in exactly the same manner he had experienced it during the traumatic event. Water treatment facilitated a spontaneous, playful experience. The use of the senses and contact with the water brought about stress release and attenuation of defense systems that on one side protected Oren and, on the other hand, sustained the trauma.

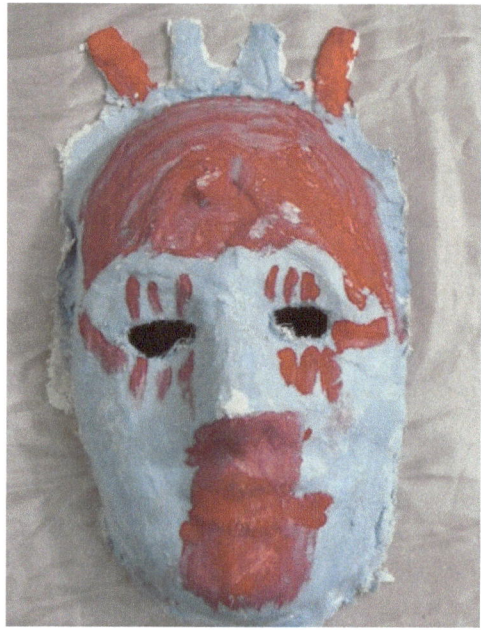

A mask made of plaster -- the Blood Monster

Birth Trauma

Otto Rank[29] was the first, back in 1925, to research the subject of birth trauma. These days, after 90 years of research, there those who consider the moment of birth as an event that has impacts the human personality. A disturbance caused during birth could be severe and often, traumatic This process was called by the psychiatrist Frank Adam, Pre-Birth: The initial split where the newborn has absolutely no control in his world. It is an event that prompts panic, fright and, most likely, we would experience birth an aggressive, invasive event. Since the newborn has no resources to cope with trauma, nor does it have sophisticated defense mechanisms, the event creates an inner schism, that manifests the sense of 'no choice.'

Hence, even the memory of the event, of the aggressive, invasive occurrence, is encoded in the baby's memory as an isolating event, since it has no former memory forms with which it could identify

---

[29] An Austrian psychoanalyst, writer, and teacher who was born in Vienna as Otto Rosenfeld. He was, for 20 years, one of Sigmund Freud's closest colleagues. Among his accomplishments, rank was a prolific writer on analytic themes, an editor of the two most important analytic journals, managing director of Freud's publishing house and a creative theorist and therapist. In 1926 Rank left Vienna for Paris. For the remaining 14 years of his life, he had a successful career as a lecturer, writer and therapist in France and the U.S. (See, Lieberman & Kramer, 2012).

trauma. Accordingly, the event is etched in memory in a focused manner and is stored deeply in its sub-conscious mind.
Frank Adam lists four levels of pressure or pain:

Ideal situation - without pain or trauma;

Tolerable Stimuli - a level of pressure that can be coped with;

Internal split - resistance and very strong pain that cannot be handled;

A desire to die - intense pain and unbearable resistance of the 'true self' creates a desire to die, in other words, the psyche works against itself because it can no longer bear the experience.

Stanislav Grof, an American psychiatrist, talks about a situation he termed "ocean" that transpires between mother and baby and the first trauma, which is a dissociation from this state under difficult circumstances. Grof argues that neurosis among adults is often caused by traumas that occurred in the early stages of infancy. Likewise, he argues that post-traumatic stress disorder (PTSD) can occur in the early years of life, at such ages as two-three, as a result of traumatic birth or an event occurring soon thereafter. The notion that infants cannot be affected by trauma, due to undeveloped mental and cognitive capacity of perception, is, according to Grof, a concept that has been proved as wrong in studies on infants who are just a few days old.

Birth trauma may be grouped with such traumas as those caused by natural disasters, war, etc., except that it occurs at a very early stage of the primary integration of the newborn with itself and his environment.

Water Treatment in Relation to Birth Trauma

It is difficult to make a sweeping generalization as to how birth trauma would appears during water treatment, as every child is very different in the manner he constructs the water world he devises, and in selecting the various components which he chooses to put in the water. However, in my experience and based on repeated observation of different children, I can nevertheless ascertain specific common elements.

The story contains elements of drowning or some other danger which elements are narrated during play or are told to the therapist while describing the water world. The story reflects real struggle for either preserving one's physical integrity or a life-threatening situation affecting the characters participating, which is related to the water or to an animal or creature present in it.

(See, Chapter 12, Trauma and Birth Trauma, Birth Trauma - A Case in Point, p.277)

The scene - Unlike other traumas there is a focusing on an occurrence in the water but which does not takes place within the boundaries of the "lake."

Characters - Most children opt for a baby, a cub, puppy, etc., which is the one in danger of drowning or whose life is threatened.

An example - a water world created by a six year old fraternal twin.
The twins are seen, each on a different flower in the same water container

The Water's Color - Some children choose colors that do not conform to the "classic" array of such colors, like blue, light blue and turquoise. A lot of the colors chosen are "womb" colors, such as red, orange, burgundy, yellow, brown, which are root chakra colors.

A six year old boy, who selected a murky greenish brown color, related a story about two small crocodile brothers who live in the murky waters and are in search for food, "and that water," he said, "is disgusting, it constantly enter the crocodiles mouths."

One can see the tank with the murky water. As part of the healing process of the trauma the patient constructed for "crocodile brothers" new environment, with food and a clean water source.

In a later conversation with the mother , following the water treatment, it turned out that both the patient and his brother were, prior to birth, immersed in meconium-stained amniotic fluid (called either "meconium liquor" or "meconium stained liquor"[30]). the color of stained amniotic fluid is may appear in various shades of green, brown, or yellow, instead of clear and colorless. It indicates that the neonate expelled feces into the fluid in utero. The meconium stained liquor is a sign of possible fetal distress (which places the neonate at a risk of meconium aspiration).

Since water treatment elicits information unconscious that floats up in a simple and accessible manner there is no need to check for the birth trauma. It will appear on its own. The therapist simply needs to be attentive and pay attention to the visual and textual information that

---

[30] Meconium is normally stored in the infant's bowel until after birth, however, on the rare occasion it is expelled into the amniotic fluid prior to birth..

comes and not rule out the presence of such trauma.

Water treatment is an effective not invasive tool in the treatment and comprehension of birth trauma. It may be the only tool that allows very young children to touch a deep and distant memory of the time of birth.

Birth Trauma - A Case in Point

Lihi, a first grader twin is a test tube baby. She arrived at treatment following a report by her parents of fears that come up by nightfall, difficulties in falling asleep, and a fear of failing in school and of not being an outstanding student.

I meet a girl with bright eyes and black hair, rapid speech and a hoarse, low voice of a mature woman. Already at our first encounter she lists for me the reasons that prompted her being brought for treatment: "I have a fear of death and of monsters."

"Besides, I want you to know that I am rather talented," she then specifies for me the talent she has. I get the impression of a very successful girl who constantly struggles to maintain her place at the top, wherever she is. These high expectations as it turns out, are of herself and these make her feel guilt, because her sister may be jealous of her. Lihi's sister is more childish, dreamy, gentle.

As the sessions went on, Lihi earned the nickname "Newton," for her mind is replete with data on so many different subjects, especially, exact science, current events, evolution and more. Knowledge represents power and control for her and with it she assumes the role of a responsible adult at home.

All the knowledge and rationality she possess, have prevented her from being able to cope with nor make sense of fears, death and monsters, since emotions and fears are, at times, irrational.

Lihi was having the time of her life while working and creating at the therapy room. She created all sorts of materials, devoted herself with much passion to the creative imaginative process and the stories that emerged from the activity.

After working in clay Lihi chooses the **wet sandbox** where she creates an island in the center of the box. I surrounded by **pink water** and she adds: "The island was created from stones that were collected, water that evaporated and sand collected from the bottom of the sea, to be shaped as a mountain."

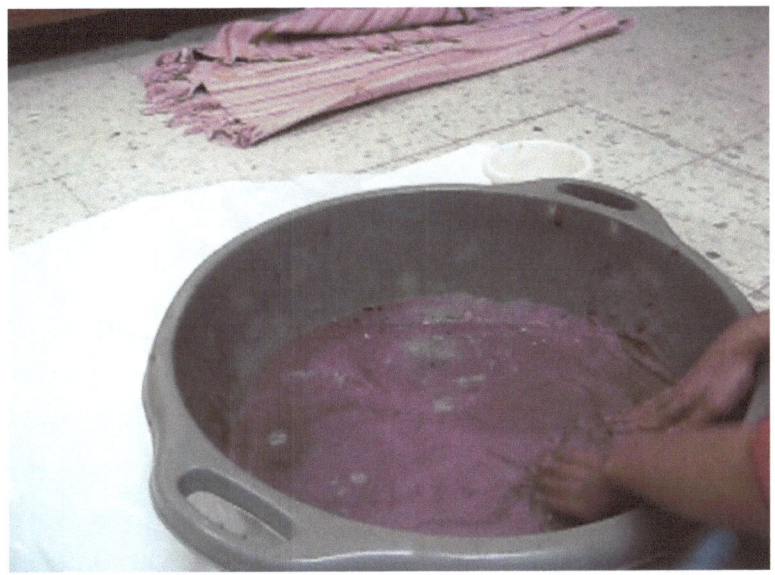

"**There was a boat that sank there were two children**, Healey and Tim, on it who were sailing with their father. **They were friends, Healy drowned and Tim had saved her**. Their father washed ashore. The children came to the island was the seals' and turtles' and the seals helped them convey a message to the rescue team that came to rescue them.

"**The seals' mother is pregnant**, she allows the children to take two pups but **she cannot give birth because she needs a veterinarian**."

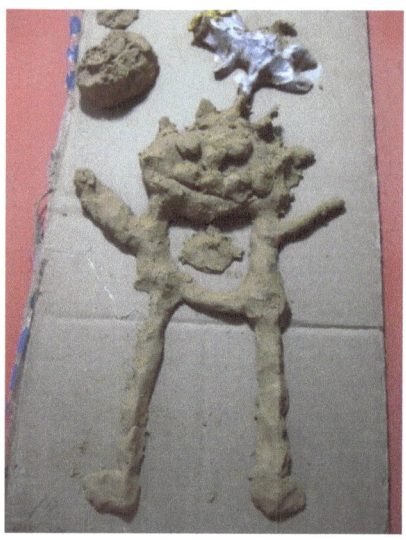

Lihi - a work with clay: a figure with a heart
and above it a small figure painted silver

During one of the encounters, following the work she did with wet sand, Lihi created a structure of a building.

"Hospital" she nimbly creates the structure out of play-dough, then an ambulance, physicians and a wounded person on a gurney. She tells me about a classmate who broke his arm. "I didn't see how that'd happened, because it didn't take place at school. He has a cast on his arm, surely it was painful, now it's not."

Interpretation: it appears, from a review of these meetings, that Lihi is busy handling anxiety that is related to physical health, and, repeatedly, there is presence of danger: First, the story of the boat depicts a risk of drowning. Then there is a threat to the well-being of the pups who are about to be born necessitating the presence of a veterinarian, i.e., a physician. Now, working with play-dough, she is focusing on the place where treatment is provided but, in effect, providing assistance of a place to contain anxiety. The matter of the broken arm simply triggers the inner experience.

Hospital

Water Treatment

The color chosen, light blue, yellow, pink.

During the session we worked with water, Lihi is very excited and curious. She picks the first color, light blue, mixes it in a jar and says: "It's okay that I sprayed out a little, right?"

She then responds to her own inquiry: "What really counts is that I'm enjoying myself! It's okay."

Her association: **Light blue** = "sky, stormy sea filled with waves" (while she is mixing the paint with her hands).

Yellow - "I know that when we'd add it to the light blue it will make green!"

Green - "Grass -- a lot, a lot and calm grass."

She has hard time picking the third color. She breaths heavily as she is looking at the paint bottles.

Yael: "Is it hard for you to decide?"

Lihi: "Silence, "pink!"

(Lihi adds the pink to the water.)

Yael: "What's the outcome? What does it remind you of?"

Lihi: "A kind of soil, full of water -- polluted land."

Part II - the Water World

Lihi opts for bright red and says: "It reminds me of lips, blood, blood has brown in it and also black. Black is really dark brown. (She sweeps up red water with her hands, than let the water drip away to the floor.)

Yael: ""Do you want us to place a soil pad on the edge of the sink?"

Lihi: "How would that help us any? (thinking) I want an island and land animals."

(Lihi now builds an island on the water, filling the base of the island with dirt.)

Lihi: "I'll call it the Air Mattresses' Island, since everybody is floating on air mattresses, I need everything to float."

(Once Lihi is done arranging the island and those on it, she is ready to relate a tale.)

Rising on Water

The floating island on the Sea of Rubella with the family on it

"Truth be told, it's a sad story ... you might think it's the biblical water-into-blood plague of Egypt,[31] no, this is called the Sea of Rubella, for it is red.[32]

"It started one day as this family sailed away, **and one of them fell into the sea -- the girl -- the brother was really worried, he dove in and rescued her**, then they lived there on the island , help each other and eventually **one day the mother went swimming and drowned in the Sea of Rubella (and died).**

"There were no cemeteries there, so what they did, was to take the baby-girl -- **the nurse cared for her instead of the mother -- 'mother replacement.' Everyone was sad because they no longer have a mother since they threw it into the water because she died.**

"The mother suddenly woke up (Lihi takes the mother figure out of the water, raises it up in the air watching it from below) and she saw written 'Mother Grezden's graveyard.' The mother then tells them, 'I'm alive. Don't worry ' the mother sings. However, one day, the baby was a little older, she fell into the water, and the family was sad

---

[31] See, Ex. 7:14–25.
[32] In Hebrew the word for rubella is *ademet* a derivative of the word *adom* which means, "red."

because she died, she was a year old, they were all dressed nicely. They took the baby, dove to retrieve her out of the water. They wrapped her in cloth and wrote a note: 'You will live again, Mom, don't worry' and put him in a cemetery in the Sea of Rubella so that she'd live again.

"'Don't worry, someone will bring you back; don't worry, if you're not alive we'll all depart, you're not *grezden* (dead) and if you're alive they'll bring you to us to the dream.'

"The turtle jumped into the water and put in it the baby who wasn't alive , the whole family left and prayed for her: '**If you live, then we will not have a disaster, just have calm and contentment**.'

"Another day the older daughter went swimming and she found **the baby covered with blood all over, unconscious they brought her back to the hospital** , buried her on the island and prayed for her: 'If you live, you come back to us through Heaven.'

"They were digging and saw something rising, watching the family from above and saying, 'Hello I'm your baby daughter. I'll never go back to life, uless God decides differently, still I will not see you, this is not really your daughter it's her soul.' They were all very sad.

"The family asked the voice:

    "'And what happens to her up above?'

    "'Why did you go up to God, does God want you there?'

"Response: 'I've **drowned, God brought me back to life!**'

"**Something awakened from the ground and the baby came back to life.**"

Lihi played the characters in the story with such great passion, it was not possible to halt the flow of words. As she was narrating, she acted and, in fact, dramatized the text.

She called the story, "The Sea of Rubella."

A few weeks later, I asked the mother whether she remembered any relevant information relating to Lihi and her twin sister's birth.

At first she said it was an uneventful birth and that she did not remember anything exceptional, except, possibly, the fact that they were small and were placed in an incubator for a few days.

I persisted: Might there have something, even if insignificant, to do with the birth itself, that may have been experienced by Lihi as momentous. At that juncture she "remembered" that by the end of the birthing -- she had a C-section, it turned out that she had a **postpartum hemorrhage**.[33]

She was rushed to the operating room for it was feared she would die. Her condition was very dangerous and there was a threat to her life. Due to the anesthesia and urgent surgery she did not see the girls for a few days after giving birth, when her condition stabilized.

"Is it possible that Lihi could remember this?" the mother asked me.

"Apparently so," I replied.

Interpretation: Lihi opts for the red color, the color of the root chakra. According to her interpretation, it is blood mixed with black and brown akin to blood found in the womb. She also describes an association she had with blood, with the word, "lips." She had started the whole account with reference to the mythological the biblical water-into-blood plague of ancient Egypt – water wellsprings which

---

[33] Loss of blood following a delivery resulting in *hypovolemia* or causing the patient to become symptomatic due to the blood loss. It is measure PPH by a blood loss of greater than 500 ml of blood following vaginal delivery, or 1000 ml of blood following a C-section. It is the most common cause of perinatal maternal death in the developed world and, worldwide, it constitutes a major cause of maternal morbidity.

are, universally, supposed to sustain life turn there into blood = unfit for human consumption, death-bringers! The experience of blood pouring out like water conforms to the mother's medical condition at the time of birth – ceaseless hemorrhaging either during or following birth.

During the first part of the story, Lihi repeats the drowning narrative, as she does during other parts of her treatment: The older brother rescues his younger sister. Lihi was born before her twin sister and always assumes the role of the responsible sibling. Moreover, in contrast to her sister, she is a tomboy. Her voice is hoarse and has a rugged texture to it. She repeated the same theme of the story, including the drowning and resurrection or rescue, which are typical themes of accounts by children who underwent a traumatic event.

The description has in it an omnipresent story teller, one who observes the event from the outside. There are emotional experiences of sadness, worry, hope and prayer, as well as practical activities of the family, sister and baby. The action involved includes: diving, burial, wrapping (a dead body), prayer. The story is a spontaneous flow of consciousness and often lacks logic and continuity; it often repeats itself.

Children who raise contents from the subconscious do not bother with the arrangement of the sentences contextually. They play in the water world and sentences float up from their minds outwardly, at times lacking order or logic, which points at the deep link Lihi had to inner information that poured out.

There is a parallel between the mother's drowning and the baby's. In fact, Lihi as a neonate, felt she was drowning and dying when she concluded that the mother died, or at least as she perceived the energy transmitted around her during birth at the hospital, that she was experiencing a life threatening event!!

The story distinctly raises the spiritual connection between the characters, including the ability to "communicate" non-verbal messages, ask God tough questions and use the term "soul." It cogently depicts the experience of the resurrection of the dead baby: "Something came out of the ground, and the baby went back to life."

It appears that Lihi's birth experience was traumatic and is etched in her memory - its oceanic. The encounter with water allowed her birth experience to rise to the fore in complete form: cues of distress, helplessness and danger had come up already during previous sessions, before the water treatment, however, it was difficult to cogently relate them to points along her life timeline regarding the reality of her personal history.

Following the water treatment, there was significant improvement in regard to symptoms of anxiety and stress, especially, the mother noted that Lihi is no longer afraid of death; she feels freer, and falls asleep on her own at night. She even allows herself to be an ordinary student in school and no longer undergoes anxiety attacks before exams and violin performances.

Chapter 13

Subject - Adoption

Maya, an Eight Year Old

Maya arrived at treatment when she was at the third grade. She is a beautiful blond, blue-eyed girl. She is introverted. She walks with a straight back, tension is noticed in the manner she holds her shoulders. Maya was adopted when she was 14 months old from an orphanage in Russia. It is not known why she ended up at the orphanage or how she was treated there. It is known that her mother is alive and that she has siblings. One of her brothers, who is three years older than her, was also adopted from an orphanage in Russia by the same adopting parents who adopted her. Her adopting parents, both in their forties, are warm hearted individuals and are well to do economically and well-educated.

They describe her assimilation in the family as being fraught with difficulties, both functionally and in the manner of connecting with her: "We have always felt the presence of a certain barrier that she never broke through." (Naturally, they compare the relation with her to the relations with her brother.)

As part of the adoption process and the need for religious "approval" her parents were compelled to transfer her from a state secular school to religious state school with different characteristics of clothing, rituals and beliefs than those she was accustomed to. Adapting was not an easy process, she was rejected by her female classmates with whom she had often quarreled. Things got worse when she was caught stealing from a teacher's locker. At home she had outbursts of rage and dominated members of the household with demands for order and cleanliness. On her free time she was at the computer, searching for her family in Russia.

The sessions with her were utterly fascinating. At first, she put me through trust and connecting tests and much time had transpired until she was actually ready to truly bond. I, too, experienced the "barrier" her parents felt. During one of the encounters we played with Native American Cards.[34] She picked ten picture cards and related them to a story: "There were these mother and daughter in a Native American tribe. Every evening the mother would bathe her daughter in a lake. One day the fish bit the daughter who screamed, "Ouch!" The mother tried to calm her down but she wouldn't becalmed. Seeing that the situation was so, *she left the daughter at the edge of the lake* and went to look for help."

Puppet-shows and role-playing brought up themes related to the reality of her life, the relation between teacher and female student, friendship and various aspects of family interactions.

Her choice of therapeutic cards (notice the bonding issue)

---

[34] This is reference to certain therapeutic cards on which scenes from tribal native American life are depicted.

The play choices Maya made were varied and provided much data about the perception of her world and different emotional experiences in her life.

It should be noted that the significant turnabout started when the water came into the picture. Not only that emotional issues came to the fore, a meaningful improvement occurred in every aspect of her life.

Treatment at the Wet sandbox. She is narrating a story and enacts the plot: "There is a lake with an island in the middle. To reach the island one has to pass by crocodiles and threatening animals. The crocodiles are like guards, one may not pass them. In order to do so, approval must be secured from one man who didn't agree yet."

Interpretation: There is reference to a source of water with an island in its middle. The island is indicative of emotional isolation felt by children who sometimes experience difficulties in bonding with their parents (difficulty in connecting with an object). Likewise, the theme of bonding proceeds to the relationship between the two "women" who cannot reach the island which is surrounded with defenses and is guarded by aggressiveness = crocodiles. The women could be Maya and I (the therapist figure) or, alternatively, Maya and her mother, for instance. At any event, the approval was not yet granted, allowing entry to the desired lonely island, which is akin to an entry to one's inner world and formation of emotional bonding.

Working at a wet sandbox

A few weeks before Passover Maya asked that we would make a "Moses in the basket." We worked with soft Play-Doh (which we softened with hot water). While Maya was forming the of scenery and the lake and building the basket, she told me the Biblical story of Moses and the basket. She made the infant, covered it with a small piece of cloth = a blanket, and said: " Now it will be warm and comfy for the baby, the blanket will protect it." In a subsequent conversation we had about Baby Moses and the Biblical story, she told me: "Pharaoh's daughter rescued him from the Nile's water and then he grew up and brought the Children of Israel out of Egypt. I replied, "You know Maya, now that you're telling me about Baby Moses in the basket, it dawns on me that Moses, too, was adopted. (I observe her eyes open wide and she ceases her Play-Doh creative effort as she stares at me). "And you know," I go on, "The Lord chose him – of all people – to bring the Children of Israel out of Egypt. Yes, him especially!"

Maya pauses then resumes breathing and, at once, I can see how her chest rises proudly and a big smile spreads over her face.

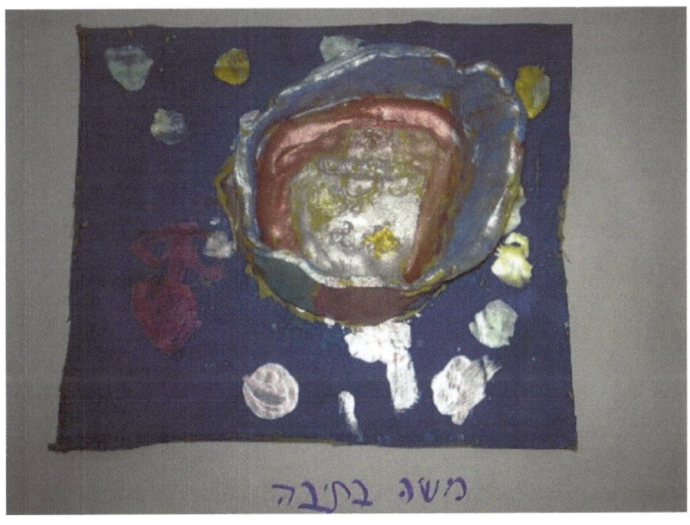

"Moses in the Basket" by Maya, a nine year old

The situation in school improved considerably and Maya began forming social relationships, the thefts ceased and her achievements were steadily improving. There were still difficulties in her functioning at home which included meticulously arranging her bed in the morning, a lot of pressure as she lives home in the morning, reaching school on time and other such situations.

The water treatment befitted the next session.

The Water Treatment

Maya chose paints in three colors and poured them into the sink's water one after the other:

Pink - "It reminds me of the good life"

Silver - "Joy and contentment"

Gold - "Shimmering"

Yellow - "Sun light" and she adds to it fairy powder, then silver glitter; we empty the sink and print.

The water world - blue: All the animals in it – a whale, shark, sea-cat, sea star, a turtle and **a little dolphin that was just born**" (she says "dolphin" with an empathetic, sweet voice).

As she is working, she says about the lake: "It's a lake that may be entered but one must beware of the animals in it," she surrounds the lake with rocks. "There is this rich man who build himself a house by the lake, there is a baby, a couple – a male millionaire and a female one (she makes baby-talk sounds: "ah, ah, ah). There is a pool outside, the baby girl and mother swim in the pool. One day the male millionaire accumulated debts and sells the house and with the money he got, he builds a huge swimming pool."

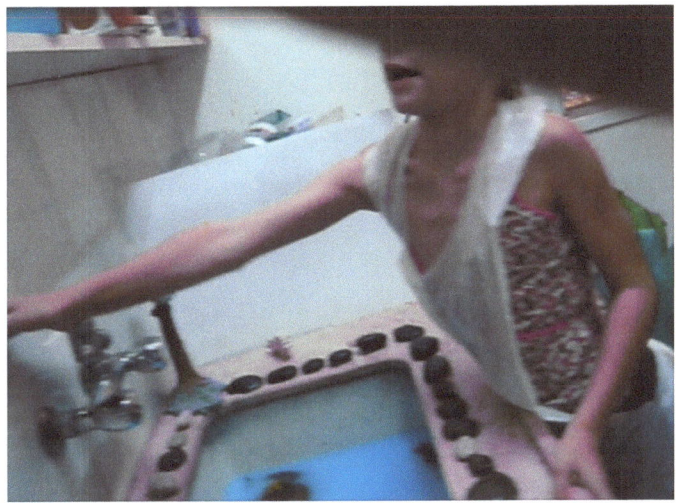

The lake where the infant dolphin lives – surrounded by rocks

1. <u>Interpretation</u>: In Maya's water world there are several interesting elements, all of which relate to her self's perception as an infant and perception of initial bonding. First, there is the new born dolphin = Baby Maya. In the enactment by Maya, the baby dolphin does not have a mother figure, it swims alone. It is possible to enter the lake, where the dolphin is swimming, but one must beware of the carnivorous animal roaming there = tenderness holding much aggression that defends it. The lake itself symbolizes her inner world which she surrounds and seals with rocks. This rocks' boundary does not allow access. There a build-in detachment between the outside world and the water world. There is separation and protection, which is how she creates a split between her inner world, where the dolphin lives – the infant, the neonate – and the rest of the world. On the outside, a different relationship occurs, between her mother and the baby girl who are together in the same pool. Here Maya relates to the relation between herself and her adoptive mother, since the mother figure here is related to the millionaire's figure (she is his wife). Accordingly, Maya identifies two types of initial bonding: the tie between mother and infant with a father figure in the background where the infant's age she describes is around one year, as indicated by the fact that the infant talks. However, in a deep layer of her

psyche there is the "Baby Dolphin" who is pre-verbal and survives on its own in a alienated and shielded environment.

She chooses to place the infant with the mother in a pool outside the natural lake, which is surrounded by rocks, and in fact indicates a kind of split – there is a baby dolphin who is found at its natural place but is detached while the mother and infant are together, but in an artificial small pool. What she is actually saying about her infant self is that though she might be with her mother, the situation however is artificial, it is a pool, not a natural spring of water. Maya thus expresses an apprehension that this state of affairs might also come to an end and the pleasant and intimate closeness between mother and daughter would also disappear, since the home will be lost and a giant pool will replace it; which is an analogy to the lake of the "Baby Dolphin."

After a few weeks during which she was treated with water, her mother reported that she found a small square of stones around the shower, which was the only way she would shower.

Maya's treatment had lasted about a year during which she greatly improved her bonding ability with her parents. They reported demonstrations of physical closeness, she began hugging and cuddling, conduct she had previously avoided. she became an outstanding student and her circle of friends grew and steadily expanded. Manifestations of anxiety, related schedules, passing exams and her compulsive need to keep her room neat before leaving the house decreased significantly. She has loosened up considerably, and she laughs and smiles a lot. She looks more relaxed and joyous and now participates in such activities as a youth movement and a dance group; she leads a rich and satisfying life.

Chapter 14

Selective Mutism

Amir

Six year old Amir arrived for treatment in the middle of winter, a skinny, delicate child with fine straight hair. His parents referred him for treatment after he stopped talking both at home and in kindergarten. The parents described Amir as a middle child, between two sisters, a kindergarten student, joyous, independent, talkative and curious. A neat child who likes to have things in good order around him; he tends to react angrily when he fails, has sensorimotoric sensitivity (**excessive sensory reactivity**, which can be expressed not only with contact, through the skin, but may also manifest as sensitivity to noise, light, traffic). A characteristic behavior, in this case, is that Amir does not wear underwear. They also mentioned that he is a compulsive collector. During the summer vacation, prior to enrolling in kindergarten, regression was noticed in his behavior. He lost his self-confidence, felt under pressure, his physical activity diminished and his gaze would occasionally glaze. The start of the school year in kindergarten went well, with no separation problems, however he would only communicate with the teacher using pantomime and she had to intermediate every task he was to perform. During the holidays, while not attending school, Amir would sink into silence and brooding anger, episodes that would last a few hours each. His condition worsened about six weeks before arriving for treatment. He had hard time leaving home in the mornings and did not bond with his peers. Instead, he would interact with younger children. He became attached to a single mate, playing imagination games for hours, at the same time his silences grow longer till he quit talking altogether.

Amir was referred to differential psychiatric diagnosis[35] which determined that he suffers from selective autism, coupled with rebellious behavior with autistic spectrum characteristic and in addition motor problems where also discovered.

Course of Treatment:

During the First Meeting Amir entered, a thin introverted child stood before me, holding his mother's hand, refusing to let go. To communicate, fe issues sounds and uses a form of sign language, moving his hands and body. He becomes really curious about the objects found in and games at the therapy room, but persists in holding onto his mother's hand. I invited the mother to stay with us and play a cards game. In order to play, Amir releases his mother's hand and loosens up, but then he approaches the drums and begins to play them. Now he closes his mouth and tries to issue sounds, which he finds hard to do. He becomes all red and angrily hits on a drum, his livid facial expression pointed at the musical instruments. Thus, as he was playing the drums, his inner conflict – between the desire and need for expression and his inability to freely express himself – comes to the fore. Already, from the start, I communicate with him by expressing his reactions, like you do with infants – a form of reflection. sometimes his reactions speak for themselves, e.g., anger, impatience, joy, etc., at which instances I would speak directly to him.

By the Second Meeting Amir, though not entirely confident, came in by himself. He opted for the drums and played enthusiastically for 20 minutes. I listen then add a few minutes of my own on the drums. Next, Amir played Pickup Sticks then we painted together. The initial stage is a warm-up for Amir, so that he would allow himself to

---

[35] Differential diagnosis is a systematic diagnostic method used to identify the presence of an entity where multiple alternatives are possible (the process may be termed differential diagnostic procedure),

participate in interactive pursuits.

Now we move to playing 'Winnicott's Squiggle Drawings.' This is a drawing game which entails the use of one page and two identical color pencil. Each participant starts at a specific point of the page and strolls wherever he wants till the color pencils meet, at that moment the game ends. The child's manner of conducting himself on the page is indicative of the way he forms ties: direct, indirect, escaping, and more. I noticed that Amir starts a line then returns to where it started thus creating a lot of "snails." This selection indicates that introversion affects his way of bonding and reveals the presence of inner paralysis.

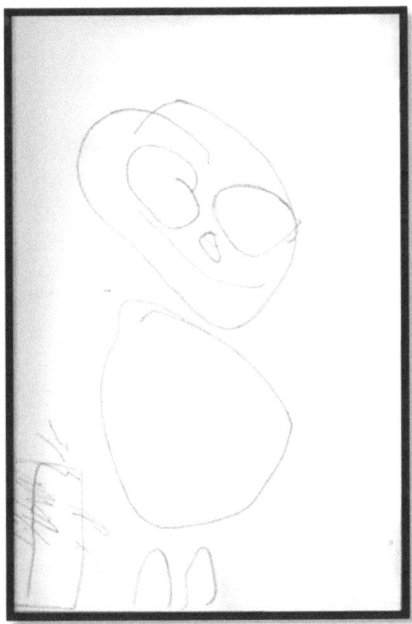

Man and tree drawing
Note, there is no physical integrity of the body parts; the head is tilted and there are no arms. The tree is smaller than the human figure, its branches are needle-like and sparse and the trunk is thick

Amir draws another sketch – a tree with a smaller tree next to it. Amir's drawings are rather regressive. He creates them based on a clear model that than is messed up in a childish manner. The theme of most of his drawings is a large figure next to a small one. Likewise,

Amir chose to excessively color the drawings which is indicative of anxiety.

Amir - a tree drawing.
Note the coil surrounding the tree, the short and distinct trunk and the motion used while coloring.

Amir arrived **at the third meeting** willingly and immediately turned to the musical instruments. This time we are playing together and I repeat his rhythms after him or create a consistent rhythmical accompaniment. I suggest that we record the music created in the process, he agrees with a nod and looks very pleased with the results.

During treatment, I often provide refreshments to the children. Amir ate some snacks and littered the floor. I used the incident to manifest play. I affected a gruff tone of voice and said: "Amir! What's that!? You littered the floor. I'm was angry! "Amir was pleased and, to provoke me further, tossed some other thing on the floor. This way I was able to work with both of Amir's layers, present in his conflict: On the one hand, listening to his own reverberation through repeat of rhythms with voice accompaniment and recording of music, on the other hand, he both mirrors and demonstrates all that conveys anger and aggression.

After the "warm up" Amir is ready for art work. He builds a container that looks like a ship and put inside small balls of clay. Then, he does two things: First, he seals the container's opening and repeating the act again and again, then he adds cannons at the walls of the container and outside of it.

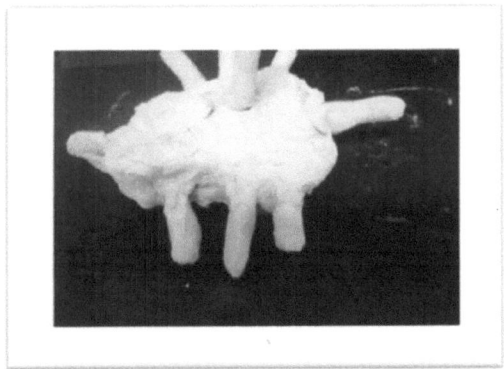

A gunship by Amir

During the Fourth Meeting Amir declares (with hand gestures) right at the start, "I don't want music instruments!" Amir begins walking around the room, he discovers the large bean bag and tries to hop on it several times. I made a suggestion that he could go inside it, since it has a zipper that would allow such exercise. He agreed and we played peek-a-boo. He enjoyed it thoroughly, his laughter reverberating his feelings. Next, we build a house of pillows; he and the beanbag hide inside the "house." I add forest music to the atmosphere. Amir takes a play snake into the "house." In reaction, I start telling a story out laud:

"Once upon a time there was toddler, nearly two years old, who lived in the forest, together with his friend, the snake. Because the toddler was small, he couldn't talk or walk for long distances, thus, the snake would go and bring the toddler food." Amir immediately began participating and begun manipulating a hand snake puppet, according to the story, as if we were in a hand-puppet show.

I go on: "... and then, one day, the snake could not find food and the little child was compelled to do it on his own. Amir comes out of his hiding place and takes some of the refreshment laid on the table. At this juncture, I add another character to the play, saying: "Parrot voices were now heard," picking a parrot hand-puppet, and add: "The parrot saw the berries (the child had found) and wanted to eat them. The child gave him berries then took him to his place and played him some tunes. Whatever the child played, the parrot sang and every sound the child uttered, the parrot mimicked." Amir was hooked and began issuing sounds akin to humming a song.

Amir's disinclination to repeat the ritual "warm-up" signaled for me that he was ready for a change of some sort. When he entered the beanbag we have shifted to an image of a womb and, accordingly, to a state of emotional regression, since Amir wanted to hide and since playing peek-a-boo are all behavioral patterns associated with very young children. The act of building a house of pillows is indicative of a child who prolongs remaining at such an early stage of his emotional development, indicated by the choice of soft materials. On the other hand, it allows a form of separateness.

Amir took to the snake (that represents the placenta) with him into the pillow house. In the story, I "compel" him to come back out and even add a new figure, "the parrot," who serves as a voice double of Amir's expression. It is, repeatedly, an external reverberation facility, voicing the expression wedged inside Amir; parrots, however, are birds who, unlike children, need not be intelligible as is required of Amir day in and day out.

During the Fifth Meeting Amir opts for playing in the the sand box combined with background music. At first, he touches the sand, investigating its qualities: he buries stones in it and then unearths them. He takes the rubber snake and buries it then finds it. He then takes the gunship he made and puts it in the sandbox in such a way that most figures in it are covered with sand. One edge of the sandbox is cleared up and its blue bottom is showing, looking like the ocean. Amir places a whale in its middle. Two superhero figures (both Batman) are laid in the sand.

Wordless :

We are looking together at a picture that was formed in the sand box and I ask Amir,

"What is the pleasant place in the world you have just created?" He indicates **water, the ocean.**

"What is the unpleasant part?" He points at the superheroes.

"Which is the place of danger?" He points at a turtle buried in the sand.

"Who, in the sandbox, would you switch place with? Amir points at the superheroes, again.

During this encounter it begins to appear that Amir desires to form an integration among the various figures. For instance, he takes the gunship created during the third meeting and places it in the sand. This vessel reflects his current state: one of being impenetrable, while the guns are indicative of his aggressiveness. Similarly, the snake, who showed up during the previous meeting, was placed in the sandbox, playing the role of "assistive ego." Most figures were covered with sand, a symbolic gesture of the hidden layer within him; and, for the first time, he turns toward water, the emotional world, with the figure of the whale as one to identify with. This image would, down the road, serve as a key, once he shall have begun working with water.

The Sixth Meeting commenced with a card game. I tried to express myself like Amir, using pantomime – he was not impressed with my attempts to communicate this way with him. While I was reluctant to keep playing, he expressed a desire to play the card game, again. He got angry at me, so I brought out the large beanbag and invited him to smack it hard. He did so soundlessly but was so frustrated that he turned to a direct attack at me, bypassing the protective beanbag. He pinched and bit me, leaving a tooth mark in the shape of a wristwatch on my arm. At this point I offered him to switch to art work and he drew a face with teeth and another figure whose throat was emphasized in color.

A figure with teeth, emphasized throat and huge ears

I thought to myself, how hard it is to be angry and voiceless. Since that day, a new "warm-up" ritual had started. It included music whose tones were repetitious and bouncy and the same tussle with the beanbag. A boundary was set, disallowing biting me personally. Whenever he felt a desire to express anger and bite, it is the beanbag that would take the wrath. Our tussle, which is the warm-up game, would usually last 20 minutes during which he would cause me to fall on the beanbag, I fall while making a great deal of noise, declaring that I have died with torment registering on my face. Each time, Amir laughs gregariously, pleased with his success in killing me.

A figure with teeth, note the sharp lines' motion

During the Seventh Meeting we worked at the sandbox. Amir created a place of water with a whale and a small crab, who was in hiding. This is the pleasant place. In contrast, the unpleasant spot is where the two superheroes are lying in the sand after a physical scuffle. Amir adds another element in the sand, a trap and whoever steps in it falls down.

It is possible to see the whale motif repeating itself as being indicative of the pleasant place and the water as an inner world, in juxtaposition to the outer one. The sand, in Amir's view, is an unpleasant place for he sees it as a place of struggle.

At this meeting Amir began to produce words built of fragmented syllables with his mouth closed.

The Eighth Meeting. Following the ritual "tussle between us," which also serves as a warm-up, Amir painted with brushes. He used yellow, blue, brown and red. He also prepared an aquarium in a bottle, having put water in it; he made a fish of Play-Doh who'd live in there. This is the first time that Amir uses water as creative material, which is a definite sign of his readiness to work with that medium.

The Ninth-Tenth Meeting is a replay of the eighth, except that Amir adds another element to the tussle, that he has to be caught after he runs away from me and, once caught, held onto tightly and not released. Only then, calm descends and we can proceed with art work. Following the warm-up, Amir prepares food for the fish in the bottle and by the end of the meeting, relaxed, we read a story on the couch.

The 11th Meeting – Water Treatment

Amir picks light blue paint for the water world. He picks whales and dolphins to be placed in there. In addition, three snakes hang down from the sink's faucet resembling a waterfall.

He plays an imaginary game by himself and conducts battles. He sings what sounds like underwater whales' songs. I then play such songs and he reacts immediately as he notices the resemblance.

Amir creates an aquarium, conducting a preservation: three whale, two dolphins and one starfish. It is possible to see in this aquarium an expansion of Amir's inner images' repertoire. It had started with a single whale. I felt there is a kind of an emotional key in there. Amir is attracted to the whale's image, which represents him on every occasion and even serves as his duplicate as he works with water. He also responds to recorded whales' songs. This gave me an idea: I acquired a nature video of a mother whale and her infant depicting how they live their life in the ocean.

After this meeting Amir's mother reported an improvement in many small ways, both at home and in school. Amir was still not talking but, more than ever before, he was making varied sounds and sounds indicating that he is getting ready to start speaking. Additionally, Amir's mother discovered on his crown a cluster of white hair that was not there before.

The 14th-15th Meeting

After two meetings in which we returned to the ground, i.e., encounters during which we engaged in expressive arts therapy, Amir returns to the water, and paints them an almost transparent, light blue color. As the sink is filling up, Amir is nodding, humming and mumbling, even speaking words to himself with his mouth closed.

During the game Amir makes a lot of sounds, akin to preying, and moves about rather energetically. The sounds he makes resemble the noise made by an accelerating car. He sprays out a lot of water and the shark moves fast in the water, jumping in and out time and again.

During the next meeting he repeated his previous action, playing the same water game with the same characters, only this time Amir makes deeper sounds, freer, and more diverse, whose intensity and tone go up and down. Once in a while he turns to me and displays the struggle taking place in the water. He creates two conservation aquariums, one with three whales, a big dolphin, a small one, a starfish, two sea turtles and three fish.

The 16h-17th Meeting

Amir played cards with me and for the first time he is pronouncing two words out loud, however, they are incomprehensible. Amir has created an alternative language, which is gibberish pronounced loudly. Then started our warm-up -- our regularly-scheduled wrestling session. Amir seems much more controlled and less angry. The strength of the physical tussle is very great, he creates situations of struggle and control but when, for example, he is at a close place to me he holds me tightly in his hands as his face appear to be threatening, then suddenly a smile blooms. He wants very much to be close as if to say: In order to love you I must first subdue you.

I set boundaries and rules for the game, and out of my physical holding of him a story emerges: "Once upon a time there was a chick that didn't hatch yet, and this was nice for it. But it wanted to hatch for it wanted to find out what's out there in the world. Then I release my hold. This kind of act corresponds to the game in which we imagined him entering into the belly of a whale. During the following meeting Amir painted faces with charcoal.

The 18th Meeting – Water Treatment

The water's color is blue and there are a lot more animals in the water than ever before. Amir adds stones, frogs and an octopus. The number of animals has increased to 16, including the three snakes hanging down from the faucet. In the middle of his work with the water Amir signals to me that he needs to go to the toilet (the manifestation of such a need is very common during water treatment). Amid the water treatment Amir makes clear sounds voices: kuku, a rubbing sound with his throat, sounds of splashing, trickling, and "*oye*," when the fish come out of the water, fly above it and dives back in.

The sounds he makes resemble warm up sounds made during voice lessons. Does he prepare his vocal cord for speech? By now, Amir has not spoken for eight months.

The 19th Meeting – Water Treatment

Amir uses new colors: orange, red, blue, black; and he is now making sounds all the time. He darkens the clear water with blue paint then he hits the animals in the water with the brush used for mixing the paint with the water. He also bites the brush with his teeth again and again. He then add flat floats on the surface of the water, like islands, for some of the animals. In addition, for the first time there are figures out of the water, they are: a soldier who at first was taken by him out of the water, but then fell into the water; and Tarzan hanging over the water from the faucet.

This scene indicates that Amir is starting to form an interaction between the world inside the water and the world outside it. The images that now appear relate to his first works in the sandbox, where there were two superheroes out of the lake water, lying on the sand after having fought physically. Also, in preservation aquariums one can see the division into two worlds, thus the creation of two aquariums. This constitutes significant progress, indicative of Amir's expanding perspective and a departure from the "sealed space" where he had previously imprisoned himself.

The 20th Meeting:

Amir talks to me only in gibberish. He went back to playing the drums but now he does it solo. In terms of the creative work's themes, it seems that we have closed a circle – he goes back to playing the drum, only this time from a place of independence and separateness. Later in the meeting, Amir works with clay and uses a lot of water. He employs a great deal of force in his work and, as he is creating, he unleashes much anger. Amir cuts the clay into smaller and smaller pieces, then puts them back together. That, initially, created a character reminiscent of an embryo, it also resembled an animal in a withdrawn posture.

The 21st-22nd Meeting: Water Treatment

Amir fills the sink with blue water then puts a lot of rocks in there. Then, he hangs the three snakes on the faucet and removes the dolphins, whales, sea turtle, fish and frogs out the preservation aquarium. He pulled stones out of the water and hit the snakes and fish with them; once again there are fierce battles between the whales and the faucet snakes.

In a new aquarium he arranges five adults dolphins and **a very small one**.

Amir's family consists of five persons. Amir's mother told me that once, two weeks after she became pregnant she had to abort, for the fetus did not developed well, "the children of course did not know a thing!" She added.

During the next session I speak gibberish with Amir, using Japanese intonation making up hacked-up and short, word-like, sounds, which, of course, have no meaning in Hebrew. Amir returns to the sandbox: he creates a pool of water and places in it two whales; he constructs a bridge above it, leading from one side of the land to the other. All around soldiers are doing battle.

The 23rd & 24th Meeting:

Amir's passion for card games gives me the idea to develop with him a card game of his own creation. The first cards he designed were sun, tree, house, flower, table, child.

The cards, from right to left: sun, tree, house, flower, table.

He paints out of concrete verbal notions, which are his own ideas. At times he fails to paint what he wants to express. He does not quit and tries over again. I encourage him to go on. These are the rules of this new card game: The cards are turned upside down. He picks a card and I ask, "What do I have here?" while showing him a white box of cards and he answers, *"koof-sa"* (box in Hebrew) expressing the syllables one by one.

This is the first time Amir speaks clearly on his own, not repeating syllables I utter. For every card he created, he said the word that names the painting, which was written on its back. Again, using the same hacked syllables that form together a word.

I breathe a sigh of relief!

The 25th & 26th Meeting:

It has already been a whole week since Amir has been talking with his parents. In the therapy room, his speech is abrupt but lucid. Now it is possible to know what he thinks, and a new world has opened up for him. Amir creates new cards: tulip, door, boat, truck, **whale, dolphin, child.**

Cards from left to right: flower, door, truck, whale, dolphin, child. Note the three central images that appear in these cards.

At the treatment room a new way of conducting things has developed. it included, first, playing with the new cards created by Amir while pronouncing the words. This is coupled with a beginning of direct speech toward me, eating some refreshment, playing drums and art work.

Thus, ten months after he had ceased talking Amir has returned to communicating with his environment, at the age of seven. Amir was now able to conduct normal life in school and at home. These days he is an adolescent, a good student, he has friends and hobbies. Among other things, he plays the guitar and practices martial arts.

Years later, when I opened the treatment file again I noticed the therapeutic effect the water had during the healing process. About a third of the meetings we worked with the water in the sink and in the preservation aquarium. In a significant number of other sessions there were symbols taken from the sea, like sea creatures, the ocean, in the sandbox, vessels, etc.

I assume that children with communication disorders of varying severity can greatly benefit from water treatment as a means to release, open emotional blockages and as an expressive medium that does not require verbal communication.

Conclusion

When I was a child, I had this recurring dream: I find myself in a nursery that has a large glass door. When it is open, blue water laps at my feet. In all those dreams I jump in, getting wet from head to toe in the cold, refreshing water. I then dive in while listening to my breath in the water and to the silence surrounding me, wrapped all around in deep blue water. The dreamed returned at the age of eight, when my parents got divorced, except that now the water outside was stormy, dark, and threatend to swallow me up, to carry me away from my bedroom. I jump into the water, fighting the waves, get slammed and finally succeed in surviving.

When I started writing this book, which deals with water, that dream recurred, once more I am standing in front of a glass door, overlooking a large garden. I go out and discover astonishing water pools, their lines hewn in soft and round lines. Among the pools meander colored stone paths and inside the blue pools float pink and white water lilies.

I had a feeling of coming home.

Water incorporate within it an ensemble of solutions; it calls us to hear the deep inner voice of our heart.

Listen to it.

Bibliography

1. Ruth Fishman, **Symbols Dictionary**, Astrolog Publication, Hod Hasharon, 2002.

2. Carl G. Jung, **Man And His Symbols**, Laurel Book Publication, New York, 1968.

3. Ellen Levine, **TENDING THE FIRE Studies in Art, Therapy and Creativity**, Palmerstone Press, Toronto, 1995.

4. Stephan K. Levine & Ellen G. Levine, **FOUNDATIONS of EXPRESSIVE ARTS THERAPY Theoretical & Clinical Perspectives**, Jessica Kingsley Publishers, London, 1999.

5. Paolo J. Knill, Helen Nienhaus Barba & Margo N. Fuchs, **MINSTRELS OF SOUL Intermodal Expressive Therapy**, Palmerstone Press, Toronto, Canada, 1995.

6. Linet McMaahon, **The Handbook of play therapy**, Ach Publication Ltd, Haifa, 1996.

7. D.W. Winnicott, Play and Reality, Am Oved Publishers Ltd, Tel Aviv, 1977.

8. Carrol E. Izerd, **Emotion Theory and Research, Highlights, Unanswered Questions, and Emerging Issues,** http://brainimaging.waisman.wisc.edu/~perlman/papers/EmotionTheory08/Izard_annualreview_2009.pdf.

9. Michael Talbot**, The Holographic Universe**, Mirkam Publications Ltd, Tel Aviv, 1997.

10. Poul Ekman**, Basic Emotions**, University of California, San Fransiciso, CA, USA.

11. Dr. Shelomo Ariel, **A Program for Training Therapists in Integrative Multi-Systemic, Culturally Competent Therapy,** 2011.

12. Ken Wilber, **A Brief History of Everything,** Shambhala Publication, Boston, 2000.

13. Sue Jennings, **Dramatherapy Theory and Practice for Teachers and Clinicians**, Routledge, London, 1994.

14. D. W. Winnicott, **Transitional Object and Transitional Phenomena in Through Pediatrics to Psychoanalysis,** Karnack Books, London, 1992.

15. C. G. Jung , **Dreams,** Dvir Publications, Tel Aviv, 1982.

16. Roy Bailey, **NLP Counselling**, Winslow Press Ltd, Oxon, 1997.

17. Judith Lewis Herman, **Trauma and Recovery**, Am Oved Ltd, Tel Aviv, 2000.

18. Juel Ryce-Menuhim, **Jungian Sandplay, The wonderful Therapy**, Ach Publication Ltd, Haifa, 1993.

19. Dr. Violet Oaklander, **Windows To Our Children – A Gestalt Therapy Approach to Children & Adolescents,** , Nord Publication, Tivon, 1995.

20. Rinda Blom, **THE HANDBOOK OF GESTALT PLAY THERAPY, Practical Guidelines for Child Therapists,** Ach Publication Ltd, Haifa, 2010.

21. Morton Chethik, **Techniques in Child Therapy, Psychodynamic Strategies**, Ach Publication, Haifa, 2005.

22. Pseudo-Plutarch **Placita Philosophorum**

23. D. W. Winnicott, Transitional Objects and Transitional Phenomena — A Study of the First Not-Me Possession. International Journal of Psycho-Analysis, 34:89-97 (1953)[36]

24. Masuro Emoto, **Messages form Water and the Universe**, Hay House, 1st ed. 2010

---

[36] Same as no.14, above but different year of publication. Needs to be reconciled.

25. J.W. von Goethe, **The experiment as mediator between subject and object** (1772)

26. c. G. Jung, **The Archetypes and the Collective Unconscious** (London 1996)

27. John D. Greenwood, **The Disappearance of the Social in American Social Psychology** (2004)

28. Avi Bouman, **The Golden Hairs of the Devil** (2005) (based on a Grimm Brothers' tale, **The Devil with the Three Golden Hairs**)

29. Riva Perry, **Rebirth** (Modan, Psycha Series) (2003)

30. Josepf L. Henderson, **Ancient Myths and Modern Man** (ed.) (London 1978)

31. Connie Zweig, **Meeting the Shadow** (1991)

32. , Audi, Robert, ed. **Cambridge Dictionary of Philosophy** (2nd edition(1999)

33. Jung, C.G. **Psychological Types. Collected Works**, vol. 6, (1921)

34. Exodus 2:1-3

35. Carlo Collodi, **The Adventures of Pinocchio** (1883)

36. Pribram, H.H. **Recollections. Neuroquantology** (2011)

37. Izard C.E., Fantauzzo CA, Castle J.M., Haynes O.M., Rayias M.F., Putnam P.H., *The Ontogeny and Significance of Infants' Facial Expressions in the First 9 Months of Life*. Dev. Psychol. 31 (1995)

38. Rizzolatti G., Arbib M.A., Language within our Grasp. Trends Neurosci. 21:188–94 (1998)

39. Ramachandran, V.S., *Mirror neurons and imitation learning as the driving force behind the 'great leap forward' in human evolution*. Edge, October 15 (2008)
http://www.edge.org/3rd_culture/ramachandran/ramachandran_p1.html

40. Patrick Casement, **Further Learning from the Patient** (1990)

41. E. James Lieberman & Robert Kramer, **The Letters of Sigmund Freud & Otto Rank: Inside Psychoanalysis** (2012)

42. Exodus, 7:14–25

www.ingramcontent.com/pod-product-compliance
Ingram Source LLC
TN
121224
00002B/4